We Also Served

*Three Generations Growing up
in the Military*

By Carolyn Clark Miller

For all those I love and have cared for, and for all the military families who continue to serve our country well.

Acknowledgements

My deepest gratitude to my husband, Ted, for reading my manuscript multiple times, for his editing and suggestions, and his long-suffering patience while I worked, on and off, on this memoir over the past 18 years. Thanks to my cousin, Clark Lincoln, whose artistic talent is demonstrated on the covers of this book. Thanks also to my friend, Jan Tarasovic, who reviewed an early version and suggested that I include a glossary to explain all the military lingo, and to Betsy Marron and my Selah Sisters who encouraged me to continue this endeavor. I also owe a debt of gratitude for all the hours my patient Mom and Dad answered my many questions in multiple interviews over the years; for saving my letters; and for the notes my brother left me. Finally, my appreciation for all the necessary lessons that I have learned on my journey, and for those in my military family who have provided many of those lessons for me to learn.

Contents

Introduction

★★★

PART I
This Brat's Life

★★★

PART II
The Third Generation of Brats

We Carry on Bravely
He Served His Country Well. We Also Served
A New Beginning
The Years Go By
The View from Near the Journey's End

★★★
PART III
Those Who Marched Before

Chapter Eight
Our Family's Irish Story   263
Our First Trip to Ireland
The Enduring Legacy
The Luck of the Irish

Introduction

We were all Brats, and proud of the title. My parents, my aunts and uncles, my cousins, my brother and sister, and my children all grew up as military dependents, nomads in the service of our country. Although I am no longer a military dependent, I will always be a Brat.

We moved so often that the military service became our hometown. So, what did we say when we were asked "Where are you from?" I practiced different answers. I experimented with saying that I was from wherever we lived last, or wherever we had lived longer than a year, or where my grandparents had been from. Or I would just make up someplace I longed to be from, Hollywood or New York City. If I said, "Las Vegas," I'd think, "Well, that was true for a short time, anyway." But I usually just gave up trying to explain. Sometimes, I'd say "I'm a Brat." If there was any spark of recognition, I'd met a kindred spirit. If the look was confused or embarrassed, I'd quickly add, "An Air Force Brat." But I finally settled on, "Nowhere in particular."

My extended family of Brats were proud of being Brats or sometimes weren't, depending on where we were living. If we were safely ensconced in military housing on Post, we were proud of it, the special few who wore the label "Brat" as a badge of honor. On the other hand, if we were living "on the economy" in a civilian world and were the new kids in one more of a long succession of new schools, we tried to avoid attention and stay alert. We Brats had much in common with each other, but little in common with classmates from the local communities surrounding military installations.

My father and one of my grandfathers graduated from The United States Military Academy at West Point. The West Point motto, "Duty, Honor, Country," clarified an important issue. Duty, honor and country, and their military careers, came first. My other grandfather joined the Army as a new doctor and practiced medicine in the trenches of World War I. For him, his patients came first but were followed immediately by duty, honor and country. My extended family also included two Naval Academy graduates and, in time, an Air Force general, two Army generals, a Navy admiral, and a naval officer killed in World War II.

Their decisions to become professional military officers resulted in three generations of children living transient, sometimes exciting, often lonely lives. Three generations encumbered with our military ancestors' aspirations, successes and failures. Three generations trying to prove ourselves worthy of our heritage, of the examples of heroism and courage set by our fathers in uniform, and by our mothers who "kept the home fires burning." We are different in fundamental ways from those who have grown up rooted in the stability of civilian life.

We find our roots in our country's history and in our fellow Brats, as much as in the many places we've lived. We cherish old photographs, genealogy charts, and scrapbooks: sentimental reminders of our family's past. Our military history has left us with exciting stories and numerous display cases filled with medals and commendations for those in uniform. There are none for the wives and children who supported their calling.

We also served, we who waited and cared for the children, kept our homes ready to welcome our husbands and fathers back; and followed them from one duty assignment after another. As did the children who kept their heads up and courageously entered new school after new school. That is our legacy, our hometown. Pat Conroy said of military Brats, "We spent our entire childhoods in the service of our country, and no one even knew we were there." No one in the chain of command, anyway.

We grew up with absent fathers and anxious, worried mothers. It is not just the experience of war that demands a heavy price, but also the ongoing anticipation of war. There is a cost to pay. The cost for families is frequent anxiety caused by moving every few months or years, rootless, from Army post to Army post, or from Air Force base to Air Force base.

Our childhoods were shadowed by close-up images of war, surrounded by the weapons of war. Every day of our fathers' lives was spent preparing for, and imagining, that awful possibility. Furthermore, when they had fought in their war, they were often emotionally exhausted, experiencing sadness, guilt, and anger on their return home, sometimes missing their fellow warriors more than they had missed their families. Readjustment to family life was a challenge.

That is not to say that we are not proud of our legacy of service. We thrill to the sound of a military band, the sight of the colors blowing in the breeze, the roar of a fighter jet overhead. We weep at the sight of the American military graves scattered across the United States and Europe, and especially at Arlington National Cemetery, where many of our loved ones lie. We revel in discussing the wars in which our brothers, fathers, uncles and grandfathers fought.

Our family's stories are of struggle and joy, but also of faith in our country, hope for the future, and love for each other. I hope my children and grandchildren will value their country even more because of the sacrifices made by the generations that came before. May they come to forgive their parents' and grandparents' failings and remember, instead, their honest commitment to service.

How It Was When I Was Born: My birth came only two decades after World War I, the war to end all wars, had come to an unstable conclusion. What was called the Spanish Flu had killed millions worldwide. Women had finally won the right to vote just fifteen years before I was born, punctuating a long and continuing struggle toward equality. Five years before I was born, the 18th Amendment, prohibiting the manufacturing, selling or transporting of alcohol, was repealed.

Sulfa drugs, the first antibiotics, were being developed and had begun to save lives. We didn't know yet about the importance of drinking lots of water, washing our hands often, or wearing sunscreen. Almost everyone smoked, and it would be another 25 years before doctors would warn that cigarette smoke, even second hand, was dangerous to our health.

The Great Depression was causing untold suffering throughout our country. The world was nervously watching Hitler taking over Europe and arguing about what to do. The United States was unprepared, both politically and militarily, to step in and help stop him. While everyone was nervous, the men in uniform, my father and both my grandfathers among them, were preparing for orders that might come at any moment. Their families were living with daily insecurity and apprehension.

Mothers stayed home with their children. Long distance travel was mostly by train or bus. Airline travel was frightfully expensive and primarily by propeller-driven DC-3s and DC-4s without pressurized cabins. There were no seat belts in automobiles, no air conditioning, no television, and we still had five-digit telephone numbers. Most home telephones were connected through party lines with the phones in other homes. Each party had its own distinctive ring, but every telephone call rang in every home, and your neighbors could listen in on your calls.

African Americans were an impoverished underclass who were educated, if at all, in poor and segregated schools despite the war that freed them some 70 years before. Most worked as laborers or farmers. On my travels through the South, I watched as they and their children picked cotton by hand in millions of acres of hot, dusty fields. Although black men had the right to vote long before any women did, they faced daunting obstacles designed to allow as few as possible to exercise that right. Civil rights, it seems, were for white Americans.

The wheels of technological progress were turning. I was five years old when Grace Hopper found ways to store, process, and search information electronically, far more efficiently than was possible before. A mathematician and Rear Admiral in the Navy, "Amazing Grace" developed the first computer language. Forty years later, I would be working for the government when I attended a demonstration of something called the Internet. From a stage in Washington, DC, I watched the internet search for and provide information from a library in Italy. I didn't imagine how fast and how far that astounding innovation would spread.

There were subjects--mainly homosexuality--that were not talked about. Until after I was married, I had no idea what certain words meant, words spoken with derision or disdain. Until a Supreme Court ruling in 2003, homosexuality was a crime in many states, punishable by arrest and imprisonment. Although research has shown that a fairly stable 10 percent of the human population feels strong attraction to members of their own sex, those feelings had to be kept secret, a secret shrouded in shame and fear.

Unwilling or unable to accept their sexual preference and anxious for the respectability of marriage, many gay men married unsuspecting women who would unwittingly stand guard at their husband's closed closet doors. I knew some of them, women in late middle age, who finally could talk about their experiences. Some of those couples became friends and successful partners raising their children. Others endured years of loveless marriages. Wives grew to believe themselves unattractive and unlovable, while their husbands tried to pretend what they didn't feel and struggled to keep their secret. These were cruel fates. Emotional and sexual attraction between two people may not always be what some think of as love, but who are we to judge?

Men ran the world: government, business, wars and peace. Despite a few brave and exceptional women, men were the politicians, doctors, lawyers, and judges. They dictated the behavior of women. In the year I was born, a woman named Helen Hulick was arrested and sentenced to five days in jail for daring to wear pants to a court appearance in Los Angeles.

Women were supposed to get married and have children. If they didn't get married, they were considered "old maids." Children were the expected blessings of marriage, and childless women were often pitied. Children arrived, or they didn't, pretty much unplanned. The birth control pill had not been developed yet and there were no reliable means available to plan or prevent a pregnancy.

For their part, children were to be seen but not heard, an oft repeated axiom of the day. Children were expected to be well-disciplined and to follow in the footsteps planned for them by their parents. Their feelings were rarely solicited or communicated. We kept our heads down. It's not for nothing that my generation has been called "The Silent Generation."

Children can now be born when their parents are ready and eager to share their love. People are less likely to be judged based solely on their gender, the color of their skin, their religion, sexual or gender preference or innumerable other variables. We have had an African American president. Almost certainly we will someday have a woman president, a Jewish president, a gay president. Over the course of my lifetime, our culture has gradually become fairer, kinder and more compassionate. I am truly grateful to have lived to see these changes.

PART I
This Brat's Life

Chapter One
In the Shadow of World War II

The Telegram

On the afternoon of July 31, 1942, there was a knock on the front door of Officers' Quarters #4 on the U.S. Army post at Fort Sam Houston. We were about to learn of the event that defined my early childhood. Heat and humidity rose from the streets of the Post and the surrounding area of San Antonio, Texas. Quarters #4 was a rambling, three-story, brick, four-bedroom home with a large screened-in porch across the front and generous maids' quarters in the rear. The sign out front indicated that Col. Arthur E. Wilbourn, who was my maternal grandfather, had been assigned the quarters. The house was randomly furnished with a few antiques and Army-issue pieces, and smelled of babies, gardenias and furniture polish. The cries of young children echoed throughout. My mother, brother, sister and I, three aunts and a cousin were living temporarily with my grandparents.

The door was probably answered by an orderly or a maid. Either would have been dressed in the proper uniform indicating the position of servant in an officer's home. There was a telegram addressed to my mother, Mrs. Albert P. Clark, Jr. When it was handed to her, I imagine that she shuddered, and might have muttered a prayer. I hope her mother and father were present. She tore open the telegram and read:

> *We regret to inform you that your husband Lieutenant Colonel Albert Patton Clark United States Army has been reported as missing in action in*

1

British Isles since July twenty sixth stop further reports will be forwarded as received. (Appendix #1)

I was three years old on that day, my brother was two, my sister an infant. Although the war itself was a great cause of alarm for all the adults around me, Dad's being declared missing in action brought the danger and fear right into my little heart. A shadow settled over my happy, carefree childhood, a shadow that would remain for three years, leaving memories of sadness that linger still.

My father was assigned to the Army's First Air Corps unit, the 31st Pursuit Group, sent to England soon after the United States entered the war. He was the second in command of the Group. Because no American aircraft had yet reached Europe, Dad was piloting a British Spitfire when his flight of four aircraft was ordered to fly a reconnaissance mission over the English Channel to the coast of France on July 26, 1942. Dad was flying in the most vulnerable position among a flight of four, called the slot. A German fighter spotted them, and a brief battle ensued, which badly damaged Dad's aircraft. His flight leader reported that Dad had crashed into the English Channel in flames, a report that was informally relayed to my mother.

That report was not true. Because Dad's compass and altimeter had been damaged and his cockpit jammed, he could not bail out, or ditch—a blessing in disguise. Spitfires were known to sink like anvils with no time for a pilot to get out. Dad spotted land and, not knowing whether he was heading for England or France, skillfully crash landed in a field next to a beach. He struggled to open the cockpit, finally climbed out with a few cuts and scratches and a bump on the head thinking he may have been lucky and landed in England. When he saw German helmets coming over a rise, his heart sank. He had landed on the coast of France. For him, the war for which he had trained for months and years, was over. It ended near Cap Gris Nez about 20 km. north of Boulogne.

When the telegram arrived five days later, I don't remember Mom crying, or explaining. But I knew that something was dreadfully wrong, and that it had to do with my much-loved Daddy. I remember worried faces turned away from me and intense discussions. Although my mother was told that no parachute had been sighted when my father went down, she says she never doubted that he was alive. My father's Aunt Anne wrote her a letter indicating that she believed that my mother was now a widow. Mom never forgot Aunt Anne's lack of faith. She wrote the following in a letter to my father's sister, Aunt Mary Lincoln, two weeks later:

> *Aunt Anne wrote me a letter of sympathy – assuming that Bub* [my father's nickname] *had gone onto another world. I'll probably be on her black books for my reply, but I couldn't just let it go. I simply told her that as long as the War Department regarded him as alive the least we could do was to hope and pray that was true.... I try to believe that Bub is a prisoner and so at least safe out of the battle.*

In this letter, given to me after my Aunt Mary died, my mother writes that she   had received a letter of sympathy and encouragement from General George C. Marshall, who had attended Virginia Military Institute (VMI) with my grandfather.

She learned that Dad was alive on August 27, 1942, his 29th birthday, in a letter from the War Department, Adjutant General's Office. It stated:

> *In accordance with the terms of the Geneva Convention with respect to interchange of information regarding prisoners of war, a report has been received in the War Department from the German Government, through Geneva, Switzerland, indicating that your husband, Lieutenant Colonel, Albert Patton Clark, Jr., O-20218, Air Corps Army of*

3

the United States, was taken prisoner of war. Mail for your husband properly addressed as indicated below will be forwarded to him free of postage. Because of the limited facilities available, no packages should be sent.

Signatories to the Geneva Conventions regarding treatment of prisoners of war had agreed that the only information prisoners of war are required to give to the enemy is: name, rank, and service number. As both the United States and Germany were signatories, that was the information my father provided to the Germans when he was taken prisoner. And that was the information that the Germans provided to the United States following his capture. (See Appendix #3, The Military Code of Conduct for American Combatants.)

My father has told the story of his experiences during the ensuing years in his memoir titled, *Thirty-Three Months as a POW in Stalag Luft III: A World War II Airman Tells His Story.* As he looks back on the experience, and retells the story, his memories of those 33 months were among the most vivid of his life. The story of our wait for his release, during a world-wide war that killed more than 60 million men, women and children (no one knows the exact number) is not as exciting or colorful, but still worth telling.

My Parents' Love Story

My parents met and fell in love in San Antonio. My mother had come with her family when her father was assigned to Fort Sam Houston. She dated a couple of young officers, including a handsome lieutenant named Dick, who painted a stunning portrait of her. That portrait was to become a major bone of contention in the family, but that story comes later. My grandmother was fond of Dick and wanted my mother to marry him. But when Mom met my father, a drop-dead handsome Army pilot in training at nearby Kelly Field, Dick was history.

4

My father had graduated from West Point in 1936 and was lucky enough to qualify for flight school, his long-held aspiration. He learned to fly at the United States Army Air Corps flight schools at Randolph and Kelly Fields, one northeast, the other south of San Antonio. He trained in P12s. Those were still the days of leather flying helmets and some open cockpits. At six feet, three inches tall with flaming red hair, he must have cut a dashing figure, tightly squeezed into the little cockpits, perhaps with a silk scarf flying in the breeze.

One day Mom and her friend Sue were gassing up her car when Sue said, "Hey, there's Bub Clark!" Mom was immediately attracted to him and didn't hesitate to mention this to a number of people. It was reported back to the handsome redhead that, "Carolyn Wilbourn is in love with you." Naturally, he was interested. A petite brunette, Mom was as beautiful as he was handsome. He told her that he planned to stay single for several years. Then he sighed and confided that he thought he was in love with her too. But there was a small hurdle ahead, his parents.

They were interested in his career potential in the military, and in factors that might advance it. They always provided their opinions of his dates. Mom was given high marks because, they reasoned, an Army Brat would understand the difficulties of a military life and would not complain as a wife from civilian life might. But Mom's nose also had to pass muster with Dad's mother. Small English snub noses ran in my grandfather's family and my grandmother hoped her children's mates would have substantial noses. The story goes, and probably it was just a story, that she always gave her opinion of their dates' noses. Mom had a lovely nose, and Dad's sister married a wonderful man with an unforgettably substantial nose.

My parents liked to ride horses together while they were courting. "Baby it's Cold Outside" was their favorite song. They were married in San Antonio on October 8, 1937, the day after my father graduated from flight school.

Dad at Selfridge Field, Detroit

Selfridge Field, Michigan: October 1937

Three days later, Dad was ordered to report to Selfridge Field near Mt. Clemmons, a suburb of Detroit. They honeymooned along the way. Dad was assigned to the 31st Pursuit Group to fly single-engine fighters. He would fly a lot of them in his career: P-5s, P-26s, P-35s, P-36s, P-40s, C-45s, P-51s, T-33s, F-86s and F-100s. He also flew some multi-engine aircraft: B-10s, B-17s and even B-26s. At Selfridge, most of his flight time was in P-39s. One day a fellow pilot, distracted while studying a map, flew right on top of him, badly damaging his aircraft and forcing him to bail out. Luckily, he landed in a farm field instead of in the lake and collect-

Mom and Dad get married, 1937

6

ed a golden caterpillar. In those days, a golden caterpillar, symbolizing the silk in the life-saving parachute, was awarded to any pilot who had to bail out to save his life.

I was born in Harper Hospital in Detroit on October 13, 1938, the first of my parents' three children. They named me after my mother, Carolyn Pierpont Clark, but decided to call me Bunny. They drove back down to San Antonio in the spring to visit her parents and have me baptized. My Godfather was Dad's best friend from childhood, fellow Brat and a 1936 classmate from West Point, Frederick Caesar Augustus Kellam. Freddy was a Major in the airborne infantry and parachuted over France during the Normandy Invasion. He was killed on D-Day, defending a bridge near Sainte-Mère-Église, now called "Kellam Bridge." An only child, he was 26 years old, married and had a son. Although I don't remember him, I haven't forgotten about him and I often wear a little gold cross he presented to me at my baptism.

Housework was hard manual labor in those days. Babies wore cloth diapers, which were washed in wringer-washers and hung out to dry. Diapers on clothes lines quickly froze solid in the cold Michigan winters. Consequently, all the officers' wives had maids, and some also had nannies. Managing her maid was a responsibility Mom took seriously and she often found herself looking for a new one as they quit fairly regularly. Years later, after I had accompanied Mom grocery shopping, she remarked that she could buy two weeks' worth of groceries for less than five dollars when they lived in Michigan. I can hardly imagine what the maids earned for a day's work.

Mom remembered those years as the happiest of her life, despite the looming Nazi menace in Europe. They had many friends on Post. There were dinners, receptions, and dances. The ladies were free to leave their children with nannies and get together for coffee, tea, lunch, bridge and gossip.

My brother, Albert Patton Clark III, nicknamed Pat, was the second baby, born on March 2, 1940. He seemed to be a healthy baby, but they soon realized that something was wrong. He was constantly hungry, cried incessantly and experienced projectile vomiting. When he hadn't gained any weight at the six-week checkup, the doctors diagnosed his condition as pyloric stenosis, a severe narrowing of the opening from the stomach into the small intestine. He was immediately scheduled for surgery. The doctors gave him a shot of whiskey, made an incision in his abdomen, and opened the passage from his stomach to allow nourishment to pass through his gastro-intestinal tract.

Pat's first months of life were harrowing for our little family. Fortunately, my mother's sister Elizabeth, whom we called Danny, lived nearby. She was also married to an Army flight officer stationed at Selfridge. She cared for me during much of that difficult time and we became close. Although Pat's incision became infected and resulted in an ugly scar, he recovered, gained weight and displayed a sunny disposition.

For me, those days were mostly peaceful and full of childhood joys and discoveries. I was cared for by many people in addition to my parents and visited by doting grandparents. The almost constant sound of the propeller-driven fighters my Dad flew was part of my world. The gentle drone of small aircraft, the sound of a push mower, the fragrance of freshly mown grass, the smooth feel of lightly starched and ironed sheets and clothing—these bring back comforting memories of my early days of bliss and innocence.

I have a few clear memories: bits and pieces before the War. I remember excitedly watching from the front porch and jumping for joy as my tall, handsome Daddy strode purpose-

Dad, Mom, Pat and me before the war

fully up the front walk. He laughed when he saw me and asked whether I had a "bee in my bonnet." A few days earlier I had been stung on a toe as I walked barefoot in the grass and was worried by his question. I worked hard to untie my crisply starched and ruffled white bonnet, pulled it off, examined it carefully. Finding no bee, I went inside to show him my empty bonnet, but he was deep in serious conversation with Mom.

I imagine that they might have been discussing the events in Europe. The Germans entered Paris in June of 1940, and by August had launched the "Blitz," bombing London and the east coast of England. Londoners were sending their children, often infants, to live with strangers in rural villages, saying good-bye for who knew how long, and for some as long as five years. Air raid shelters in the cities were filled day and night. Lights were prohibited after dark or allowed only within homes with dark coverings over the windows. My parents must have feared that it was only a matter of time before the United States would be at war and Dad would be off to fight.

In July 1940, Dad was sent TDY to gunnery training. So Mom, Pat and I flew to Texas to visit my grandparents. My grandfather had been transferred to Ft. Brown, near Brownsville, Texas. Mom said the flight took 12 hours. We stayed for three months. Mom's brother, Bobby, was a teenager living at home. He told me years later that I drove him crazy with my joyful screams as I ran up and down the street in front of the quarters.

When Mom became pregnant with my sister a few months later, the dark clouds of war were directly overhead. Dad disappeared for long periods of time for "maneuvers." Mom's other sister, Anne (nicknamed Tooty, for my family delighted in nicknames!), and her brother Bobby both came from San Antonio to help care for us when my sister was born on October 29, 1941. Aunt Danny, pregnant with her first child, had already left Selfridge for San Antonio when her husband Eric had been ordered TDY. My sister was named after my father's mother, Mary Gannon Clark.

Dad was in Indiana preparing to move the 31st Pursuit Group to a new base at Ft. Wayne when the Japanese bombed Pearl Harbor on December 7, 1941. The Germans formally declared war on the United States a few days later, aligning with Japan to form the Axis Powers, soon to include Italy. When he heard the news, Dad telephoned Mom from Ft. Wayne and told her to leave Selfridge and go home to her parents as soon as possible.

The Army wives on the Post began a flurry of activities necessary to pack and ship household goods, clear quarters and go home to parents or relatives to wait out the war. Mom packed our belongings for shipment to San Antonio and cleared quarters within a week. What to do with our large and gentle German shepherd, Mike, was a big problem. Mike and I loved each other.

Mom decided that Mike had to be put down. Of course I had no idea what that meant. She invited me to accompany her when she took Mike to the vet. I remember looking at her silently hunched over the steering wheel of an old Pontiac, smoking furiously while I sat in the passenger seat. Mike sat on the back seat, with his head on the console between us, panting and licking my face. "Where are we going?" I asked. "We're taking Mike to heaven," she said. "Where's that?" "In the sky," she said. "When will he come back?" "It will be a long time." I begged to go with him, but she wanted no guff from me. I patted him and put my cheek up against his. Mom and Mike got out of the car, and I stayed in the car with a heavy heart.

By this time, my grandfather had been reassigned

Me as a toddler, with my best friend, Mike.

from Ft. Brown back to Ft. Sam Houston. We flew out on a C-47. Our trip was interrupted by the same winter storm that Dad would contend with. We sat in Chicago for several days with Aunt Margaret and Uncle Charlie before flying on to Texas.

Dad had been ordered to lead a flight of seven P-39s to Paine Field near Seattle to prepare to defend the West Coast against possible attack by the Japanese. The huge winter storm in the middle of the country forced him to fly east and south. P-39s had a range of about 500 miles, requiring frequent stops for refueling. He remembered that this trip was lengthy and difficult. The route to avoid the storm took them south and east to Louisville and Jackson, Mississippi. Then they turned to the west, making many refueling stops, including in Dallas, Albuquerque, and March Field in California. They lost several days due to thick fog over the mountains before flying up to Sacramento.

A large flight of P-39s had recently crashed in the Cascade Mountains, which they would have to cross if they flew directly north to Seattle from Sacramento. Dad decided to fly east to Elko, Nevada, then north to Boise, Idaho, before flying over to Spokane and finally across to Seattle, thus avoiding the mountains known for unpredictable weather at that time of year.

The airplanes were old and worn. Somewhere on this trip, Dad's aircraft developed an oil leak and his radio conked out. As he approached the field to land, an observation plane cut him out of the landing pattern, forcing him to go around. About three-quarters of the way around the field his engine quit. At that point, an airplane was taxiing on the runway on which he was planning a dead-stick landing, and he was forced to crash land. He went into a ditch and broke off the front end of the airplane, but fortunately was not injured.

A Refuge at Fort Sam Houston: December 1941

We arrived in San Antonio on December 14th, one week after Dad's telephone call. We were welcomed into the large brick quarters where my grandparents lived on the Post. Our grandfather was a full Colonel by then. We always called him, Pappy, the name of a character in the comic strip "Lil' Abner," and the moniker attached to him by his disrespectful daughters. We called our grandmother Granny.

In those days, the profession of military officer was one of prestige and status equal to that of doctors and lawyers. Only 25 percent of Americans had graduated from high school. As most military officers had graduated from college, they were among the educated elite. Military families may have felt privileged but, perhaps due to the extreme upheaval of the Great Depression, my military family didn't feel wealthy and was always careful with money.

Still, Robert J. Gordon tells us that, "In 1940, about 40% of homes had central heating, 60% had flush indoor toilets, 70% had running water, and 80% had electricity" (as in the Washington Post 01/18/16). Growing up in the military service, both my parents enjoyed all those modern comforts in military housing, and the occasional civilian quarters.

Like our last, our new home with my grandparents on Fort Sam Houston had all the modern conveniences. In addition, there were maids, drivers, cooks, orderlies, and gardeners. Some of them were white, some were black, and some were brown, and I was totally oblivious to differences in skin color. The kitchen where the children ate meals was large and always full of people taking good care of us.

Mom soon left by train, joining Dad in Seattle where they were together for a couple of weeks before he was ordered to New Orleans. Over the next five months, Mom followed Dad, only rarely reappearing in San Antonio. My sister was eight weeks old and I remember Pappy pacing the floor with her when she cried. I frowned a lot, and they began

13

to call me "hot cross Bun." But we adjusted, as Brats learn to do, and I was generally content with the loving attention from my grandparents, my aunts and "the help."

There were light moments recounted frequently over the years. One evening the adults were in the dining room when Jose, a dark-skinned Mexican, came in laughing. He said that while he had been feeding us in the kitchen, Pat had licked his finger and tried to clean the black off Jose's skin. He said he told Pat, "That ain't dirt, Sonny. It ain't gonna wash off!" That story always elicited loud guffaws for which Pat took proud credit.

Mom's sister, Danny, gave birth to a little girl shortly after we arrived. The new baby was named Elizabeth after Granny, quickly shortened to Lisbeth. Danny's husband, Eric, was serving on a mysterious assignment in the Caribbean. Mom's youngest sister, Tooty, was a teenager living at home.

Bobby, age 20, had recently married and was a Second Lieutenant stationed at Fort Bliss, Texas, with the last mounted unit in the Army, the First Cavalry. He had left the University of Virginia and joined the Army when it became clear that war was imminent. The First Cav would soon ship out for Australia to fight in New Guinea and throughout the Pacific before participating in the largest naval battle of the war. The Battle of Leyte Gulf regained the Philippines from the Japanese. They fought heroically and made it possible for Gen. Douglas MacArthur to keep his promise to return. Bobby's new wife, Mary Randolph Truscott, was also living with us for a time.

It was a full and bustling household, a worried household. The help cared for the children, and the adults talked about things we did not understand. For the next two years, Americans would not know whether this war could be won, or whether America was facing Europe's fate: bombs and Nazi occupation.

I remember the radio announcements and the serious faces as the adults gathered and listened. To this day, a high-pitched male voice with a certain tone and intensity brings back the memory of that mute, uncomprehending sense that something was terribly wrong and none of those I loved and trusted could fix it. Edward R. Murrow's Columbia radio news broadcasts, and those of the other war correspondents, were to become the background sounds of my life over the next three years.

Pappy, a fervent Republican, had isolationist sympathies, as did many other influential Americans, including Charles Lindbergh. Pappy later wrote that his major concern was that the American military was totally untrained and unprepared for war because the services had so quickly demobilized at the end of World War I. Pappy didn't believe that we could win another war in Europe. Dad told me later that the isolationists shut up after the bombing of Pearl Harbor and the country united behind the Allies in determination to defeat the Germans and the Japanese. Sixteen million signed up to fight, about 12 percent of the total population (135 million) of the United States in 1942. Eight million women joined the effort.

Orders to War

Several weeks after my Dad and all the aircraft in the 31st had arrived in Seattle, his commander decided to divide the Group into two organizations, equal in experience and numbers. On the flip of a coin, half the Group was assigned to fight in the Pacific with orders to New Guinea. That unit of the 31st took severe losses. Fortunately, the coin flip assigned Dad to the unit going to fight in Europe.

In March 1942, with Dad in the lead, his group took off to fly to New Orleans. Dad decided to fly due south over the mountains. When they arrived at what is now Edwards Air Force Base in southern California, there was panic. Reports had come in that our forces had spotted, and lost track of, a large Japanese Task Force off the West Coast. Suddenly his flight of eight P-39s was ordered to get weapons ready and launch as quickly as possible, fly west up to 30,000 feet, find the Japanese and bomb them. They never found the Japanese Task Force and concluded that the spotting was in error, a result of the hysteria sweeping the West Coast. The fear was not unfounded: a few weeks earlier, an attack by the Japanese on the coast near Santa Barbara had caused light damage but triggered panic among the population.

When the group arrived in New Orleans, they were instructed to crate the aircraft for shipment to Europe. The airfield in New Orleans was on Lake Pontchartrain. Aircraft had to take off over a dike, making take-offs rather "sporty," as Dad put it. While they waited for final orders, their mission was to patrol south of the Mississippi along the coast and watch for German subs. The Germans were raising havoc in the Atlantic and we feared that they might enter the Gulf of Mexico. While in New Orleans, Dad remembered hearing a rumor that a German submarine commander had come ashore and had been seen in the French Quarter. To tense Americans near the coasts, nothing seemed beyond the capabilities of the German subs. They had sunk 226 of the Allies' merchant ships in the first six months of 1942 and were laying mines at the mouth of the Chesapeake Bay.

Orders to pack the aircraft never came. Instead, the Group was ordered to fly to England. The P-39s were fitted with belly tanks and flew test flights over the Atlantic to see if it was feasible to make the trip. The plan was to fly to Labrador, Greenland, to Iceland and finally to Prestwick, Scotland. All the ground support equipment was loaded into C-47s and C-54s to ferry across the Atlantic. But days before they were to deploy, there was a report that the Japanese were planning to attack the Aleutian Islands. Plans to get the aircraft and pilots to England were scrapped. The B-17s and cargo aircraft that were going to carry the equipment and lead the P-39s to England were unloaded and deployed to the West Coast instead.

The unit was ordered to report to Grenier Field in Manchester, New Hampshire. Following a brief trip back to San Antonio in May 1942, Mom drove with three other wives to Buffalo. The wives had been told to wait in Buffalo for a call saying that they could join their husbands in New Hampshire. It was feared that German spies might be watching where wives traveled as a clue to their husbands' movements. Mom and her friends were apprehensive because they knew their husbands expected orders to Europe any minute. The call to the wives waiting in Buffalo finally came and they drove to New Hampshire to spend another five days with their husbands. Mom remembered that on the way, they were stopped by the police and ticketed for driving over 35 miles per hour, the speed limit due to gasoline rationing.

The top-secret orders came. The pilots of the 31st Fighter Group were to sail on a British ship to England. Because they would be a prime target for German subs, two passenger ships from the Peninsula Line would travel in convoy. The ships had been designated auxiliary cruisers and outfitted with guns fore and aft. The holds of the ships were filled with ping pong balls so that if they were torpedoed, they wouldn't sink immediately, giving passengers a chance for survival. The ship that the 31st was to travel on was the Rampura. The other ship was the Queen of India, which carried the Canadians destined to make the disastrous raid on Dieppe where more than 4,000 men were killed, wounded or taken prisoner.

As final preparations were made for the journey, Mom and her friends left New Hampshire hoping for another chance to be with their husbands in New York City before the farewell. Mom and Dad had agreed on a signal if Dad was ordered to sail for Europe. He was to call and say, "I ran into Bunny, Pat and Mary the other day. They want to see you very badly."

Before their husbands could join them for a last hurrah, the signal telephone call came at the hotel where they were staying. When two of the wives collapsed in hysterical sobs, Mom angrily shushed them, fearing that a spy might hear and guess that their husbands were on their way to Europe. Sad and silent, they went to breakfast and then headed south by car from New York. They dropped one woman off in Memphis, and another in New Orleans. Mom took a train from Little Rock to San Antonio, and the fourth woman drove on from there to her family in Enid, Oklahoma. Little did my parents know that the five days in New Hampshire were to be their last time together for three long years.

Moving to Civilian Quarters: October 1942

We spent almost a year living with my grandparents at Fort Sam. My mother, her two sisters, and four children under four filled the spacious quarters. The children played and the adults worried.

In the fall, the Army ordered Pappy to Dallas, assigned to the Army's Eighth Corps Headquarters, Office of the Inspector General. Granny and Pappy asked us all to come with them as they would again be assigned large quarters, but Mom decided to stay in San Antonio. In retrospect, I think I would have been happier with my grandparents, and maybe Pat and Mary would have been also, for the stress on my mother would have been reduced.

So Mom had to find a place to live. There were few rentals, so she decided to buy a house. The only money she had to make the purchase was $2,000 in war bonds. She found a house at 215 Young Street (renamed Claiborne Way), in Alamo Heights, but when she went to the bank to close the deal, she was told that she could not cash the bonds without Dad's signature. They would make no exception. She wrote a desperate letter to the Secretary of the Treasury, Henry Morgenthau, Jr., who quickly responded giving her permission to cash the bonds. She remembered that the bank manager was stunned when she returned with a letter from the Secretary.

Our family suddenly shrank. We were an anxious single mother with two small children and a baby still in diapers. Mom bought a Great Dane who was not friendly. She said she didn't want a friendly dog, she wanted protection. The dog's name was Freya, and I never grew attached to her.

I don't know whether Mom had a gun in the house, but I certainly thought she did. I have a crystal-clear memory of her pointing it out the upstairs bedroom window one night at a man who was standing in the front yard yelling, while we three cowered in the background. But Mom insisted that never happened. Apparently, I had overheard her telling a friend what she would do if a drunk came around and bothered us. My active child's imagination had created the scene, or maybe I dreamed it.

I missed Dad, longed for his return, and believed that only his return could bring laughter and joy back into our lives. I paced up and down the hall in our little house, repeating my mantra, a prayer before I had learned how to pray, "Daddy come home. Daddy come home. Daddy come home!" I remember those days as bleak and filled with my silent worrying. I was timid and shy, and I'm sure I didn't speak up about what was on my mind, and Mom had too much on her mind to notice.

In December 1942, four months after Mom had received word of Dad's downing and capture, she finally received a letter from him. His letter makes clear that he was unaware that Mom knew that he was a prisoner of war. He is very concerned about that and about his not having received any letters from her. He writes:

> *Have patience my love. Wars never last forever, and although sometimes the news is not encouraging, we all expect to be home soon. Remember, do not worry*

19

about me ever. The only thing that concerns me is whether or not you are aware of the fact that I am alive and in good health. If you think the war will last long enough to justify it, please send me some books on American history. I desire to prepare myself to raise our children to be intensely patriotic and good citizens. Obtain the "Warsaw Concerto" and think of me when you play it. There is, I believe, a message in it for you.

Mom found a recording of "The Warsaw Concerto" and played it over and over, trying to find some hidden message. When Dad came home three years later, he reassured her that the message was simply the beauty and emotion in the music itself. Someone in the POW camp had a recording and the Germans often played it over a loudspeaker. It always brings tears to my eyes.

All of Dad's letters from the prison camp, Stalag Luft III, and our family's memorabilia from those tumultuous war years, are in the Air Force Academy Library. It is a treasure trove of our family's history during that time and includes, in addition to Dad's letters, some of my mother's letters and family photographs.

Many families of servicemen fighting the war were living in San Antonio, and the wives soon established a support network, talking on the telephone and meeting frequently. Dad was the first American Army Air Corps pilot to be shot down and taken prisoner by the Germans after the U.S. entered the War. As more Americans were taken prisoner in Germany and Japan, Mom became active in a support group for those whose husbands, sons, and brothers were in enemy prison camps. She and other families of POWs were often interviewed by interested newspaper and magazine reporters. The photo on the next page and an accompanying story appeared in a San Antonio newspaper in 1944. I think you can

The worry shows on our faces in this 1944 photo.

see the anxiety on all of our faces, though Mom is trying to put on a brave smile.

Working with Bea Patton, Gen. George Patton's daughter, Mom formed an organization called "Relatives of POWs" with chapters in Washington and in San Antonio, the two locations with the largest number of prisoners' relatives. They published a newsletter for all relatives of POWs being held in Germany and Japan, sharing information of general interest from POWs' letters. Germany allowed relatives to write three letters and four postcards a month to POWs. Writers had to use pencil so that our military censors could easily black out any information that was deemed inappropriate. The POWs' letters home were also limited and censored by the Germans. There were no letters to or from the POWs in Japan.

In the early days, most of the prisoners of war being held in Germany were British, and they were receiving care packages through the Red Cross. The American prisoners received nothing. Mom began working with the Red Cross to allow families to send care packages to the American prisoners. When they were finally allowed, Mom went twice a week to the Red Cross to help wrap packages that included cigarettes, soap, chocolate, powdered eggs, powdered milk and vitamins.

When Dad arrived in England, he was trained in a code that would be used if he were captured and became a POW. After his capture, all his letters to Mom were decoded before they were forwarded to her. When the American POWs finally began receiving packages, a top-secret organization located in Ft. Hunt, Virginia, called MIS-X coordinated with code-trained POWs through these coded letters. Techniques and tools to help the POWs escape and evade were developed. MIS-X staff hid such tools, cameras, film, compasses and radios in game boards, pipes and food. *The Escape Factory*, by Lloyd R. Shoemaker, who worked in MIS-X for the duration of the war, describes these activities. Dad never discussed this part of his experience because it was highly classified. All MIS-X records at Ft. Hunt were destroyed within days of the Japanese surrender.

One of the biggest issues facing the POWs' families was the disparity between the treatment of the POWs in Germany and those in Japan. Mom told me about one meeting when the mother of a POW being held by the Japanese became angry with her because she felt that the group was not paying sufficient attention to the more desperate plight of prisoners in Japan. Mom was in tears when another mother of a POW held in Japan spoke in her defense. Mom remembered sadly the news that came much later. The son of the first woman died. The son of the second eventually returned home.

In a lengthy interview I held with Mom shortly before she died, she spoke with gratitude of the many people who helped her during those difficult years. When she discovered that her roof leaked, a roofer gave her a new roof for the cost of minor repairs. When the car began to rust, the service station down the road patched and painted the car for $200 instead of the original estimate of $1,000. Americans were all in the war together, buying war bonds, cursing the Nazis, cheering on the Allies, turning in their bacon fat and aluminum foil for ration tickets to use to buy food and even for toothpaste. They were glued to their radios as the Allies landed in Africa, Italy, and finally in June 1944, on the coast of Normandy. The whole country listened with bated breath as the Allies slowly and painfully advanced, from the east, south and west, toward Germany.

Critters, Accidents and Misadventures. With these important concerns occupying much of Mom's time and many of her thoughts, she was often away during the day and we were left with a disparate array of sitters. On one of those days, a Mexican woman who spoke no English was caring for us and walking around the yard with us. I noticed what looked like a string of colorful beads coiled around the base of a tree, partially obscured by fallen leaves. I reached down to pick it up. The sitter started screaming in Spanish and running toward the house. Pat and Mary hesitated momentarily before following her. With my hand poised to grab it, I realized that I was being left alone and didn't know why. I regretfully left the beads behind and followed them as they fled.

When Mom came home, I learned that the colorful "beads" were a coral snake, plentiful in Texas, and very poisonous. Mom changed clothes and called a handyman who had worked for Pappy at Fort Sam. I remember the three of us kids, noses glued to the screen door that opened into the back yard, watching as they paced around the yard looking for that snake. They found it, killed it with a hoe and showed it to us before hanging it on the fence.

After our discovery of the coral snake, Pat decided to put poison around the yard to prevent any further incursions by such dangerous critters. He persuaded me to help him collect piles of Freya's poop in a bucket, into which we were to pee. I declined, but Pat emptied his bladder into the bucket, and we stirred the concoction with a stick before carefully pouring it around the perimeter of the back yard. Pat was satisfied with his ingenious solution to the problem when we saw no further snakes.

I never developed a fear of snakes. I did, however, develop a phobia about cockroaches. Texas cockroaches are huge and dark and many of them lived in the basement of that house where the washing machine and laundry sink were located. If a maid had not been there for a while and Mom had to do laundry, she would station me on the stairs to watch for cockroaches as she pulled the clothes out of the washer and put them through the wringer before taking them outside to hang on the clothesline. I was to warn her whenever I saw one. I wasn't very good at that task, losing interest and thinking of other things. I failed to warn her one day when a particularly large cockroach was crawling on the wall right above her head as she bent over the laundry tub. When she looked up and saw it, not having been warned of its menacing approach, I was soundly scolded and sent to my room.

By now I was five years old and, as the oldest, Mom depended on me to be her helper. I strived mightily to meet her expectations but simply was not up to the task. I was a dreamer, disappointing her over and over again. My sister, a sweet, impressionable toddler, noticed that I was always in hot water and must have decided that I was a bad girl. She went after me, mimicking Mom's scolding, slaps and spankings. Pat quietly watched and tried to stay clear of Mom when she was upset.

As I think back to those years, I feel deep compassion for all well-meaning little kids who try so hard to please the all-powerful, all-knowing, and often struggling and preoccupied adults upon whom they depend: a universal story of childhood. And the universal story of old age is adults looking back with regret for the lost opportunities to simply cherish their children. Just before she died, Mom sadly mentioned a particularly harsh slap and how hard she was on me during that difficult time. I quickly told her that I understood completely what a terrible time the war years had been for her, and that I had long since forgiven her.

Not only were Texas cockroaches plentiful and large, but there were also tarantulas, wasps, hornets, red ants, chiggers, ticks and prickly heat. We had them all! Chiggers are tiny insects that burrow under the skin and itch ferociously. I remember the terrible chigger itch that lasted all summer, and the stinging burn of the prickly heat rash that inevitably circled our necks, under our arms, and between our legs.

The aroma that filled the house in the summer was of the dank, musty, wet basement. It wafted up the stairs, hovered inside, begging for a breeze to find the open windows. In my childhood memory it was always summer in Texas. I remember no balmy springs, no brisk colorful falls or snowy winters. Only humid, hot, breathless summers provide the context for my memories of those four years in Texas. The difficulties of childhood often make a stronger impression in our memory files. They are sharply recorded in bold and italics, unlike the more frequent days of quiet contentment.

We played hide and seek in the house when we tired of the hot, smelly back yard. One day, I ran into the only bathroom, shut and locked the door. When Pat found me, he complained to Mom who commanded that I open the door at once. I tried, but I couldn't turn the lock and open the door. I put towels in the tub and determined that I would be fine because I had water to drink, a potty, and could sleep in the tub. Through the door, I suggested that they could all find a bush in the back yard when they needed to pee. Mom panicked and called the fire department. A fire truck came into the yard, and a long ladder was propped against the side of the house. I watched a fireman climb up the ladder, open the window, and laboriously hoist himself through it. He quickly and easily unlocked the door, sighed, and gave me a disgusted look.

Pat and I were sick frequently. He suffered bouts of croup, and I suffered ear infections. Mom found a woman doctor named Dr. Bonnet who provided the support and encouragement she so badly needed. The fact that I remember the doctor's name is an indication of how important she was to my mother. The ear infections were terribly painful. Although they discussed double mastoid operations, I fortunately avoided surgery. I remember Mom lighting a match under a teaspoon full of mineral oil, warming the oil, and dropping it into my ear with an eye dropper, often in the middle of the night. Fortunately, Dr. Bonnet did not recommend the latest treatment for repeated ear infections. Mom's younger cousin, Betty Cobb, had radium capsules inserted in her ears to end her infections. Betty died of cancer as a young woman, leaving her small children orphans.

One day I was waiting outside the Fort Sam Houston PX while Mom shopped. I was alone, singing quietly to myself and watching a blond young man dressed in grey clothing who was working on the grounds. He began to talk to me in heavily accented English, and I tried to understand and respond. We talked awhile, until Mom came out, angrily grabbed me and pulled me toward the car. When I later heard her describe this incident, I learned that he was a German POW.

Rationing During the War. Food was a big issue for us during the war. Meat was rationed and there wasn't much food around that I liked. I was frail and puny and ate mostly under duress. My child's memory reports that we always had spinach for lunch and corn meal mush for supper. I'm sure that is not true. But I remember throwing up in my bowl at the dinner table on more than one occasion and sitting for hours in the kitchen with a wad of chewed food ballooned in my cheek, gagging often and loudly.

We lined up in the evenings after our corn meal mush, and Mom gave each of us a large tablespoon full of cod liver oil. We had to stand there until a wide-open mouth attested to the fact that we'd swallowed it. I still remember how it tasted and running to the bathroom to rinse my mouth out after I'd swallowed the foul stuff. Because I was so sickly, someone told Mom that I needed goats' milk. She went out in search of a farm with goats and brought some milk home, which was offered with a wheedling voice. I didn't like it and she soon gave up on that remedy.

Gasoline cost 18 cents a gallon in 1940, but there wasn't much available during the War, so we didn't get out for car rides very often. When we did it was a special event. We had an old dark blue Pontiac with running boards, no seat belts, and no automatic turn signals or brake lights. Rain or shine, when a turn was coming up, Mom rolled down the window and put her arm out to signal a turn: straight out meant a left turn, arm out and raised toward the roof from the elbow meant a right turn, and arm down with hand turned back toward the cars behind meant that she was slowing down or stopping.

Mom left us in the car while she shopped. One day, as she shopped in the Piggly Wiggly, a woman in the parking space next to us scraped our fender as she backed out. She quickly looked at the damage to our car and fled. Ever the responsible eldest, I ran into the grocery store and told Mom who came out with fury in her eyes and called the woman a bitch. I think I remember that incident because I'd never heard that word and didn't know what it meant.

Shopping for new shoes was a special, once-a-year event. We each had a ration card, which we needed to buy shoes and many other commodities. I think we were each allowed one pair of shoes a year. They were brown leather high-top Buster Brown lace-ups and were bought with plenty of extra toe room. Every shoe store had an X-ray machine to allow proper sizing. We would put on new shoes and stand with our feet inside the machine, looking down through a glass window to see the bones of our feet inside the shoes to make sure they fit properly. And while the rest of the kids were being fitted, we could stand with our feet in the machine admiring our bones and wiggling our toes. I'm not sure when such cavalier use of X-rays was determined to be dangerous, but the machines disappeared soon after the war ended.

Fat, for some reason, was important to the war effort. All bacon fat had to be carefully collected in cans to be turned in for ration tickets. It was very mysterious, but we knew it was important. The aluminum foil wrappings inside packages of cigarettes were also saved, rolled up into balls and turned in. Everything seemed to be saved. "Waste not, want not," we were told, "Use it up, wear it out, make it do, or do without!" Maybe it was the war rationing or maybe it was because our parents and grandparents had experienced the Great Depression, but we were a thrifty bunch and some of us still are in small, weird ways.

My Best Friend. Pat was my best friend. I loved him, played with him, made him laugh and took his toys away with impunity until one day he protested by hitting me over the head with a Lincoln Log. My sense of superiority was offended but I took a lesson from it: "We're in this together, Pat and I." There were no more squabbles between us from that day on.

Bunny (me) and Pat have a tea party.

Pat sucked his thumb and twirled a cowlick that stuck up at the crown of his head. Another cowlick swept fine red hairs from his forehead up into his hairline. I admired his easy-going nature. He was adventurous and he was fun-

28

ny, he never hurt us and didn't pout from hurt feelings. He was a born comic and excelled at making people laugh. He had an uncanny way of recognizing and enjoying the small ironies in life. Pat had a peculiar habit of putting himself to sleep by rocking back and forth, sometimes against the wall next to his bed, making a racket. I was used to hearing this rhythmic banging and only woke up if I heard a hollered, "Pat, stop rocking!" There would be silence of a minute or two, but then he'd begin again more quietly.

Pat and I were frequently left to our own devices, playing alone on a linoleum floor in the bedroom upstairs, or in a bramble-filled, weedy, dusty back yard, where we often unsuccessfully dodged piles of Freya's poop. We had no friends except each other, and we never left the yard. The neighborhood was rural; a small farm was just on the other side of the rusty wire fence. There were chickens and horses, and an occasional tractor or dump truck.

Pat was always drawn to big machines and thrilled at the sight of a dump truck. When asked what he wanted to be when he grew up, he would invariably reply, "A dump truck driver!" a response greeted with great hilarity. The laughter pleased and perplexed him. He wasn't sure why it was so funny. Maybe he just wasn't up to acquiring such remarkable skills? But he was determined. He would smile, raise his eyebrows and his chin, and look sideways indicating his determination, and declare, "I'll show 'em." And did he ever!

Pat and I were trundled off to kindergarten at the same time, and my only clear memory of my first school is when a little red-headed boy named Zachary derisively announced that, "There is no Santa Claus, you silly! It's your mother and father who give you the presents." I tearfully disagreed and went right to Mom when I got home, asking for her assurance that what he had told me was untrue. She shushed me and told me that this was a secret that I must keep from Pat and Mary since I was the oldest. I was quite downhearted at this revelation, but I kept the secret.

29

Our wringer washing machine was the top of the line in those days and was interesting to watch. After soaping and scrubbing the dirty clothes on the washboard, Mom loaded them into the washing machine to be rinsed. Then she lifted the dripping clothes and carefully fed them into the electric wringer mechanism, two rubber rollers rolling toward each other. The clothes came out the other side flat, no longer dripping, then dropped into a laundry basket placed underneath.

One day, Mom was outside hanging up the wash and had left the wringer turned on. My curious little brother stood on tip toes and put his finger onto the surface of the wringer. Into the wringer went his finger, his hand, and then his arm. Mom came in to find him dangling from the wringer up to his arm pit, his feet several inches above the ground. Pat was whimpering and struggling. I heard Mom's exclamation of alarm and came running down the basement stairs just in time to see her reverse the wringer, which then slowly turned in the opposite direction and dropped Pat to the floor.

This mishap resulted in a trip to the hospital at Fort Sam Houston. There the doctors decided to admit Pat to the men's ward where Pappy was undergoing his retirement physical. Pat was about four years old and entertained the guys on the ward, keeping them laughing for the next couple of days. The doctors finally reluctantly sent him home, reluctantly because he was raising the morale of the many wounded troops on the ward.

Pappy Retires. About two years after my grandparents left for Dallas, Pappy retired from the Army. They returned to San Antonio with Danny, Lizbeth and Tooty. Granny fondly remembered the farm in Connecticut they'd lived on when she was a teenager, so they bought a small farm with a frame house outside the city. There was a sand box and a swing that hung from a huge oak tree out front. They kept a horse and little chickens called pullets. I remember collecting eggs with

Granny. Sunday dinners were in the middle of the day. We would sit around the table watching Pappy carve a roast or a turkey. The days after my grandparents returned to San Antonio were full of companionship with those who loved us. The fear for my prisoner-of-war father faded. The news reported daily that Gen. Patton was advancing farther into Germany and I sensed optimism in the family.

Mom said that Pappy had been a harsh disciplinarian when she and her siblings were young. Granny once said that she wished Pappy had had as much patience with his children as he had with horses. Although he mellowed with the years, he was never able to establish a warm relationship with his son, Bobby. Trouble between military fathers and their sons seems to be fairly common. I saw it often among my military Brat friends, and it was certainly reflected in the three generations of my own family.

But to us, his grandchildren, Pappy was a kind and loving grandfather, although an irascible driver. Our few trips in the car with him were punctuated with comments such as, "He ought to be horse-whipped!" and with epithets yelled at fellow drivers, the most benign being "scoundrel, "gutter-snipe," and "skunk." At that, I would look around with great expectations of seeing a skunk coming down the road. And I've never figured out what a "guttersnipe" is.

The closeness of this family, which I remember with some nostalgia, formed the blueprint in my mind of what a family should be; big, laughing, loving and supportive. When the three Wilbourn sisters got together there was often hilarious laughter emanating from the kitchen as they washed dishes and talked. The sisters shared a laugh, a rather raucous cackle. Today, when I hear such laughter, sometimes my own, I am reminded of Mom and her two sisters.

They would sing together some of the popular songs of the day. The most puzzling was a song entitled, "Mairzy Doats and Dozy Doats." It was years before I learned that the song was a playful way of saying, "Mares Eat Oats and Does Eat

31

Oats." It goes on: ". . .and little lambs eat ivy. A kid'll eat ivy too, wouldn't you?" I still find it puzzling, along with another topic of conversation. They often teased Pappy, and I remember the teasing and laughter about Pappy conducting "short-arm inspections," which I thought must have something to do with short weapons of some sort. When Mom explained many years later, I was left with a raunchy and bizarre image still in my memory files.

I was always close to Danny. I remember her using the newspaper to teach me to read. She also took me to church and to my first movie, "Snow White and the Seven Dwarves." By that time, her husband had written and asked for a divorce. Danny decided that he would never see Lisbeth again, and gave him the divorce. He later married an Army Brat who gave him four fine sons and supported his successful military career. He retired a full colonel, and Lisbeth did see him again before he died. Years later, Danny finally remarried, a much-older friend of Pappy's, Marion Knight.

Bobby's wife, Mary, had left San Antonio some months after Pearl Harbor and moved to New York City, where she worked as a secretary. An Army Brat, she was the only daughter of General Lucian K. Truscott, who led the allied forces in North Africa, and at the landings in Sicily and Anzio. Mary never communicated with her in-laws during those years. We later learned that she never wrote to Bobby, either, during his nearly two years in combat. He confided years later that he came home wounded in spirit as a result of seeing his buddies receive V-letters from wives and sweethearts while he received none from Mary. He did receive many letters from his parents and sisters. After he returned from the war, Bobby and Mary reconciled and lived together for another ten years before divorcing.

The last letter I have from Mom to Dad's sister, Mary, was dated December 18, 1944:

Here it is almost Christmas again, and I was so sure Bub would be home this year by now. This makes the fourth Christmas without him. That's a lot of Christmases for him to miss with his family. I just hope we can somehow make up for it all someday . . . one more bleak Christmas in Germany . . . it's been so long now I wonder if it will ever, ever end, but surely this next year will see the end at least in Europe and I just don't look any farther than Bub's return now.

Four months later, Mom dreamed that my father told her he would be home soon. Within days, the news came that Gen. Patton had liberated the huge prisoner of war camp at Moosburg in Bavaria where Dad had spent the last months of his imprisonment. Most of the POWs in Germany had been marched through heavy snow and freezing temperatures to Spremberg the previous winter, then put on squalid boxcars, packed together so tightly that they couldn't sit. Over several days and nights, they traveled to Moosburg, where Hitler had planned to use them as hostages. Many died on that journey.

Daddy Comes Home: May 1945
Although I don't remember Mom saying so, I must have overheard a joyful conversation because I knew that some momentous event had occurred, and that my Daddy would be home soon. But it took almost three weeks for him to find his way from Bavaria, across Europe to Paris, finally to New Hampshire, and back down to San Antonio. Mom received a telegram in June from the War Department saying that Dad had been returned to Allied Control. By that time, he had been home for several days.

Dad flew from Paris to New Hampshire and found a ride to Kelly Field near San Antonio. A generous WAC drove him from the flight line to our house. Mom had dressed us in our Sunday best and lined us up on the front porch. We watched expectantly as Dad climbed out of a military staff car in full uniform, put on his hat, and grabbed a duffle bag from the back seat. I could hardly contain the impulse to run toward him and grab his leg, hoping for a toss in the air.

For some reason, Mom had turned the sprinkler on to water an unkempt front lawn. I watched quivering with excitement as he hesitated momentarily, then ran right through the sprinkler and embraced Mom. I looked up at this father that I had longed for so helplessly, whom I had prayed for before I knew of either prayer or God. He didn't look like anyone I'd ever seen before in my life. "He will hug me," I had thought, "and throw me up in the air with the joy and happy laughter I remembered in my dreams." My beloved Daddy had been full of wide smiles and exuberant energy. But this was not the Daddy who had left me, and I was not the toddler he'd left behind.

My disappointment was overshadowed by my concerted effort to hide the fact that I hadn't recognized him. He rather awkwardly patted us each on the head after his long embrace of my mother. My sister ran under the baby grand piano with a scowl on her face and hid. For our little family, everything had changed.

Although I had spent hours looking at Dad's black-and-white photo, I had no memory of how tall he was, or of his red hair. When he came home, he was rail thin, gaunt, and hungry, very hungry. My mother had prepared a banquet. We sat together at the dining room table, and I eyed the pile of lima beans on my plate with dismay. Within a few minutes I was predictably gagging between tears, as he urged us to clean our plates. "There are so many hungry people in the world," he scolded, "especially where I just came from!"

Finally, Dad told me to come to the head of the table where he sat. Not knowing what he was going to do, maybe force the food into my mouth, I walked slowly in fear and trembling. He quickly scraped my plate onto his and began to devour the lima beans and everything else that had been on my plate, except the chicken bones. My brother tentatively stood up and followed me. Then came Mary. Dad licked his lips and, with a huge grin and exaggerated gusto, dug in and cleaned the plates in quick order before asking for more. He ate all our scraps and leftovers for months.

We had cleaned all the chicken off the bones when Dad instructed us to bite the ends off the bones and suck out the marrow. He demonstrated, licking his lips and loudly proclaiming, "Yum, yum, yum." This began a family ritual, carefully followed when we were served chicken, whether we were at home or in a restaurant. We must have been a sight, little kids chomping the ends off chicken bones. If we were in a restaurant, Mom would look around and blush. When she saw that we were being watched, she'd mutter, "People must think we're starving these children!"

My sister spent much of the next several days under the piano eyeing with great suspicion this stranger who had suddenly walked into our lives. Her close connection to Mom

The Clark family reunited after Dad came home from the war.

suddenly changed as Mom turned all her attention and affection toward Dad. This must have been a shock to Mary, who was only four and had enjoyed the extra attention and love that is often lavished on the baby of the family. Pat had no memory of Dad and accepted his return with amiable curiosity.

I watched Dad with an intense and discerning eye, learning to brush my teeth the same way he did, drinking water to rinse my mouth from a cupped hand instead of a glass. I lifted my cereal bowl up and slurped the milk down. I watched his every expression, mimicking his laugh, his walk and his way of climbing the stairs, two at a time. I couldn't jump that far yet, but the day would come.

Dad quickly bought many cans of Spam and large tins of KLIM (milk spelled backwards and powdered), which were in the Red Cross parcels he'd received during his imprisonment. He was not successful in convincing us to love these items as much as he did, so he devoured all of it by himself.

An Adventure on the Way to the Beautiful Sea. After a month at home in San Antonio, Dad was ordered to a military installation near Fort Lauderdale for top-secret debriefing. It may have been at this time that he provided material that would be used in the Nuremburg Trials. Mom's uncle, Evelyn Cobb, made their cottage in Fort Lauderdale available to us for a month and we drove down to Florida in the old blue Pontiac. We had a flat tire somewhere between Lafayette and Lake Charles, Louisiana. Dad quickly changed to the spare but within a couple of minutes back on the road that tire also went flat. I remember the incident well because Mom was so upset, and I quickly realized that we were alone on the side of the road a long way from the nearest town.

Dad got us all out of the car, lined us up by the side of the road in order of our heights, reflecting his flair for order and maybe a sense of humor about our predicament. He showed us how to put out our thumbs to hitch a ride. When an old pickup approached, he ordered, "Thumbs up and out!" The pickup stopped, and Mom warily eyed the unsavory-looking driver. Offering his thanks, Dad cheerfully climbed into the front seat while the rest of us crowded in the back. Mom told me years later that she noticed a tire iron on the floor in the back and picked it up in order to be ready for the mugging she fully expected. Happily, we were delivered to a large old Victorian house with a wrap-around porch and a sign in the front yard that read "Rooms to Let."

Dad walked down the street to the tire store and tried to buy tires. He was quickly told that if he didn't have any ration tickets, he was out of luck. The war was still on. He came back and informed Mom of the situation. I heard her sigh and mutter that we'd be spending a long time here. I chose a comfortable rocking chair on the porch and prepared for this to be home for a while.

Then Dad went to the filling station across the street and began to tell his story, "I'm a POW from the war in Europe, on my way to a TDY assignment with my wife and three small children, two flat tires, no ration tickets." A man standing nearby overheard his story and said, "Sir, you go right back to that tire store and tell Mr. Whatever his name was that Mr. Hudgins said to sell you two tires right now, and you won't need no ration tickets!" Dad bought the tires, and someone gave him a ride back out to the car, helped him put the two new tires on, and we were on our way to Florida again in the morning.

I clearly remember that joyful month in Florida. Mom was happy and laughing again, and it was the first time I saw the ocean. I loved everything about it, but particularly swimming in the surf and sun. I can still summon, in quiet moments, that feeling of freedom and joy swimming in the light-filled waves.

While we were in Florida, Dad taught us to pray the "Our Father," the "Hail Mary," and the "Salve Regina," the prayer that he said had gotten him through the four long years that he had been away from us. It goes like this:

> *Hail holy queen, mother of mercy, our life our sweetness and our hope. To thee do we cry, poor banished children of Eve. To thee do we send up our sighs, mourning and weeping in this vale of tears. Turn then most gracious advocate your eyes of mercy towards us, . . .*

The Country Rejoices. We ate out frequently in Florida and Dad dubbed our favorite restaurant "Brown's Eat Joint." He always wore his uniform when we went out. I don't think he had any civilian clothes that fit him, or that he considered proper attire for eating out. One evening we were eating dinner at Brown's. A radio was on, mounted high up on a wall. Suddenly a news announcement boomed throughout the restaurant. I watched, astonished, as people jumped up out of their chairs. Some were weeping; many came over to my father and shook his hand or saluted. Dad smiled broadly and told us to stand at attention behind our chairs and showed us how to put our hands over our hearts. He held a salute as the strains of "The Star-Spangled Banner" filled the restaurant.

I wondered why there was so much excitement, and so many tears. Well, it was August 15, 1945, Victory in Japan (VJ) Day. Dad must have explained that the Japanese had surrendered, and the War in the Pacific was over, but I didn't understand. For me, the war was over when he came home.

Moving on With Our Lives. When our stay in Florida ended, we drove back to San Antonio. In the fall, I was outfitted in a school uniform--a dark green skirt and white blouse--and sent off to second grade at Incarnate Word School. Not having been indoctrinated in Catholic ritual, I was mystified by the frequent recitation of prayers I didn't know. I began piano lessons with a kindly nun who taught me the rudiments of reading music. I clearly remember the moment when the music notes on the page began to make sense.

Dad was away more than he was home for the next few months. He eagerly looked forward to flying again but needed re-training to become proficient. When he was home, he would take us to Mass on Sundays. That's when I learned of a terrible disease. Polio was claiming 50,000 victims annually, many of them children, leaving them crippled if they didn't die.

On the way to Mass, we would often pick up Mrs. Kimball, a friend of my parents, married to one of Dad's best friends. One Sunday, she had trouble walking and needed to lean on my father for balance. She complained that she had not been feeling well for several days. The next day she was diagnosed with polio and sent away to a sanitarium where she stayed for the next three years. She walked laboriously with crutches and a leg brace for the rest of her long life. For those who didn't experience the scourge of polio, it's hard to imagine what a hero Jonas Salk was when he developed a vaccine against it in 1955.

In February 1946 Dad received orders to report to Barksdale Field, Louisiana. I remember walking through the house on Young Street after it had been emptied of all our belongings. My footsteps echoed across the bare floors. I saw marks on the walls where pictures had hung, dust on the baseboards behind where furniture had stood, gouges on the hardwood floors, and marks where wet galoshes had rested beside the front door. It was no longer a home, our home. It was just an empty house and I was not sad to leave it.

My father came upstairs and saw me reflecting on the empty rooms. Without further ado, I heard his oft-repeated command, "Attennnnn-shun, fall in troops, forward march! Hut, two, three, four!" I marched down the stairs and happily out to the waiting car.

Walking empty rooms became a ritual over the ensuing years, a necessary step in saying good-bye to a place.

My walk-throughs marked an ending and a preparation for moving forward to a new home. I have slowly walked through so many empty houses--no longer familiar once they were empty, but still the locations of important memories. I wonder if there are bits of my DNA still scattered in cracks and crevices of houses around the world.

Over the years, I would file my memories by location, a more accessible cue than date. We moved so often during the next ten years that we came to remember *where* we were when specific events took place and were much less sure exactly *when* they had taken place. As Pat Conroy, also a military Brat, wrote, "My wound is geography. It is also my anchorage, my port of call." And so it has been.

A new beginning lay ahead. The moving van drove away packed with our belongings, and we ventured into the unknown with little concern for all we left behind. We looked forward to the adventure, confident that somehow it would all be fine despite the sadness at leaving Granny and Pappy, and Danny and Lisbeth. I didn't know how little I would see of them over the remaining years of my childhood. For the next thirty years of my life, I would not live in any one place for as long as the four years and two months we lived in San Antonio.

Chapter Two
Reporting for Duty, Sir!

On the Road

We left San Antonio in February and drove to Barksdale Field, near Shreveport, packed into the old blue Pontiac now referred to as "Car Clark." The car wouldn't go much faster than 45 miles per hour. When we stopped for the night, we slept in our clothes. Mom and Dad would carry us out to the car before dawn, still sleeping. Dad liked to get an early start, so we watched many sunrises from the back seat as we sped along trying to make time ahead of the traffic.

How many hundreds of hours have I ridden back and forth across our beautiful country, passing through small towns and cities, across the prairies and over the mountains! I was always intrigued by the abandoned houses, surrounded by trees that had been planted for shade, shutters hanging askew, broken windows open to the elements and the imagination. I would compose stories in my head about the families that had lived there, and wonder what had driven them away, and to where. There were clues: an old tire hanging from a rope tied over a low-hanging branch meant that children had surely lived there. A rusty old truck leaning on three tires; a broken plow; a hand-lettered for-sale sign slouching toward the street; a small clump of trees apart from the house, maybe shading an ice- house, an outdoor privy or a few fallen gravestones. My musings happily occupied me for many hours.

We would compete for permission to ride in the back window well where there was just enough room for one of us to lie down. We had picture books, coloring books and crayons, and nothing else to entertain us. Dad had no patience for frequent potty breaks. We had a white enamel potty with a handle, a necessary part of our travel gear. We would each take a turn when nature called, an easy feat for my brother, but trickier for my sister and me. When we had filled the potty, Mom would roll down the window and quickly empty it as we sped along. No matter how far she tried to thrust it out the window before dumping it, pee always splashed back along the side of the car. I remember more than one filling station attendant asking, "What's that splashed along the side of your car? It don't look like mud!" We would suppress grins and listen for our parents' vague responses. "Not sure what that could be," they'd say.

Learning About Military Life
Dad stopped the car when we arrived at the front gate of Barksdale Field and I watched, hugely impressed, when the soldier at the gate saluted him and he saluted back. We moved into a large set of brick quarters down the street from the Officers' Club.

Although Mom had never allowed us to leave our yard in San Antonio, we had the run of the Post at Barksdale. Everyone believed the Post to be a safe environment for children to roam. But Mom and Dad solemnly announced that we'd better behave because if we didn't, it would always get back to Dad's boss. Reports of our misbehavior would be certain to ruin Dad's career. To ruin our father's career would be one of the worst things we could do, and we shuddered thinking about the punishment this would incur. We learned that we must never, ever create a scene in public. We were not to draw attention to ourselves except by our polite and obedient behavior. If something didn't go our way, we were to "suck it up."

We started back to school the end of February. I remember nothing about school in Louisiana, perhaps because there were so many other new experiences overwhelming me. We spent the summer, as we did most of the summers of my childhood, at the Officers' Club swimming pool. In a letter that I wrote to Granny and Pappy in May

1946, I reported that: "Daddy says to tell you how big and fat and brown I am and how my teeth are coming in."

When it rained in Louisiana, it poured buckets. One day, in the middle of a deluge, Dad told us to put on our bathing suits and come outside. He was in his bathing suit, with a bar of soap. He ran out into the yard and started soaping himself all over, taking a shower in the rain. We followed his example, running around whooping and shrieking with joy while Mom watched from the kitchen door. "Come on, Sweetie! God's giving us a free shower!" Dad urged. It was a joyful moment. I wonder whether this was a replay of the best showers Dad had enjoyed in the prison camp.

The sacred rituals of life on a military installation quickly became an important part of our daily lives. We heard a distant bugle announcing Reveille in the early morning. At five minutes before 5:00 every afternoon, a bugler sounded "Colors." Then we heard a cannon roar, the bugle call for "Retreat," and the "Star Spangled Banner" played as uniformed soldiers lowered the American flag on the parade grounds. This ceremony was followed by the bugler playing "Carry On."

If we were outside playing in the late afternoon when we heard the bugle, we immediately stood at attention with our hands over our hearts. If we were in a moving car, the driver pulled to the side of the road until the music stopped. If Dad was with us and in uniform, he got out of the car and held a salute. Near bedtime, we could sometimes hear Taps from the direction of the barracks.

My parents had an active social life and there were many gatherings at our quarters where there was a lot of drinking of what Dad called "bug juice." We were each given a big swig of Scotch or Bourbon or some other of the awful stuff to ensure that we wouldn't touch it again. We were banished upstairs to "mind our Ps and Qs" when my parents had company. I never minded because I had discovered books. I remember crying as I read Dad's old copy of "Black Beauty."

In late August, Dad took several weeks off and drove us to Colorado. On our way through the South, we passed field after field of white cotton filled with black pickers, entire families including many small children. Every filling station where we stopped had a sign that read "colored" over a dilapidated rest room door, some of which were off the hinges and didn't close completely. There were often two water fountains, and invariably the one that didn't work was labeled, "colored." When I asked why there were such signs, they didn't answer my question, or I didn't understand the answer.

When we arrived in the Rocky Mountains near Denver, we stayed in a little cabin with a wood-burning stove. We hiked and picnicked and were supremely happy. In September, we rode horseback into the mountains, walked on rocks across gurgling streams, ate freshly caught trout cooked over an open fire and awoke in the morning to snow weighing down the walls of our tents. When I asked Dad to read an early draft of this book 60-some years later, he agreed that this was an especially happy time for him too. The fragrance of fir trees and the sound of the wind in the evergreens still brings back those wonderful memories.

We didn't arrive back in Louisiana until late October, long after school had started. Dad was soon reassigned to the Armed Forces Staff College in Norfolk, Virginia. We never went back to school. Maybe my parents already knew that he was on the list before we went to Colorado, and therefore knew that we'd be uprooted again after only a couple of months in school in Louisiana. We left for Virginia in early January 1947. I was eight years old.

A Hard Six Months for My Dad: Armed Forces Staff College, Norfolk, Virginia

The best and the brightest officers from all four uniformed services were selected to attend the Armed Forces Staff

College. They were the most highly decorated officers from World War II. It was a feather in Dad's cap to be selected. But it turned out to be one of his most challenging assignments.

I have since learned that Dad suffered from stage fright when he was required to make oral presentations to his class, and he was unhappy about his war record. He believed that his shoot-down and crash landing was a great personal failure. He had surrendered to the enemy and was embarrassed among a class filled with heavily be-medaled war heroes to have only one medal, a purple heart. Mom told me later that he felt that his military career was over, and he struggled to keep his head up and survive the competitive classroom experience. Little could he imagine that, in time, he would be promoted way above most of his classmates.

Mom gave up on sending us to school for that year. She wrote to the Calvert School in Baltimore, obtained materials, and began to home-school Pat and me. The Calvert School third grade course focused on Greek mythology. I studied diligently, but Pat had difficulty applying himself. He would have to start the second grade over when we were transferred again seven months later.

On the Norfolk Naval Station, we were living in a second floor, three-bedroom apartment in an old wooden building that had been Navy barracks. The barracks had two stories of covered porches along which were the entrances to each apartment. There was no guard railing, only a handrail that was attached about three feet from the floor to the columns that held up the roof. The second-floor porches were dangerous. While we were living there, a child fell from one and was badly hurt. Dad was concerned.

I remember that my sister had begun defying Dad soon after his return, sticking out her tongue behind his back when he scolded her. They often had harsh words for each other, shocking my goody-goody soul but amusing Mom, who laughed when my spunky sister took on her father. The conflict between my father and my little sister added to the challenges associated with becoming a family again. My father was short on patience, as he struggled with the demands of the school and tried to put his sense of embarrassment about his wartime imprisonment behind him. As the youngest, my sister had enjoyed more than four years of full-time affection from our mother, and now she had to share it with our father. The tension lasted for some years, and our mother seemed at a loss as to how to diffuse it.

Among our downstairs neighbors were the Kurtzes, and they had a beautiful baby girl they had named "Swoosie" after her father's B-17 bomber, called the "Swoose." There was a large painting of this aircraft hanging proudly in their living room. Swoosie Kurtz kept her name and went on to become a well-known Broadway and television actress.

The neighbors who lived right below us had several children, one of whom was a baby. One night, close to bedtime, we heard the baby crying incessantly. After an hour or so, Mom asked me to come down with her to investigate. The apartment door was open, but the parents were not there. The older children were quietly entertaining themselves and ignoring the crying baby who had dropped his bottle out of the crib. Mom picked it up, filled it with milk from the refrigerator. When she gave it back to him, he immediately quieted down. Mom was highly indignant, as we walked back upstairs, angrily muttering criticism of the parents whom, she sniffed, were Navy.

I had my first asthma attack while we were there at the Armed Forces Staff College. The place was dirty and dusty, and I don't think Mom was able to find a maid. A doctor came over from the dispensary across the street. He told my parents that asthma could have a psychological component and they decided that my asthma was a bid for attention. I remember lying there for what seemed like several days struggling to breathe, a harbinger of many similar episodes to come.

Dad always took us to church on Sundays. As I sat beside him during Mass, I felt the presence of a God I didn't understand but who urged me to always do the right thing, to always try my best. This was a demanding God who watched over me on my journey and saw every misdeed. Only years later would I feel loved by a God of mercy and compassion, a love that would surprise my tense and fearful soul.

After church Dad would often take us down to the Norfolk Naval Base shipyard and we would stand in homage before the great Battleship Missouri. He would tell us the story, again and again, about how the Japanese had surrendered to Gen. MacArthur on board shortly after VJ day. He recounted the story of the surrender and how, just as the surrender was signed, 500 B-29s roared over the ship to celebrate the end of the war. Accounts of the ceremony report that the surrender was otherwise a brief, businesslike affair. The battleship Missouri just looked to me like a big old grey ship, but I was impressed by his opinion of its importance. Dad's reverence for the ship, and my memory of the announcement over the radio on VJ Day in Brown's Restaurant in Fort Lauderdale, made lasting impressions. That war, like those to come, left a mark on my soul.

Most of the families living at the Staff College had only recently been reunited after the war. There must have been a lot of older children around and there was much telling of dirty jokes, which I didn't understand. I remember their ridicule when they realized that I didn't understand what they were talking about. I heard the "F" word for the first time. I asked Mom what the word meant and she said, "It's just a bad word that some people write in toilets." I was eight years old and immediately thoroughly inspected the toilets in our apartment. I did not find the "F" word and figured that she had not told me the whole truth.

On moving day, a few days later, the apartment was filled with packers and movers. I sat myself down and began singing loudly every word I could think of that rhymed with the "F" word, e.g., luck, muck, shuck, tuck, buck, etc. From time to time I slipped in the "F" word. When Mom heard this raunchy ballad, she came running in and angrily told me to be quiet, but not before I had noticed several of the movers laughing. It was a long time before I understood what that word meant, and I didn't learn it from her.

By the spring of 1947 Mom was experiencing a great deal of abdominal pain and her doctor insisted on a complete hysterectomy. Dad's classes and our brief studies with the Calvert School ended, and Mom had the surgery. She was thirty-one years old. We knelt and prayed the rosary for her and went to sit outside the hospital in the car while Dad visited her. She waved to us once from a window in the hospital. When Dad sneaked us up to see her, she had a huge bandage around her mid-section. She was finally released after three weeks and gradually regained enough strength for our next move.

We all Loved Langley

Toward the end of July 1947, we moved about 20 miles away to Langley Field near Hampton, Virginia. Our new home was in the brick duplex officers' quarters located at 38 B Bryant Avenue. At least fifty years old, the building had four floors with a full attic, a full basement, and a maid's room off the kitchen. A metal sign that read "Lt. Col. A. P. Clark, Jr." soon appeared in front of the quarters.

Two important events in the military service occurred while we were at Langley. First, President Truman signed an order to desegregate the military. Mom remembered that Leonard Drennan, a classmate of Dad's, was a driving force behind this important event. A controversial proposal, it generated ominous predictions of trouble like those made decades later when women entered the military academies. However, segregation in the military ended quite smoothly and few of the dire predictions became a reality. In time, Americans would become familiar with the stories of the black fighter pilots from Tuskegee, Alabama, the courageous U. S. Army 422nd Combat Team of Americans of Japanese descent, the Navaho Code Talkers, and the many other soldiers, sailors and airmen of color who served during the Second World War with valor and distinction.

Dad celebrated some months later, in 1948, when Congress created the Air Force as a separate service. Despite several onerous conditions demanded by the Army and the Navy before they would agree to this new branch of service, the Army Air Corps became the U.S. Air Force. Langley Field was no longer an Army Post.

When winter came, the old coal-burning furnace in the basement of our quarters was activated. A truck came around to the back and dropped a load of coal that thundered loudly down a metal chute into the furnace room. For the rest of the winter, a soldier would come very early every morning including weekends, descend the stairwell into the basement and strike the fire in the furnace. The soldiers assigned this task were called "strikers" and they had free access to all the quarters. There were radiators in every room that gradually warmed up by the time we rose for breakfast. Winters at Langley were cold, and we were out of our minds with joy when we woke on Christmas morning to see the ground covered with snow .

School Days at Langley. In the fall of 1947, we entered the Base school, a five-minute walk across the parade ground behind our quarters. I started fourth grade, Pat began second grade again, and Mary entered first grade. We walked home for lunch. The first day of school, I suffered one of the major embarrassments of my life. It was bathroom break time. We lined up, and I was behind a boy. I followed him into the boy's restroom; looked quizzically at the urinals; lifted my dress, pulled my panties down, perched precariously on the edge of one and peed. It only took a couple of seconds before the boys saw me there and began pointing and hollering and running out in the hall yelling that there was a girl in the boys' bathroom. My teacher, Mrs. Rowe, came in, shushed them and took my hand, kindly showing me that the girls used a different restroom further down the hall. I wonder how I could have been so ignorant.

Shy and timid, I studied hard to please this teacher, whom I adored. We sang from our song books every day, accompanied by Mrs. Rowe on the piano. One day I wrote her a note upside down on the bottom of a paper saying, "I love you, Mrs. Rowe." She wrote me back saying that she loved me too. I came across that note recently in my "saved" file.

During the summer of 1948, there was an outbreak of polio on a part of the base called "Lighter than Air," or LTA, because that was where the dirigibles had been launched many years before. The enlisted airmen and their families lived at LTA. No one knew what caused polio, but LTA was quarantined. The swimming pools where we spent our summers were closed, and the kids who lived at LTA were not allowed to begin school for several months. There were only ten of us in my fifth-grade class and I was the only girl until sometime late in the fall.

One day, there was an assembly in the school auditorium. Every child in the school was required to attend. The room was darkened, and a movie screen set up. We were told that we were going to see something terrible, and that we needed to see it so it would never happen again. I gaped uncomprehending as black and white pictures of American troops finding and liberating the Nazi concentration camps appeared on the screen along with captured photos of the camps during the war. I looked in horror at the piles of bodies, the emaciated men, women and children as they were herded into the ovens, the stunned and expressionless faces as they stared at the camera. I had nightmares that continued for months. I have never visited the Holocaust Museum. I don't think it was necessarily wrong to show the films to such young children, but I didn't understand, and I don't remember that we talked to our parents about it.

We were not a communicative family. We kept our concerns to ourselves and worried privately. When we came home from school, Mom was usually either upstairs engrossed in her sewing, writing a letter, or deep in a book. Our parents had their jobs and we had ours, school. When I received a good report card, I might be told "Don't let it go to your head!" or "Don't get too big for your britches!" When Pat's grades weren't good, he caught the "dickens!" Parent and teacher conferences had not yet become an established practice and there was no Parent Teachers Association.

My parents' childhood experiences had been similar. Their apparent lack of interest in our daily lives reflected their parents' and their generation's attitudes about raising children. Our grandparents had always had household help who played an important role in raising their children, but they usually didn't help the children deal with the emotional struggles of childhood.

Learning Military Discipline. We were allowed to go anywhere on Langley provided we could still hear Dad call for us with his loud and distinctive whistle. On numerous occasions I heard the whistle and went running home to find that the summons was meant only for Pat. He must have forgotten to empty the trash or some such chore. His punishment would usually be restriction to the yard. The other boys would taunt him from across the street and he would hurl threats vowing to make them sorry. During his early childhood, Pat took his punishments "like a man" as he was directed. He was getting the treatment military fathers often visited upon sons to "toughen them up."

There was no doubt that we were a military family. At Langley we first were drilled on how to stand at attention—with shoulders back, chins tucked in, back against the wall, responding "yes sir" or "no sir," and staring straight ahead while Dad delivered a lecture. If my lips trembled, or tears began to come into my eyes, or heaven forbid I cracked a grin, I was quickly told to, "Wipe that look off your face." My hand would come up to sweep slowly across my face, bringing my expression to an acceptable solemnity.

We were taught early on that punctuality was an important virtue. When Dad said, "Wheels in the well at 0800," we knew we'd better not be even one minute late. When we were told to do something particularly important, we heard a firm, "That's an order!" We dared not do it slowly or sloppily. If we were suspected of not telling the truth or were asked to make a promise, we were told to, "Give me your word of honor." If we looked like we might "talk back," we were told to "bite your tongue!" The greatest compliment Dad could give me was, "You're a real trooper, honey!"

We also learned how to eat a "square meal," which required that the fork or spoon move down to the plate, up to the mouth and back again tracing a perfect square. Sometimes Dad required us to sit on the first four inches of our chairs at meals and keep our eyes on our plates. He had learned this particular disciplinary technique as a plebe at West Point. We had to focus on eating and keeping our balance so as not to fall on the floor as we ate. This invariably interrupted and quelled any complaints about the food.

I don't resent these experiences. Life is hard and I needed to learn to be strong and disciplined for the years that lay ahead. I tried super hard to follow Dad's orders. But Pat and Mary often had difficulty not giggling, or silently and angrily pouting, which brought down more paternal harassment on all three of us. Our plates were to be cleaned, and we learned that "there are no excuses, sir!" Pat and Mary learned to carefully drop unwanted food into their laps and surreptitiously deposit it on the generous-sized brackets under the table that secured the corners. I was not let in on this trick. They both knew that I would have tattled on them.

Bunny No Longer. By this time, I was developing a serious over-bite and wore unattractive pink-plastic-framed pre-scription glasses to correct my nearsightedness. It was my siblings who first decided that my nickname, Bunny, was appropriate because I looked like Bugs. That's when I decided I would only answer to my given name, Carolyn, which Mrs. Rowe called me. I simply stopped answering unless I was addressed as Carolyn. It took a few months but eventually they all began to call me Carolyn. I may have still looked like Bugs, but I felt better not being called Bunny anymore. I wonder whether we weren't a disappointment to our parents. We were ordinary in appearance while they both were strikingly handsome. None of us inherited her glossy dark hair or his beautiful red hair. We all had straight, mouse-brown hair, fair skin, crooked teeth and freckles.

A New Best Friend. Granny and Pappy had found a rickety girl's bike at the farm outside of San Antonio and presented it to me. It was tied onto the back of the moving van each time we moved. When I finally found my balance, I rode all over Langley Field with my best friend, Margie. We were often riding hurriedly away from a gaggle of small boys, usually including Pat, chasing us as we yelled for our lives. Truth be told, we had deliberately attracted their attention, forcing them to start the chase.

We joined the Brownies, and then the Girls Scouts, earning merit badges together. Margie's parents invited me to join them on a trip to New York City when I was 10. What an experience lay ahead for me! We checked into the Astor Hotel on Times Square and bought lunch from an automat. We saw the Rockettes at Radio City Music Hall, the Ice Capades, and the rodeo at Madison Square Garden. I was deeply impressed by the crowds still in the streets at midnight, which is clear in this excited letter to my parents:

"We got back from the ice review last night at Twelve and it is still like day. The lights were on and crowds of people were on the streets. Police on horses and foot were all around. Last night lots of people were carrying signs with Vote for Wallace on them." [That would have been Henry Wallace in 1948.]

But the Bowery left the most lasting impression. General Fitzmaurice took us on a walk through the Bowery because he felt that we were old enough to learn that others were not as fortunate as we were. I'll never forget the sight of the men passed out in the gutter, the rank, fetid smell of the place, the trash and empty bottles strewn everywhere, and the man who came after Gen. Fitzmaurice with a rope. Gen. Fitzmaurice responded firmly but kindly. I loved the Fitzmaurice family and am still in touch with Margie. I visited her parents several times before their deaths many years later.

Go Play, Kids. What did kids do back in the olden days before television, video games, cell phones and computers? When we weren't in school and the sun was shining, we played outside. I spent hours climbing trees, building forts under the bushes and recreating scenes from the many books I read. I devoured *The Little Colonel* and *Anne of Green Gables* and borrowed Margie's *Nancy Drew* books. Mom read the classics to us in the evenings. Our favorites were Howard Pyle's *King Arthur*, Robert Louis Stevenson's *Robinson Crusoe*, and *The Adventures of Robin Hood*. These were old editions and our vocabulary was enhanced by all the words she had to explain.

Mom was an expert seamstress and taught me to embroider. I embroidered doilies when I wasn't reading or outside playing. Sometimes we would try to catch "The Lone Ranger" on the radio, or "Bobby Denton of the B-Bar-B Ranch," "Little Orphan Annie" and "The Shadow." And I played with my dolls. We rarely played board games or cards.

We were too competitive, squabbling over the rules and accusing each other of cheating. Since I was the oldest, I tried to settle arguments by invoking the military RHIP rule, but it never worked. When our parents had to intervene in our battles, we were all punished.

The summers at Langley were filled with the delicious fragrance of the flowering privet hedges. Our lawns were trimmed by airmen assigned the task of cutting the officers' grass with push mowers. The lawn was a motley growth of crab grass and clover, neither sprinkled nor fertilized, and often scattered with random piles of dog doo as all our dogs ran loose. We spent most of the summers at the Officers' Club swimming pool. When we could swim the length of the pool three times without stopping, we could go alone. Pat and Mary accomplished this feat in no time. I was afraid to try, and consequently stayed home until Dad made a bet with me that I could swim three lengths if he swam right beside me. He won the bet and I was joyfully as free to go swimming as my brother and sister.

One day, Mom and Dad brought home a Boxer puppy, the runt of the litter with a large burn scar on her back leg. Did we ever love our frisky new pet! Mother named her Freya, the same name she'd given her dog in San Antonio. But she was hard to house train, and our carpets were permanently stained. She ran away every chance she got. We'd chase her calling hysterically, afraid she'd be hit by a car. She'd wait until we had hold of her, wagging her little cutoff tail at the end of a butt raised high in the air. Then she'd leap out of our arms barking with joy. Our new Freya came with us on every move until we left France for Germany ten years later.

On Farms and Ranches. Uncle Charlie and Aunt Margaret had left the stressful life of a corporate attorney in Chicago and bought Headwaters Farm in Virginia, near Staunton. They had chickens, horses, pigs, and an apple orchard. We visited them several times while we were at Langley. I loved the farm, which always smelled of apples, skunks and manure. (By now, you may have caught on to the fact that I remember a lot of places by their smells!)

Soon after the war ended, Granny and Pappy sold their San Antonio farm and moved to Santa Fe with Danny and Lisbeth. They wanted to be closer to Bobby, who had taken a job as foreman of Banded Peak Ranch on the Colorado/New Mexico border near Chama, New Mexico. They bought an adobe house and Pappy set to work turning the property into a little farm. Granny and Aunt Danny decided to become Christian Scientists, which would have a major impact on both their lives.

In the summer of 1949, Mom and Dad decided to take us out west for a month. We traveled by train, coal-fired in those days. I was fascinated as we watched the miles go by and oceans of prairie dogs as far as the eye could see, popping out of their holes to watch the train pass without so much as a

The three Clark kids at Banded Peak Ranch, Colorado, 1949

blink. They are endangered now and are mostly seen in zoos. The trip took three days and we slept in our seats. When my grandparents met us in Santa Fe, we were black with coal dust.

On the ranch with Uncle Bobby and Aunt Mary, which lay at the southern edge of the Rockies, we hiked and picnicked, picked wild-flowers, raced each other along the split-rail fence, and rode horses around the yard. Dad and Bobby rode horseback to the top of the Banded Peak. One day Aunt Mary brought a live chicken home from the market. The grown-ups discussed who would kill it and how. We were intrigued and wanted to watch but were banished to our rooms while someone, they refused to say who, wrung the chicken's neck. I suppose I should be grateful that we missed it. The three-day trip back to Virginia seemed to last a year.

I was only vaguely aware of the presidential campaign of the summer and fall of 1948 but my ears were always open, and I did know that Thomas Dewey and Harry Truman were fighting it out in a close election. I remember my parents' satisfaction when they heard on the radio that Dewey had been declared the winner. In the morning, I was in the kitchen when Mom picked up the newspaper from the back porch and registered dismay. The headlines read, "Truman defeats Dewey!" She was furious. "That bastard Truman stole the election!" she called up to Dad.

Granny and Pappy came for a visit just before we left Langley, and there was a lot of talk about Communists, Whitaker Chambers and Alger Hiss. I remember something I didn't understand until years later, "A pink is a punk who's too yellow to be red." Senator Joe McCarthy would soon be railing away on the radio about all the "commies" in Washington and Hollywood. The Cold War was beginning.

Uh-Oh, Moving Again. One morning I awoke to hear something flying by my window and thudding onto the ground below. I looked out and saw piles of books, magazines and other items falling from the attic window into the back yard. I ran downstairs. There were my parents' collections of the *Saturday Review of Literature*, *Life* magazine, and the *National Geographic*. "Uh oh," I thought, "Looks like we're moving again!" Lots of stuff was thrown out before every move in order to keep our total household weight within the limits prescribed by the government. Weight overages were expensive, and Dad was not about to pay extra.

When we unpacked at new homes there were always things missing. We never knew whether they had been quietly jettisoned before we left or lost by the movers, and the answer was probably both. The jettisoned belongings from military families on the move often wound up in the Base thrift shops, or at the Salvation Army and Goodwill stores. Few hoarders could survive life in the military.

Packing and clearing quarters was complicated because we always had some pieces of government-issued quartermaster furniture. We were responsible to return the furniture and the quarters to the government in the same condition as when we moved in. Making sure that the government's stuff stayed, and our stuff went, could be a challenge when movers were all over the house packing and carrying furniture and boxes out to the moving van.

Dad would get out the list and use masking tape to mark the tables, dressers and whatever else belonged to the government that should stay in the quarters. Another last-minute chore was to fill in the holes in the walls where pictures had hung. Since the walls in quarters were inevitably painted off-white or pale green, we filled the holes with toothpaste. Before Dad had clearance to leave the Post for his new assignment, staff from the Quartermaster's Office would arrive to inspect the quarters and the furniture. When the inspector removed the leaf in the dining room table, he discovered the mounds of moldy food my siblings had hidden in the corners, which were then quickly removed by my embarrassed mother.

Packing for our departure from Langley, the movers mistakenly took a government-issued kitchen table. We didn't discover that the table was missing until the moving van was on the road. After studying the description of the table on the government-issue checklist, Dad went down to the local lumber yard, bought lumber and scrounged tools and paint from neighbors. He built a table while Mom fumed, and we waited in the car. Sure enough, our quarters passed inspection and we were on our way. It was January 1950.

Mom was particularly reluctant to leave Langley and I heard her muttering mixed-up lines from a Kipling poem that I would hear again and again.

> *"Oh, it's Tommy this and Tommy that and Tommy go away! But it's "Thank you Mr. Atkins," when the band begins to play! Then it's "Yes Sir, Mr. Atkins, anything you say!" For it's Tommy this, an' Tommy that, an' "Chuck him out, the brute!" But it's savior of 'is country when the guns begin to shoot."*

In time I learned that Tommy was the British nickname for their soldier boys. "Tommy Atkins" was their "G I Joe."

Hard Times and Local Bullies

Dad had been ordered to Mitchell Field on Long Island. There were no quarters available, so he rented a house in nearby Baldwin and put us in a Catholic school. The next six months were unhappy for Mom and me. Mom's sadness may have had something to do with her early hysterectomy and the end of her friendships at Langley.

I was miserable when I found myself in a class of 75 students, half of them in sixth grade and the other half in seventh grade. There was one nun to teach us, Sister Robert Girard. In the sixth-grade half of the class, I was seated in the back and unable to see the blackboard because I needed new glasses. I was either ignored or viewed with suspicion by my classmates and the neighborhood kids. This was an established blue-collar neighborhood. We were different and the kids didn't like us. Pat and Mary took them on while I hid inside, and begged Mom to drive us to school so I wouldn't have to take the city bus.

The sixth-grade kids, like all the kids in St. Christopher's, were studying the Baltimore Catechism. Catholic school *modus operandi* for religious education was memorization. I worked hard to memorize all the questions and answers. We were assigned several each night and drilled the next day. One evening my catechism homework included the question: "What are the three sins that cry to heaven for vengeance?" The only sin that I now remember being on the list was sodomy. I had not the slightest idea what that was, or even how to pronounce it. I called down the stairs, "Mom, what is "sodomee?" There was a sharp reply, "What did you say?" I repeated the question and she called me downstairs. She said that sodomy was when two men pretend they are married. I said, "Like what do they do?" and she said, "They hold hands." I was puzzled that holding hands could be such as awful sin.

The Catechism also taught us about the Cardinal Sins, and the first was "pride." I wondered why it would be a sin to be proud when I got good grades or helped Mom in the kitchen. In time, I learned that the "pride" that is sinful is the refusal to apologize when I've hurt someone, and the refusal to forgive when I've been hurt.

The stress of those months in Baldwin took a toll and I finally got sick, running a temperature so high that I became delirious. A civilian doctor came to the house and prescribed Aureomycin, which was a new wonder drug not available through the military dispensary. It was expensive, a dollar a pill. That was a lot then and Mom thought that the drug store was "gyping" us.

The New York Board of Regents required all sixth graders to pass exams to be promoted to seventh grade. I took the exams and dropped out of school for the rest of the year while I recovered from my illness. When I returned with Mom to pick up my report card, I learned that I had scored an unheard-of 98 percent. No question that the little base school at Langley was superior to St. Christopher's.

60

While we were on Long Island, my brother and sister pulled a stunt that earned its way into family lore. One day we were left in the car, parked on a busy street while Mom and Dad shopped. We had been sitting there for a long time when Pat and Mary hatched a plan to ease their boredom. Pat grabbed his beat-up old black felt cowboy hat and they hopped out of the car. Holding out Pat's hat they began begging, telling people their parents had left them and they needed money for food. Embarrassed, I hid on the floor of the car. My parents arrived back to see a hat full of change and people "tsk-tsking," at these poor abandoned children. I expected big trouble, but Mom just laughed while Dad blushed and quickly drove away.

Yay! A Home on the Base

We jumped for joy when Dad was assigned quarters on Mitchell Field. The Officers' Club and swimming pool were nearby, the neighborhood kids invited us to join in their games, Mom was happy, and I found another best friend. Liz Thatcher and I played endlessly with our dolls, which we put on rigorous schedules, taking them to the playground on a regular basis. Liz's mother was a concert pianist and found a piano teacher so I could take lessons again. We could walk to the Base movie theater and see movies for a quarter. Before every movie started in the Base Theater, we stood at attention with our hands over our hearts as "The Star-Spangled Banner" boomed across the auditorium.

Danny and Lisbeth came for a visit and Danny gave me my first permanent. I was thrilled to have my stringy, straight brown hair turned into frizzy curls. When we started school in the fall, we attended public schools in Hempstead where there were many other military kids. Life was good again. As an additional benefit, it snowed a lot on Long Island.

But it wasn't to last. The Korean conflict was heating up and Dad believed that he would be ordered off to war again. Within weeks he got orders. Instead of Korea, he was ordered to Colorado Springs to open Ent Air Force Base and help form the Continental Air Defense Command charged with defending the U.S. from Soviet attack. Work would soon begin on building Cheyenne Mountain to house the secret operations.

We left New York in late December 1950, traveling slowly across country to Colorado battling snow and ice the whole way. We stopped in Kansas City for a visit with Dad's sister, Mary and her husband, Abe, who headed the Army's Corps of Engineers' efforts to flood-proof Kansas City. We got to know our cousins—Anne, Jim and Clark Lincoln—all of whom were close to our ages. I was highly impressed with Anne, whom I thought looked just like Marilyn Monroe. I was now 12 years old and I wanted to be just like Anne.

At the Foot of the Rockies

When we arrived in Colorado Springs, there were no rentals available, so we moved into the Broadmoor Hotel. Dad bought us ice skates and we began learning to skate while he and Mom looked for a house. A month or so later, they bought an old frame farmhouse with two sets of stairs to the second floor and a covered front porch.

We began our new school sometime in February, making for a difficult adjustment. We walked the ten blocks to school, even when there were several feet of snow on the ground. Although we all faced episodes of being bullied, as military Brats and new kids often do, Pat had a particularly hard time. While I learned to withdraw and not fight back, Pat would take the bullies on, even when he was outnumbered.

One of his worst experiences was when Mom accidentally placed him in the wrong grade in the public elementary school in Colorado Springs. As a result, he was mercilessly harassed as a "retard" by the sixth-grade boys. Pat finally figured it out and asked to be put back into the fifth grade, where he'd been when we left New York. It was a blessing for Pat when we moved again a few months later.

Freya escaped frequently. One day, Mom looked at her and disgustedly muttered, "That damn dog is pregnant!" Eyes wide, we watched as Freya gave birth to seven beautiful mutts. How we loved those puppies! Playing and laughing with them took over our lives for a couple of months. We lovingly named and found homes for each one. My favorite was "Ferdie," short for Ferdinand. His twin was Isabella.

In the spring, Dad's name appeared on the list for the next class at the National War College, located in Washington, D.C. This would be another move only seven months after arriving in Colorado! The assignment was a feather in Dad's cap, but we had hoped to be in Colorado for a long time. "Stop complaining and just suck it up like a good military Brat," they told us, but I think Mom was disappointed too. My parents finally sold the house for less than the $10,000 they had paid. It is now worth more than $800,000.

When school was out in June, Mary went to visit Granny and Pappy in San Antonio, and Dad took the rest of us on a hike to Bear Track Lakes in the Rockies. We would march up the trail with packs on our backs filled with canned food and toilet paper until Dad called a halt. I would be so out of breath that I'd drop right where I was, lying on my pack like marching soldiers did in the movies. Then Dad noticed what he thought were mountain lion scratches on trees near the trail, and we looked around nervously. There wasn't another soul to be seen.

As it grew dark, Dad was so concerned about lions and bears that he put the three of us in the tent while he slept across the entrance. He had a big stick handy and stayed awake all night. The trip down was more demanding than the trip up, which I've found to be true on subsequent hikes. When we stopped for lunch, the Rocky Mountain Magpies ate breadcrumbs from our hands. As I look back on our camping experiences, and how happy Dad was out in the wilderness, I understand why the outdoors calls so strongly to me.

We were sad as we packed up and headed south to visit my grandparents and pick up Mary before heading to D.C. It was hot, very hot. There was no air conditioning in Car Clark #2, a Pontiac "Woodie" station wagon. I carried our pet canary, Timothy, in a small cage on my lap. Freya slept on the floor. We knew better than to ask, "When are we going to get there, Dad?" So we would begin scouting out motels in the mid-afternoon saying, "That looks like a nice one!" while Dad drove on and on until dusk before he'd finally stop.

Our Home in the Nation's Capital

Mom and Dad rented a house in northwest Washington at the end of the summer of 1951. Happily for us all, Uncle Bobby and Aunt Mary left the Colorado ranch for Washington at about the same time. Bobby had tired of ranching and decided to finish college. He used the GI Bill to take classes at George Washington University from which he graduated three years later. Mary worked as an executive secretary for the editor of *Changing Times* Magazine.

Horace Mann elementary school was around the corner for my brother and sister. It was decided that I should attend eighth grade at Immaculata, a Catholic girls' school located about a mile away. After my experience at St. Christopher's in Baldwin, I was leery of this idea but was not asked for an opinion. Mom outfitted me in the uniform of the school, white blouse and maroon jumper, and off I went.

The other girls had been together for years and didn't welcome the new girl. I was shy and plain, and many of the other girls had reached puberty and wore bras and make-up. I secretly bought a tube of lipstick and put it on while I waited at the bus stop, taking it off on my way home. Aunt Mary took me shopping for clothes and helped me buy my first bra after I complained that the girls at school were teasing me. But I remained friendless throughout the eighth grade. The only bright spot was Sister Bridget, who gave me piano lessons. I practiced hard and made good progress, winning the St.

Cecelia Medal at the end of the year. Even today, I regret leaving her. This was my last chance to learn to play the piano well.

My eighth-grade teacher, Sister Mary Joseph, drilled us every morning on the Baltimore Catechism and I can still quote some of the answers verbatim. We stood if we were called on and, if we didn't quote the Catechism exactly as worded in the text, we were immediately told to sit down. I remember being furious when I was summarily seated for what seemed to me to be a minor difference. I gave sister the "evil eye" that I'd learned from Dad and walked home in tears in the middle of the morning.

Despite my misery, I was developing a powerful interest in the teachings of Jesus. This foundation in Christianity was something important that I shared with Pat, who was to spend eight years with the Jesuits. I enlisted Pat and Mary to say the rosary with me several nights a week during Lent. My cousin Anne says that it was I who introduced her to the Rosary, to which she is still devoted. On Good Friday, I spent the hours from noon to three o'clock on my knees in my room and then walked two miles to church and back. I was quite the fervent Catholic girl.

But by the end of the school year, I had had enough of Catholic schools. I insisted on going to the public junior high school, my tenth school in nine years. It wasn't easy to change schools again, but each time we started over in a new school was a chance to reinvent ourselves. I decided to pretend to be outgoing. I faked the gregarious behavior I'd watched in the popular girls and I made some friends.

It was when I was in the ninth grade in 1953 that I became aware that the Russians were considered a serious threat to our survival. People were building air raid shelters in their back yards, equipped with food and water to last the months they'd have to stay underground to survive a nuclear attack. We began to have air raid drills in school. At the sound of the bell we dropped to the floor and crawled under our desks, covering our heads with our arms.

I wasn't particularly frightened by all this, maybe because my parents weren't. Besides, I had more important things on my mind, preoccupations of the teen-age years: boys, clothes, grades and popular music. I turned my little radio on the minute I got home from school and began my homework. I learned where every song ranked on the Hit Parade.

Every day before classes, we stood, faced the American flag and recited the Pledge of Allegiance. Then someone would read a Bible verse. There were sock hops in the school gym in the afternoons, which I finally got up the nerve to attend, although I don't remember ever dancing with a boy.

I studied Latin and Algebra, and memorized lines from Shakespeare. I learned to take my glasses off except when I needed them to see the blackboard, squinting nearsightedly the rest of the time. Finally, Mom took Pat and me to the dentist, who installed single-wire braces, with hooks for rubber bands to pull our teeth back into line.

A new friend, Mariana (Mike) Woolnough, and I joined the Junior Army Navy Guild Organization (JANGO), a group of military wives and daughters who volunteered in local hospitals. We proudly donned red, white and blue uniforms with JANGO patches on our sleeves and worked weekends and after school at Doctor's Hospital, a busy hospital in downtown Washington. We spent most of our volunteer hours responding to patients' bells and emptying bedpans, and we loved it. I was fascinated by anything relating to the practice of medicine. I decided that I would be a nurse when I grew up. If I'd been a boy, I might have aspired to be a doctor like my grandfather.

Mom enrolled Mary and me in ballet classes taught by an old friend of my grandmother's. We worked hard, and both of us performed as little swans in the first National Ballet

66

production of "Swan Lake" at Lisner Auditorium. I led the line of little swans onto the stage, leaning into a graceful pose, looking over my shoulder away from the direction we were traveling on our toes, and felt a pubescent boob pop out of my costume. I must have blushed red as a beet, but I held the pose. I wanted to be a beautiful dancer to please Mom, but it was not to be. As hard as I tried, I couldn't build up the necessary strength with only one class a week.

Toward the end of ninth grade, I managed to attract a boyfriend. "Punchy" had red hair. He called me on the phone and rode his bicycle over to see me. One day he rendered me speechless by kissing me suddenly on the lips before fleeing and riding wildly off on his bike. When his father was transferred a few months later, Punchy left town and that was the end of my first romance.

Mom and Dad had a wonderful time at the numerous social events that accompanied attendance at the National War College. They were invited to the White House and to the Coronation Ball for Queen Elizabeth II.

The campaign for president featuring Adlai Stevenson and Dwight Eisenhower was a big deal. Pappy was backing Eisenhower and we were horrified when Granny announced that she would vote for Adlai Stevenson. Residents of Washington, D. C., did not have the right to vote until 1961, so Mom and Dad couldn't vote. Dad surrendered to the modern age and bought us a black-and-white television, which only received signals in my bedroom. We sat up most of the night watching the returns. Eisenhower won and we joyfully attended the Inauguration parade, peering over the crowds with cardboard periscopes.

The official family portrait for the National War College, 1951

When the nine months of classes at the National War College ended, Dad was deeply disappointed to be assigned to the Pentagon. He was to head up the section in personnel that would be responsible for reducing the size of the Air Force following the end of the Korean War, an unpopular task. He wasn't happy about it, and neither was Mom.

The dinner table sometimes became a battleground, and the arguments were often petty. I remember one over whether rice or potatoes had more calories. Fortunately, we had an Encyclopedia Britannica, which could offer some answers. But these sessions could end with Mom running upstairs to lie on her bed crying and smoking in the darkness. Depression would haunt her from time to time for the rest of her life. She had few friends in Washington and spent her days reading, sewing, and knitting with only Freya for company. It took time and effort to make friends—a major effort for introverts in the military, with another move already on the horizon. Dad wasn't happy either and feared he'd be a "desk weenie" until he retired.

Because Mom seemed so unhappy much of the time, I decided that I would grow up to be like Dad. I believed Dad to be strong, calm, focused, productive and unemotional. I fantasized about being a pilot in the Air Force, which seemed to be what he admired most. I played a question/answer game with myself. "Who are you," someone would ask. I would proudly reply, "I am the daughter of Col. Albert Patton Clark, United States Air Force." The questioner would be duly respectful of my important identity.

Pat was 11 years old when we arrived in Washington and was given the partially finished attic for a bedroom. One day Dad sent him to his room for the weekend. I don't remember what he was being punished for. Since he couldn't come downstairs, Pat told me that he peed out the window. It was hot up there and he finally began angrily pounding on the wall. This went on for hours while Mom and Dad ignored him. Somehow, he managed to sneak out the back door and was gone all night. He found a large bush a few blocks away and hid until morning. He came back, hungry for breakfast since he'd been denied food the previous day. Mom and Dad never revealed whether they knew that he'd been gone all night.

Pat loved baseball and spent countless hours listening to games on his radio. Eager for a friendly ear, he'd describe the games to me. To this day, I remember the names of all his favorite players. The Yankees were his team, but he admired a lot of stars from other teams, too, even the Dodgers. His favorite players were: Joe DiMaggio, Yogi Berra, Allie Reynolds, Peewee Reese, Mickey Mantle, Jackie Robinson, and Roy Campanella. He could quote all the batting averages, runs scored, runs batted in, etc. He tried to talk me into going with him to the playground where he would organize games with any kids he could find. He was disappointed that I wouldn't play, but I didn't see well, and was never any good at sports.

My parents would sometimes deliberately set up competition among their children as a motivational technique. When they lined Pat up against me, they seemed to want to embarrass him if he were beaten by a mere girl. I think they felt that Pat was too easy-going and needed a more competitive spirit. Pat remembered more clearly than I did the times that he lost to me. He felt the competitions were stacked against him. In fact, they were, so I didn't give beating him any credence. Over the ensuing years, Pat and I had plenty of time to talk about what we considered to be our parents' child-rearing mistakes, and how we were going to avoid repeating them. But, as parents, we both made plenty of our own.

Hiking and Traveling. While we were in Washington, Dad decided that we would walk the Appalachian Trail together in sections. In 1948 a World War II veteran named Earl Shaffer first walked the entire Trail in one trip and that inspired Dad. We would go up into the Blue Ridge Mountains, stay in little cabins along the trail and walk for a day or two.

Dad asked me to plan a family vacation for summer of 1953. Mom wanted to revisit places in New England that had been important to her and find family graves, and Dad wanted to camp in Baxter State Park in Maine and climb Mt. Katahdin, the northern point of the Trail. Dad suggested that I write the various chambers of commerce, identify historic sites along the way, and make reservations at inexpensive motels. I was pleased that he felt I could undertake this important task at the age of 14.

We visited Cohasset, Massachusetts, where Mom's grandparents had lived their last years. She found the house where she had visited them when she was seven years old and where her grandmother had died. We found the grave of a distant Wheelwright ancestor who had outlived three wives and fathered many children. I was intrigued to learn that we were descended from his second wife, whose name was Silence Tower. I wondered whether she might have been mute.

When we arrived in Baxter State Park, we pitched tents and camped for a week. We swam in the nearby river, pooped and peed in the bushes, battled voracious flies and mosquitoes, and somehow survived a large moose walking through our little camp in the middle of the night without stepping on any of us.

One hot day as we swam in a creek, Pat and Mary simultaneously screamed, "Leeches!" and frantically made for the shore. I had taken my time getting into the water and found only a couple of leeches on my lower legs, but they had them all over their bodies. We had seen "The African Queen" earlier that year and were terrified, while Mom and Dad laughed at the sight of our panic. The leeches were harmless, and we got them off without any difficulty.

Dad and Pat climbed to the top of Mt. Katahdin, but Mom gave up when the rock climbing started. Finally, Mary and I also gave up and returned to join her on a ledge about three-fourths of the way up, where we waited until Dad and Pat came back down.

On our way home we passed through a small town with an antique gun shop. Despite Mom's objections, Dad

71

went inside. In a few minutes he returned to the car and told Mom that there was a gun inside that he simply couldn't pass up. We had only $18 left for the trip home, and the store would only accept cash. He bought the gun for $18. Years later he repaired and refinished it. Today it is part of his collection that hangs in the stairwell of the Air Force Academy Library, a collection of every long gun carried by an American soldier since the Revolution.

After spending our last dollar on the gun, Dad called friends who were summering on Nantucket. He had enough gas to drive to Woods Hole and get on the ferry, promising to pay for the tickets when the ferry docked in Nantucket. We were a hungry bunch when we finally arrived. Their friends loaned us enough to cover the roundtrip ferry tickets and gas back to Washington and put us up for a week in their house on the beach in Quidnet, which had been a coast guard station. We loved Nantucket and Mom and Dad began to dream of owning a place on the island.

Another Move: July 1953. When they realized that we were likely to be in Washington for at least two more years, my parents decided to buy a house a couple of miles away from our rental. We moved in the middle of the summer, doing most of the packing and moving in Car Clark #2. It was not fun. The heat and humidity were insufferable and there was no air conditioning. Pat was again assigned to the attic and Dad set about installing insulation and turning it into a combination boy's room and sewing room for Mom.

During the next two years, I saw my family mainly at the dinner table. As soon as I returned home from school, I closeted myself in my room to do my homework, study, read and listen to popular music on my little radio. Mary and Pat were both attending the public junior high school and Pat was struggling. Dad decided to let the Jesuits straighten him out. Without complaint, he donned white shirt and tie and began ninth grade traveling out to Georgetown Prep. When Dad said years later that this may have been a mistake, Pat kindly reassured him that in his opinion, his time at Georgetown Prep was well spent.

High School Shenanigans in the Fifties. I began the tenth grade at Woodrow Wilson High School in Northwest Washington. Sororities and fraternities were a big deal there, and rush week was held sometime late in the fall. The girls dressed up in hose, heels, white gloves and hats, and went to teas held in the homes of members of the various sororities. Mothers watched and provided opinions of the rushes to the sorority members. The seven sororities were informally ranked by the perceived attractiveness and popularity of their members. I hoped to get a bid into one of the top four but was invited to join sorority number five.

As I look back on it, I am appalled that the school allowed sororities and fraternities, which were the cause of a lot of unhappiness. The rejected kids, if they hadn't fled to the library, sat alone at lunch tables on the periphery of the cafeteria, looking uneasy and getting the cold shoulder from the rest of us. I am ashamed to say that I put all my energy into making sure I'd never have to join that unhappy crew. I had sat there myself much too often, the new kid in so many different schools.

We pledged for a week. I had to braid my hair into a dozen braids, paint my face blue, and roller skate on one skate around a traffic circle for an hour. Then we were taken to some girl's basement, blindfolded and told various disgusting tales about diverse substances we were told to squeeze or hug or kiss, such as, "This is a dead decaying fish," or, "These are pigs' eyeballs," or "Drink this! It's dog pee." Then awful smelling stuff was dumped on us and rubbed into our hair and clothes. If we managed to take all the harassment without freaking out, we were accepted into the sorority.

My sorority sisters soon informed me that I needed help with my hairdo, my makeup, and my wardrobe. They taught me how to curl my eyelashes and put my hair up in pin curls, which I slept on for many years thereafter. I learned to give myself Toni home-permanents and pluck my eyebrows. I was told to ditch my glasses except in the classroom because, "Boys never make passes at girls who wear glasses."

Full skirts over crinoline petticoats were the fashion. Hemlines had dropped to 10 inches above the floor. Cashmere sweaters and silk scarves tied at the neck were "de rigueur." Mom didn't approve of the new styles so I often shared clothes with my new best friend, Andy, whose mother helped her buy clothes at a thrift shop nearby. Mom bought my clothes without me, often on sale. I hid some of them, which she didn't seem to notice. But she made me a beautiful white silk evening dress from a World War II parachute Dad had brought home after the War.

As I began to spread my wings, Mom and Dad clamped down with a curfew of 11:30, insisting that they meet and question any boy that I wanted to go out with. I found this embarrassing. Whenever I could, I'd spend the night with Andy, going out and coming back to her house at her curfew, which was 12:30. I got away with it for several months.

Then one evening, Mom was suspicious and called Andy's mother and asked to speak to me. I wasn't there. Andy's mother gave her the address where I had gone to a sorority party. Dad showed up outside honking and demanding that Carolyn Clark come out immediately. It took a while before anyone paid any attention to him but finally, someone told me that some guy was going nuts outside asking for me. When I realized it was my father, I slunk out to the car, frightened and embarrassed. I was sent to my room and not allowed out except to go to school.

Strangely, I was still allowed to date Annapolis midshipmen and West Point cadets. My parents considered them to be "safe" to date without their oversight. How crazy was that! If my parents had known how unsafe the cadets were when they took girls for a spin on "Flirtation Walk," or the middies, when they cajoled a girl to go downstairs to the "Passion Pit," they'd have stopped letting me go to either of the service academies. Those guys were much more dangerous than high school boys. But I was a good Catholic and determined to stay a virgin until I was married, although I think Mom believed I was a time bomb about to blow up and get pregnant any minute. I traveled down to Annapolis with other girls to weekly tea dances designed to help the "middies" find dates. I also went up to West Point, where Uncle Abe's brother was a professor, and stayed with the Lincoln family.

My cousin Anne was dating a cadet from Columbia who introduced me to a friend of his from Panama. I fell in love with Julio and went up to see him several times during the last year we were in Washington. I was hungry for approval and affection. Julio thought I was beautiful, and he was expressive and affectionate.

When I was finally allowed to attend a sorority meeting again, the girls decided to hold a "truth court." For this lovely ritual, they turned off all the lights, disguised their voices, and said things about each other. I was upset when a couple of girls said I was "stuck up." I cried and went home. As I think about it now, I realize that I could easily have appeared to be unfriendly as I didn't wear my glasses and couldn't recognize faces in the halls. But I quit that sorority and quickly joined another.

The new sorority talked me into having the next meeting at my house and I somehow convinced Mom and Dad to agree, not realizing that I'd been set up. The night of the meeting came, and boys started arriving. Pretty soon the house was full, and a loud party was underway. Mom and Dad were upstairs watching out the window with Pat and Mary. When some boy slugged the son of the Mexican Ambassador, knocking him down in our living room and breaking a lamp, Dad called the police. With the cops outside, Dad came downstairs and told everyone to leave. By that time a couple of boys were passed out in the basement and someone had thrown up in the laundry sink.

Everyone left and I went quietly to my room to ponder the punishment that was in store for me. Dad and Pat started picking up beer cans, and whiskey bottles, and claimed that they had walked a three-block radius around our house until 5 o'clock in the morning to pick them all up. That was the end of my social life. I was restricted until we left for Europe three months later.

Dad Gets a Command. Dad was overjoyed when he received orders to take over command of the 48th Fighter Bomber Wing based at Chaumont, France. I think my parents saw this assignment as an excellent career opportunity and a chance to work together as a team. They were happy again as they prepared for the move. But I was distressed to learn that I would be yanked out of Woodrow Wilson, the eleventh school I'd attended, just before my senior year. They decided to leave Pat at Georgetown Prep as a boarder. Mary and I would go to a girls' boarding school in Switzerland.

I developed a rash over my entire body, wept and pleaded and begged to be allowed to stay with Andy, whose mother said that I could spend my senior year with them. In a particularly theatrical moment, I feigned an attempt to dive over the banister headfirst down the stairs. Granny, who by this time had embraced Christian Science, wrote and chided me for allowing my emotions to cause my rash. She went on to tell me that, as a good child in the military service, I must gracefully accept each new assignment. She exhorted me to "buck up," saying that my current attitude did not pass muster.

My parents sent Pat to San Antonio to spend the summer with the Lincolns. He was 15 and still small for his age. As soon as school was out, he left for San Antonio, changing buses in Raleigh, North Carolina and Shreveport, Louisiana, a trip of almost two days. Years later, Pat told me about that two-day bus ride through the Deep South. He got off the bus at one stop needing to go to the bathroom. Sleepily following the man in front of him into the men's room, he was gently admonished, "Sonny, you ain't supposed to be in here." Confused about what he'd done wrong, he got back on the bus. His bladder was about to burst by the time the bus finally stopped again. This was how he learned that there were different rest rooms for "coloreds" and "whites" in the segregated south of the 1950s.

In early June 1955, just before we left for Europe, Mom and Dad relented and allowed me to go up to June Week at West Point to say good-bye to Julio. I thought I'd be gone for only a year. I still planned to return to the United States to pursue a degree in nursing. My parents were not interested in this idea, expecting me to get married, preferably to an officer in the military, have children and be a good service wife. I think they also felt that the money, which seemed always in short supply, should be spent on Pat's education.

The moving van came and left. We went to Nantucket to spend a couple of weeks with our friends before sailing for France. During the two weeks on Nantucket, I spent long days sitting on the beach watching the waves, and gradually came to terms with my predicament. As a new chapter in my life was about to begin, I let go of the past and accepted whatever the next year was to hold for me. But I was still determined to come back and go to college.

Chapter Three
Living in Cold War Europe

On the Sea to Chaumont, France: July 1955

We left for Europe from New York Harbor on the S. S. United States, accompanied by 14 pieces of luggage and Freya. Dad had contributed to the excess, so he chuckled indulgently about all the suitcases. We counted off our own, military style, each time they were transferred – from the taxi to the hotel, back to a taxi a couple of days later, and then to the loading dock, and finally onto the ship. Freya was put in a cage below deck next to the foghorn, along with numerous other dogs and a few cats. When the fog descended a couple of days after we sailed, the dogs added considerably to the volume of the horn.

We sailed while a band played patriotic music, and we waved farewell to the Statue of Liberty. I contemplated throwing my passport overboard and actually held it in my hands hanging over the stern of the ship but couldn't get up the nerve to toss it to the waves. I had accepted my fate but continued to let my parents know how angry I was to be forced to leave my friends and face another new school. I spent great amounts of time dressing in Mom's hand-me-downs, applying makeup, and donning high heels. I copied movie stars' sexy walks and airs of sophistication. But I was much less mature than I pretended to be.

I managed to conjure up a couple of adventures on the high seas. Victor Mature, a big movie star who had recently starred in the movies "Sampson and Delilah" and "The Robe," occupied a stateroom not far from ours. I found a compatriot and we surreptitiously watched the door to his stateroom as a variety of women entered, then left after an hour or two. We snickered at each exit until someone heard us and slammed the door.

Arriving in France on the S.S. United States, 1955: Mom, our dog, Freya, Mary and me. I was 16 years old; Mary was 13.

I agreed to kiss a young porter in an elevator one day so he would help us sneak down to third class to see how the lower classes traveled. They were having much more fun than we were. They danced and partied while first class was stiff and sedate. Still, our food was sumptuous and plentiful. We celebrated the Fourth of July 1955, with fanfare and toasts, dressed in formal attire. I was 16 years old.

Late one evening I looked out our porthole and saw that we had entered the port of Le Havre. The harbor was lined with the typical round glass globes that topped the dim streetlights found in Paris and the cities of France. It looked like another planet compared with the gaudy lights of New York that we had left behind five days earlier.

Dad's classmate, Chuck Billingslea, met us when we disembarked and took us to visit the palace at Versailles, built by Louis XIV. I was appropriately impressed with Paris but not eager to climb into the little European vehicle that was to be our family car for the next two years. We roped the luggage on the back and the roof, wedged ourselves in with a patient Freya and headed southeast for the American Air Base at Chaumont in the French department of Haute Marne.

As we drove the 250 kilometers to Chaumont, we passed numerous signs of the War and the German occupation of France that had ended only ten years earlier. Many of the train stations in the villages had been bombed and few buildings had yet been rebuilt. There were no rest stops and few gas stations. Indoor plumbing was rare in the villages. Toilets were outhouses or "Turkish" holes in the floor. "Honey" wagons, pulled by horses or donkeys, were a frequent sight traveling from farms and villages, as workers cleaned the outdoor privies. Chuck had warned that if we needed to relieve ourselves, we should be prepared to squat in the bushes along the road. We saw numerous stopped cars and people calmly squatting with total disregard for passers-by.

We traveled with a picnic lunch. Stopping at a café in the little towns was said to be risky. When we arrived on base, we were cautioned to boil water, and disinfect fruits or vegetables bought "on the economy." The Americans believed that the honey wagons deposited their payloads on the farm fields to fertilize vegetable gardens and fruit trees. Consequently, we were strongly discouraged from buying anything locally and told to stick with good old American food—the canned and packaged products and wilted produce found in the commissaries located at the American bases scattered throughout Europe.

There were elementary schools on the American bases in France, but the American high school was a boarding school in West Germany. My parents had heard reports of American girls becoming pregnant in the dependents' high schools in Germany and decided there wasn't enough supervision. An unmarried pregnant daughter was Mom's worst nightmare. As soon as Dad's orders had been posted, she had found an advertisement for La Chatelainie, a girls' school in Switzerland, in the back of a magazine. Mary and I were enrolled by mail before we left the States.

The American Air Base. Chaumont was the home of the 48th Fighter Bomber Wing, which Dad had been chosen to command. One of 11 American air bases in France, it was surrounded by farmland and was one of the largest of our bases in the country. It was also the most prestigious because the American aerial acrobatics team, the Skyblazers, was stationed there. I already had an eye for a uniform. I watched the fighter pilots in their flight suits. They appeared to be a happy bunch with jaunty attitudes, easy-going manners, and frequent laughter. My father admired them, so I did too.

Chaumont Air Base was a part of NATO, the North Atlantic Treaty Organization, formed in 1949 as a strategic alliance to defend Europe against the Soviet Union. All of Berlin was located in East Germany and thus it was surrounded by the Soviets, an arrangement agreed to at Yalta by Roosevelt, Stalin and Churchill. Hanging onto West Berlin was a priority for the United States. The Russians occupied East Berlin.

The U.S. military bases in France and Germany were among NATO's primary defenses. I wondered whether nuclear weapons were hidden somewhere on the base at Chaumont. However, the President of France, General Charles De Gaulle, refused to allow any nuclear weapons in France. For that reason, the pilots stationed in France regularly spent alert duty in West Germany, where the nukes were kept. This required that each pilot spend a week a month in Germany, a hardship for their families in France, which were widely scattered in villages as far as 60 miles from the Base.

A few days after we arrived, there was a change of command ceremony at the flight line. A small band played as three squadrons of airmen marched by in formation. We stood at attention as the colors went by and the National Anthem filled the air. An order was read, and a few words were spoken. Dad, up front and center, was saluted, and the men now under his command marched by again, eyes right as they passed by their new commander.

We stayed at the only hotel in town, L'Hotel Terminus, across the street from the bomb-scarred train station, while Mom and Dad looked for a house. Freya slept in our room and sat under the table in the dining room where we ate. The French love dogs and never spoke a word of complaint about Freya. Mary and I were given a room with a double bed not connected with my parent's room. A very difficult couple of weeks followed. I complained in a letter to Pat written August 16th that Mary and I were trapped in a stuffy hotel room with absolutely nothing to do, not even a radio.

I sneaked out and wandered over to the USO Club, which provided a place for enlisted personnel to socialize away from the Base. I met an interesting Englishman who had a job on the Base and was into Esperanto, a language that had been developed from all major spoken languages. He told me that Esperanto was to be the world's common language and would bring peace. Sounded like a good idea to me so he began to teach me the basics of the new language. But my excursions to the USO didn't last. My parents frowned on the Base Commander's daughter fraternizing with enlisted men.

Traveling Alone. Bored out of my mind, I persuaded my parents to let me go to Germany to visit my friend and fellow JANGO, Mike Woolnough. Mike was the daughter of an Army General stationed in Augsburg. After my week with Mike I would travel by train to another base in Germany to visit Aunt Tooty and Uncle David. Upon my return to France, Mary and

I would leave within a couple of days to attend school in Switzerland. In a letter to Pat, I wrote:

*"I leave about 7:00 at night to change trains about 9:00 in a small French town and catch the night train to Munich. And I have to carry three different kinds of money with me: MPCs [*Military Payment Certificates, the money used by Americans in Europe*], French francs and German marks. I have to go through the German customs at the border and I have to cross through a little Communist country called 'The Saar Valley.'" It's going to be a great experience. But if you don't hear from me again, you'll know the Commies got me!"*

I was properly dressed for a young girl traveling in the 1950s—in a suit, hat, gloves, and high heels—and I carried three suitcases. I had no idea that I would have exactly two minutes to change trains in the dark in Dijon. Furthermore, I would have to find the right track with my rudimentary French and haul the suitcases over several tracks and up onto the train by myself. Fortunately, or so I thought, an American airman was standing there. He saw my predicament, picked up the suitcases and pushed me on board the train as it began to move.

Then he hopped on the train after me, put his arm around me, told me his name was 'Frenchy,' and tried to kiss me. "Oh my God," I thought. "How am I going to get rid of him?" I tried to get his arm off me and avoid his open-mouthed kiss. The French conductor quickly assessed the situation and ordered the guy off the train. The airman complied as the train pulled out of the station, throwing an insult my way as he jumped. I thanked the conductor and handed him what I thought was my ticket.

He looked at it and launched into a long discourse of which I understood not one word. Finally exasperated, he put me in a stateroom and locked the door. I lay down on the bed and regretted my determination to undertake this adventure. All night I listened as we pulled into and out of station after station, the loudspeakers announcing our locations in German. I was frightened by the sound of German. Chilling memories of the War and Dad's incarceration clung in the air.

In the morning there was a knock. As the door slowly opened, I expected to be thrust from the train. An American Army officer stood there with the conductor. He asked me why I had gotten on the train with only a reservation for a sleeper, and no ticket. I told him that I thought I had a ticket, and that my father was an Air Force colonel stationed at Chaumont and would reimburse him if he could bail me out of this situation. He gave me his address and paid the conductor the 42 marks, about $10, for my passage. Dad paid him back and fired the French clerk who had made the reservation and who probably assumed that we knew we'd have to buy the ticket at the station.

I enjoyed the visit with the Woolnoughs, who lived in an old German mansion with plenty of help—cooks, orderlies and maids. We ate together as a family and had serious discussions at the dinner table. I remember once quoting a Biblical proverb in response to a point that had been made, "Even a fool may be counted a wise man if he keeps silent." Gen. Woolnough considered this for a minute and told me that was not the case. He said that people had to speak up because those who remained silent when they knew better were responsible for a lot of trouble. I think this incident stayed in my memory because he was taking me seriously and responding to me as if I were an intelligent adult. I stayed in touch with Mike for the rest of her life, and I visited Gen. Woolnough shortly before his death. I found him still the warm, kind man that I remembered so fondly.

My visit with Aunt Tooty and her husband, David Goss, was spent playing with their two little boys. They took me to the Officer's Club and tried to show me a good time. I've always regretted the distance that grew between the Goss family and ours. Over the ensuing years, Mom was busy as the General's wife, having less and less contact with her sisters and their children.

To School in Switzerland

In September, Mom drove us to the Swiss village of St. Blaise outside Neuchatel not far from the French border and about a five-hour drive southeast of Chaumont. Switzerland looked like the pictures in my imagination when I read "Heidi": snow-capped mountains, quaint villages, cows grazing contentedly on the hillsides, blue lakes reflecting the azure sky, flower boxes filled with colorful blooms below every window. Switzerland was a pristine and orderly place.

Mary and I were housed on the second and third floors of a narrow, three-story apartment building named Petit Beau Site several blocks down a steep hill from the school. Mary was put in a room with four Americans on the second floor. I was put in a room on the third floor with a Dutch girl, a German girl, and a Colombian girl. When my Dutch roommate left at Christmas a Danish girl took her place.

   Our building had no central heat. Each morning, one of the school staff would put several chunks of coal in the small stove located in the hall on each floor. The stove would burn for a few hours, go out and not be relit until the next morning. There was one bathroom on each floor. We had to sign up for the once-a-week baths each girl was allowed. Hot water was scarce. We were locked in each night at 9:00 p.m. There was only one telephone at the school, and it was located up the hill in the main building. The heavy down comforters

Mary and me at La Chatelainie, 1955

on each bed were our saving grace. We kept our clothes and pajamas under our pillows and dressed and undressed under our comforters. By late November, a glass of water would freeze on our bedside tables overnight.

I was determined to work hard and learn to speak French. There were several levels of instruction. I was placed in the third level and happy to be in the tenth level by spring. In addition to French, I studied English Literature, Chemistry, Algebra II, and Modern European History. These courses were taught in English by a motley group of teachers: a couple of Americans, a Canadian, a Russian, and a Brit.

The most popular teachers were two attractive Swiss men, one of whom taught French. The other was responsible for physical activities such as skiing and ice skating. Both were popular and constantly besieged by students. The French teacher ultimately married one of the American teachers. The ski instructor had affairs with many of the students, a fact known to all of us but apparently unknown to Monsieur Jobin, the director of the school.

In early November, our minds were briefly taken off the cold when it was time to harvest the grapes for the small vineyards on the hills around St. Blaise. Students were let out of classes to pick the grapes by hand. We learned quickly why so many boys were watching as we crawled along the ground cutting the clusters of grapes and dropping them in buckets. If we missed a bunch, the boy who found it was allowed a kiss. I was careful not to miss any grapes unless it was the ski instructor who was watching. The harvest was an opportunity for folks to dance, sing and drink wine. A bunch of rowdy boys came after us that evening as we walked from dinner to our rooms, their hands moving over our chests. We screamed. One of the girls saved us by grabbing her high heel shoe and clobbering them in the face.

My letters home whined that we were never given milk or fresh fruit. Potatoes were the main course at most meals. I told my parents that I hadn't seen an egg since I'd been there and begged them to send me some vitamin pills. Of the four meals a day—breakfast, lunch, tea and supper—my favorite was tea, with fresh-baked bread, delicious butter and homemade jam. When we were served salad, we stirred it carefully until the little green worms crawled out and inched slowly around the edges of our plates. We'd have little competitions to see how many we could scare up before our salad plates were removed. I'm sure we ate a lot of worms at our meals in those days because we were too hungry for fresh produce to refuse the salads.

Today, whenever I hear church bells ringing in the distance, I am reminded of that year in Switzerland. The Catholic Church at the bottom of the hill rang bells to announce the hours as the day passed, and the cows were collared with bells. Each family's cowbells had a different ring tone. The cows were walked down the main street to pasture outside the village each morning and back again in the evening. The herders were often young Italian immigrants who worked for the families that were wealthy enough to own or rent cows and fields for them to graze in. We had to walk the same route several times a day to classes and meals. Although we dodged a few cow pies, most were cleaned up by the herders following the cows to field and home and deposited on the family gardens.

Most of the students at La Chatelainie were English, German or American, and there were a lot of unhappy girls. As I gradually learned their stories, I heard that many had been sent there for their parents' convenience. While some were enjoying the benefit of a year at a Swiss "finishing school" to broaden their education, others had sad stories of divorces, uninterested stepparents, deaths, and parents' desires to travel without their adolescent daughters. One girl cut her wrists and swallowed a bunch of pills before someone found her and called for help.

My Columbian roommate was the only Spanish speaker and had no friends. On numerous occasions I found her crying into her pillow and tried to console her. She spoke no English and, although she spoke French better than I did, she had a heavy Spanish accent that I had difficulty understanding. She had been in the school for three years and wanted desperately to go home. Her mother had died, and she wrote her father almost daily, begging to be allowed to come home, but she rarely received letters. When she did, they never told her she could come home.

A daughter of the popular black American singer, Billy Daniels, attended the school. Diane and I were cordial but she didn't seem to have any close friends. She had gorgeous green eyes, was tall and stately with light golden skin. This was the year after Brown vs. Board of Education had passed in the States desegregating public schools. There was no need for such laws in Switzerland, but some of the American girls were uneasy about how to act toward Diane. Given the era, I don't imagine she was surprised.

We tried to speak French all day so we could sign Le Livre D'Or, The Golden Book. This book was kept up in the main building on a formal stand and was to be signed only by those who spoke French for an entire day without any words in their native language. French was still one of the most widely spoken languages in the world and the official language of international diplomacy. We walked around with our little French dictionaries, looking up words and struggling to engage in conversations with girls from other countries. The effort paid off as we learned to speak and, eventually, to think and dream in French.

I made friends quickly with my Dutch roommate but remained at odds with the German girl for several months. I didn't like the Germans. They were loud and cliquish and spoke only German. One day I discovered that Monica was pilfering from the meager store of goodies that I kept on my closet shelf. When I confronted her, she became irate and began to tell me how badly she had been treated by the Americans during our occupation of Germany. She was five years old when the war ended and clearly remembered how hungry she and her mother had been. She said the Americans threw scraps to them as if they were dogs begging at the table, and that her father had been sent to the Russian front. They never saw him again and had no idea what had happened to him. There are still 72,000 American service members missing in action from World War II, and there must be millions more of all nations still unaccounted for.

I was shocked and felt guilty for confronting her about my missing instant coffee and chocolate. Then I told her about my father having been in a German prison camp for three years and weighing only 120 pounds when he came home (I exaggerated a little). Tears welled up in our eyes and I reached out and hugged her. We immediately became fast friends and corresponded for many years afterwards.

The German girls must have felt the negative vibes from everyone and maybe guilt for the War. One day a couple of them invited me and a friend to come to their rooms. When we arrived, we found a spread of food and wine that they had prepared just for the two of us. Although they spoke little English and we spoke no German, we stayed for several hours and spoke in French with the help of a dictionary. They told us that they liked Americans because we help people, while Germans look the other way if someone needs help. I began to recognize my unreasonable prejudice.

As they had been children growing up in Germany during that terrible war, I should not have been surprised by their indictment. What horrendous things happen during war! As I look back on my brief time in Europe so soon after the war that killed so many people, I wonder at my ignorance. A brief ten years earlier, Germany and much of Europe had lain in ruins smoldering from Allied bombing raids. The horrors the German girls had experienced in the war were beyond my imagination.

My Dutch and Danish roommates had lived through brutal occupations by the Germans. The English girls had also suffered, many of them having been sent away from their families as toddlers to live in the countryside with strangers for the duration of the war—as many as five years of separation from their families. But we didn't talk about the War. Monica and I touched on the subject only briefly.

Mom's letters exhorted me to watch out for my sister. Mary had her 14th birthday after we arrived at school. I think she was too young to be separated from Mom, who wrote to me about how unhappy Mary sounded in her letters. I was writing to my parents twice a week, and once a week to Pat. I felt a huge responsibility to stay in contact with him and to watch over Mary. In one letter, I told my parents that Mary had been to the dentist and that everything went fine, and that the pimple on her neck, which she had feared was cancer, was gone. I faithfully reported on Mary's progress in my letters to Mom and Dad. She appeared to be happy, and one of her roommates told me that Mary was one of the happiest girls there, which I duly reported to my parents.

By late November, it was dark, cold and wet in Switzerland. Thanksgiving Day arrived and was going to be just another day at La Chatelainie. But we had decided to make it different. I got out of bed at five o'clock and took a shivering group down the hill to attend Mass in the village. The priest was stunned when he came onto the altar and saw so many more than the usual two or three people in the pews. After Mass, he came down and asked me what the occasion was. I told him that in America it was our day to give thanks to God for our many blessings. The 30 or so American girls had prevailed upon M. Jobin to have his cook prepare some turkeys that we bought in the village with our pooled resources. It was a wonderful feast.

My first and only attempt to ski was such a disaster, I never tried to ski again. On a Saturday, a bus took a large group of girls to a nearby ski resort for the day. I put the heavy wooden skis on, practiced some snow plows and followed the girls as we rode to the top of a long mountain on a t-shaped ski lift. When I reached the top and looked down, I couldn't believe the run. Straight down as far as I could see without my glasses. I slowly sat down and decided to go down on my butt.

A young man quickly approached me and asked me in Swiss-German and then in French what I thought I was doing. When I admitted that I didn't really know how to ski, he scolded me soundly for coming up the advanced run and asked incredulously, "Do you want to die?" Then he told me to stand up, lift my left ski and pole three feet off the ground, align my right ski with his, and put my arm tightly around him. He put his arm around me and skied me all the way to the bottom. It was an exhilarating ride, but I endured days of teasing from the other girls who accused me of engineering the whole escapade to get the attention of the ski patrol.

About this time, Dad was TDY to Wheelus Air Base in Libya, or to Nouasseur, a base in Morocco. The weather was better and more predictable in North Africa than in Europe. The pilots practiced gunnery and honed their skills in combat operations and instrument flying. Dad was in his element, enjoying every minute of flying T-33s and F-86 Sabre Jets and commanding a bunch of rowdy fighter pilots.

Mom was isolated in Chaumont several miles from the Base during a snowy winter and was lonely. One day a letter from her announced that she wanted to adopt a baby. There were plenty of babies available for adoption in both France and Germany and many American couples were adopting. Only 40 years old, Mom was feeling her nest emptied too soon. But maybe Dad was opposed to adopting because she never mentioned it again. Eventually, Mom found friends who were free to travel and make the rounds of the various Army and Air Force post exchanges scattered throughout France and Germany. Europeans were hurting from the years of war

91

and were selling furniture, antiques, linens, china, crystal, silver and knick-knacks at low prices. Both Mom and Dad had an eye for beautiful things and were particularly attracted to antiques. One of my favorites among their many purchases was an old French grandfather clock that they bought from the side of the road for the equivalent of about eight dollars.

The Cold War was filling our hearts with fear of the Russians and the nuclear weapons that we knew were pointed toward the American bases in Europe. In the event of an attack by the Russians, there was a plan to evacuate the American women and children who were scattered at our military installations all over Europe. Every family was to have an evacuation kit packed with food, water and first-aid supplies in their automobiles. In the event of an emergency, the women and children would leave in caravans for the west coast of France, to be picked up by a U. S. Navy ship. Mary and I didn't worry too much about ourselves because we were in Switzerland, which was neutral, and we felt that we'd be safe. But we worried about Mom and hoped the escape plan would work if it needed to be activated.

Our Home in France

Mary and I traveled by train back to Chaumont for Christmas. Mom and Dad met us at the station with Freya. The reunion was happy for all. But I missed Pat and felt guilty thinking of him back in Washington having Christmas with friends of our parents and spending some of his Christmas vacation alone in the dormitory at Georgetown Prep. Back then, we made no long-distance phone calls, which were expensive. All communication with our loved ones back in the U.S. was via what we now call snail mail.

Although Mary and I were "home" for Christmas, we had never seen the house our parents had rented at number 17 rue Decres in Chaumont. It was at least 300 years old and had no central heat, just a little coal stove in the dining room and another in a central bedroom on the second floor. We hauled buckets of coal to fuel the stoves several times a day in the winter, which was frigid in that part of France. There was hot water, but not much, heated by a tiny propane tank in the bathroom. The house was a duplex. The landlord lived in the attached house with his family. They were rarely seen outside, and kept the shades and shutters drawn. He never spoke when we saw him in the front courtyard.

Mom discovered from Blanche, the French maid she hired, that the townspeople believed that our landlord had collaborated with the occupying Germans during the War and the family was shunned. When my parents rented the house, the locals had raised eyebrows and clicked tongues in disapproval. My parents worked hard to overcome Chaumont residents' suspicion of us. Blanche helped considerably in representing us favorably to her friends. Then something happened that caused Dad to suspect that our landlord may have been a communist working for the Russians. Someone rifled through our many boxes and trunks stored in the attic and it could only have been our landlord. I don't think Dad discovered anything missing, but it was unsettling.

Blanche spoke no English, but we had long conversations when I was finally able to understand her rapid French. Her stories about her experiences during the War have stayed with me. I can see her in my mind's eye as she described it, a young woman pushing her three small children for many miles in a baby buggy with all the belongings she could pile on top of them. She told me that she walked weeping through the night looking for a place where she felt they would be safe from the bombs of the invading Germans. I thought of Blanche again when I read Irene Nemirovsky's book "Suite Francaise." She described the roads to the south from Paris, and all the large cities in the north of France, clogged with fleeing refugees as the German Army swept in and German planes strafed and bombed them.

Dad had studied French at West Point and was able to speak a few phrases. Mom had studied French for several months before we left the States. Their enthusiasm for France was quickly recognized. Dad gained points for sending us to school in Switzerland to learn French and he delighted in showing off our growing fluency. My parents spent a lot of time socializing with the French people in the surrounding communities to improve the relationships between them and the Americans who had so recently descended upon them.

For the most part, the French were happy to have us because we brought jobs and money. But there were unpleasant incidents: automobile accidents, chickens killed on the village roads. Worse, several local girls found themselves pregnant and subsequently abandoned by the American airmen who had fathered their babies. When I visited Chaumont in 2005, a handsome French woman in her seventies cried on my shoulder about the American pilot who left her pregnant and had refused to ever see their daughter who, she said, had learned to speak English fluently in hopes of one day meeting her father.

The base's French liaison officer reported to the local newspaper that my grandfather, also named Col. Albert P. Clark, had lived in Chaumont during the First World War when he was a medical officer on General Pershing's staff. The headquarters for the American Expeditionary Forces was just outside Chaumont in the 16th century Chateau du Val des Ecoliers. Dad made much of this important link to Chaumont, as did the French. We were honored to be invited to visit the Chateau, hidden at the end of a long cypress-lined drive.

On Christmas Eve it snowed as we walked down the street to the 15th century Basilica of St. Jean for midnight Mass. A choir was singing in French "Lo, How a Rose Ere Blooming" as we entered and sat down on the rickety cane chairs that served instead of pews. After Mass, we were invited to attend a traditional "Reveillion" celebration at the home of the town's doctor, Monsieur Bonnet. I had never seen

94

such a spread of food, served in at least ten different courses. We were seated at a long table with all his family and many friends. They wined and dined until 6:00 AM on Christmas Day, when we said au revoir and walked home in the snow.

Life on the Base. When Mary and I were not away at school, we spent a lot of time on the Base. It was surrounded by a heavy barbed-wire-topped fence, with 24-hour guards posted at the gates. There was a small hospital, a commissary and a BX, all housed in metal corrugated Quonset huts or tents covered with black tarpaper. Most of the families lived on the economy in the villages scattered around Chaumont, often in quite primitive conditions. A few lucky families got to live in trailers on the Base that were slowly arriving from the States. There was very little grass or vegetation. Mud was simply everywhere.

With the men gone on TDY so often, or on all-night alerts at the squadron headquarters, many of the wives were unhappy. Alcohol was the anti-depressant of choice. There were social events at the Officer's Club, where alcohol flowed liberally from the hands of the French bartenders into the glasses of the pilots, their wives, and teenagers like me. There didn't seem to be any concerns about underage drinking or drinking by pilots scheduled to fly the next day, or by their pregnant wives. While there were numerous auto accidents related to drinking, I particularly remember one tragedy. One of the wives found herself unhappily expecting her fourth child and drank so heavily during her pregnancy that she delivered a son with fetal alcohol syndrome.

At one of the many cocktail parties during the Christmas break, a handsome pilot that I had met briefly during the summer tentatively approached me and struck up a conversation. I chatted with him and tried to put him at ease. His name was Bud. He was one of the four pilots who flew on the American aerial acrobatics team. I learned that he flew left wing, considered a difficult position for a right-hander to fly, and that he was the only bachelor on the team. These four pilots were the heroes of the Base.

When the Skyblazers practiced their acrobatic maneuvers over the Base, everyone would congregate outside to watch. They would sometimes buzz the Officers' Club at 300 feet. One day I was outside watching this, and they came over the horizon flying so low that it looked like they were going to fly right into the Club. I ducked to the ground along with several others. The pilots in the group stood upright and laughed at those of us who ducked. The Skyblazers performed all over Europe in air shows that served to enhance the prestige of the United States and the Air Force.

Bud and Mom had already struck up a friendship and she had encouraged him to make my acquaintance. He asked me out on a date but failed to show up. I pointed that out the next time I saw him but decided not to hold a grudge. I agreed to have dinner with him and go for a ride in his red Austin-Healey. Mom was delighted, and I was happy to delight her. An American friend of mine from La Chatelainie came to spend the holidays with us and Bud set her up with dates. We roared around having a good time and drinking rum and coke as if we were old enough to drink. At midnight on New Year's Eve at the Officers Club party, I noticed that Bud kissed Mom, or maybe she kissed him.

Back to St. Blaise. One night, one of the girls in my apartment building became sick and vomited for hours. We had already been locked in when I decided she needed a doctor. In my pajamas and with my hair up in pin curls, I put on a jacket and climbed out the window, walked carefully across the red clay tiled roof, and shinnied down the drain spout. I went to the next building, which housed students and teachers, and banged on the door, shouting in French and English that we needed a doctor. A teacher called the village doctor, who gave my friend a shot. Soon she stopped vomiting and went to sleep. I learned afterwards that there was a trusted girl in the house who had a key that no one knew about, but she had not been aware of the medical crisis that was unfolding. I enjoyed being the heroine for a while.

When the rest of the girls left in January for two weeks skiing at Gstaad, I stayed behind to study for the SATs, which I planned to take in the spring. I was determined to attend college in the fall. I was lonely at the deserted school but studied hard, reading entire textbooks so I could take the Advanced Placement tests in French, History and English in addition to the SAT. This intensive studying paid off when I took the train to Geneva and spent a long day taking the tests. I was told later by the dean of students that I had high scores. But scores were mailed to parents and teachers, not to students. I never saw my scores. By the time I finally did go to college 18 years later, the community college had no interest in my SAT scores.

I was accepted by both Duke and the University of Pennsylvania Schools of Nursing contingent on personal interviews at the schools. My parents didn't want me to go back to the States and there was no one that I could turn to for help, so there would be no interviews, and no nursing school. An alternative was suggested by one of my teachers. I could go to Paris and study at the Sorbonne. The only other option was to attend the small campus of the University of Maryland in Frankfurt, Germany. But it didn't have a very good academic reputation, and not enough supervision to please Mom.

Like many young girls in the fifties, I felt enormous pressure to meet my parents' expectations. Although Pat was expected to graduate from college, preferably one of the military academies, Mary and I were expected to marry and have children. Mom, her two sisters and Dad's sister had all married young. While Dad's mother had graduated from nursing school when few women went on to higher education, maybe it was because she was poor and Irish. She was a tall, handsome woman, but was not considered beautiful. Perhaps she was uninterested in marriage, remembering that her mother had borne five children in seven years and died at the age of 25. My grandmother was nearing forty when she finally married my grandfather.

One day at La Chatelainie, I was sick in bed when a message came that I had a visitor in the main building. I dragged myself out of bed, got dressed, and trudged up the hill to find that Bud had come with a letter from Mom giving him permission to visit me. The head mistress told him that I had to go back to bed and that he couldn't visit with me until I was well. He went into the village and booked a room at the hotel. The next day, I went down to the hotel for breakfast with Bud. I was 17 and he was 26, and I felt oh so grownup to have an older man interested in me. After he went back to Chaumont, we began exchanging occasional letters.

There were a few single American women at the base—elementary school teachers and employees of the Department of Defense. They did not approve of my dating the pilots. A couple of them firmly told me that I was too young for these guys and should date boys my own age. But I thought that if my parents didn't think I was too young, then I wasn't.

Italy, May 1956: Since I hadn't be able to go to Gstaad, I was allowed to take a school trip to Italy. In May, ten other girls and I traveled by train to Florence with several teachers. Then we went on to Rome and Venice. Italy was still recovering from the War, so the hotels and restaurants were inexpensive, and there were few tourists. Forty years later, Ted and I went to see the hotels I'd stayed in and found them to be among the most luxurious and expensive in Italy.

While I was in Rome, Mary Wilbourn contacted me. She had just arrived after separating from Bobby, who was stationed with the CIA in Athens. We talked for hours, and she cried on my shoulder. I was with her when she applied for a job at the American Embassy. I loved Mary and I believe she cared for me. She never hinted that she had left Bobby for another man, a liaison that would turn out to be a disaster.

We visited the Sistine Chapel in the Vatican and found it dark and empty. By the light of votive candles, we were able to barely make out Michelangelo's famous figures on the ceiling, dim and darkened by age. When I visited the Vatican in 1996, the ceiling paintings had been cleaned and blazed with color. We were exhorted over a sound system in four languages to respect the sacred space by not talking and not using flash cameras. The din was deafening, and cameras flashed all around us.

Our Chatelainie contingent was a bunch of silly schoolgirls of several nationalities, wearing our crinoline petticoats under full skirts and making our naiveté obvious. The Italian men were sneaky and aggressive, pinching our behinds everywhere we went. They followed us and invited us on dates. We giggled and tried to ignore them. A handsome waiter at the Bauer-Grunwald Hotel in Venice asked me to marry him and gave me his address. When I told Mom, she had a fit and refused to let me write to him.

While I was fascinated by all the beautiful art and historic sites, I remember just as clearly a couple of terrible incidents. On a crowded bus on our way to visit St. Peter's Basilica, I was holding onto a ceiling hanger when suddenly I felt a hand inching under my panties. I jumped with a loud intake of breath, pushed my skirt down and turned around to see three men behind me staring impassively out the window. I had been forewarned. Worse was ahead.

In Venice, four of us decided to take the vaporetto (water bus) across the Laguna to the Lido, the public beach located on another island. We'd seen little sun over a long cold winter in Switzerland and were in good spirits looking forward to sunning on the beach. We didn't know that nice

Italian girls did not go to the beach and we didn't notice their absence when we got there. We trotted up onto a long wooden dock and walked to the end of it, smiling and ignoring the wolf whistles that accompanied us.

As we dove into the water, a group of men dove in after us, separated and surrounded us, and began tearing at our modest one-piece bathing suits. I was a strong swimmer. When I realized what was happening, I let out a couple of loud gasps, coughed, went limp and sank. I knew a little Italian and heard one of the guys warn the others away from me as I sank. I swam underwater back to the beach. When the other girls got out of the water, they were sobbing, and their torn suits barely covered them. We were a traumatized and silent group as we headed back to the hotel, and we never told our chaperones what had happened.

Summer 1956. When school ended, I wrote to Pat, "Well, here I am out of high school. No graduation ceremony, no diploma, no senior prom, no graduation present, and no way to get back to the States to college." I was not looking forward to summer and couldn't imagine what I was going to do with myself. When June came, Mom picked us up and drove us back to Chaumont.

Shortly afterwards, Pat arrived. He was sixteen and was given a job tending bar at the Officer's Club. I was offered a job running the youth center on the base. Few children came to the youth center, and I was not an interested director. I tried half-heartedly to gin up some enthusiasm for activities but without much success. I spent a lot of time stressing about what to do with the rest of my life. I made tentative plans to attend the Sorbonne in the fall but had no place to live. Eventually I learned of a woman who took in students to share rooms and arranged by mail to live with her and attend the Sorbonne. I would study in the French Civilization program for foreign students. I felt trapped but had no alternatives.

During that summer, the whole family went to Berchtesgaden, a German resort in the Alps that was the site of Hitler's famous "Eagle's Nest" retreat. We stayed in a beautiful hotel and prepared for an adventure. Dad wanted to climb to the top of the Wachsmanspitz, which is the second highest mountain in Germany. Perhaps wisely, Mom and Mary declined to make the climb, choosing instead to sit in the sun by the swimming pool. Pat, Dad and I set out early with packs on our backs to climb half-way up the mountain on the first day out, not daring to attempt getting up and down in the same day. To assure the opportunity for some rest and recuperation, we had reservations at the half-way hostel for dinner and the night.

The Germans love to hike. They would sail by us in large numbers wearing lederhosen and saying "Grus Got" as they passed. The stay in the hostel was uncomfortable. We were served a huge dinner of potatoes and corned beef and cabbage, which I couldn't eat. The next day, Pat climbed all the way to the top-most pinnacle of the mountain. Dad and I

Pat and I climbed the Wachsmanspitz with Dad in Germany, 1956

stopped near the top when we came upon large rocks and sheer drops of several hundred feet on all sides.

On the way down, exhausted, I dropped in the middle of the trail and insisted that I couldn't go another step. They picked me up, each supporting an arm at my elbow, and half-carried me the rest of the way down the mountain. The next day I couldn't get out of bed. I lay there all day, moaning and groaning. Mom and Mary laughed as I whimpered for the next month going up and down stairs.

A Statue of Liberty. A very exciting event took place at Chaumont that summer. One of the officers who lived in a small village off the Base made a stunning find. He lived near the foundry where Bartholdi had worked and cast his first models for the Statue of Liberty. Under dirt and hay lay a nine-foot mold that Bartholdi had used to cast one of the smaller statues prior to creating the large one that now stands in New York Harbor. Dad decided that a good way to foster better relations with the French would be to cast a statue from this mold and give it to the French as a gift. None of the funds could come from the government, so the Base personnel set about raising the necessary $1,500. Bake sales, car washes and a car raffle raised the money. The French community got wind of the project and contributed.

Finally, the big day arrived. On July 4, 1956, a nine-foot Statue of Liberty was installed on a six-foot pedestal in front of Base Headquarters. High-ranking American officers, along with noted French politicians of the Haute Marne area, arrived to dedicate the Statue. Dad gave a short speech in French. A parade followed, the French and American flags were raised, bands played both the Star-Spangled Banner and La Marseillaise, the Skyblazers performed their acrobatic air show, dignitaries met to drink a ceremonial toast (a Vin d'Honneur) in the Officers' Club, and to sign Chaumont's Livre D'Or. For Dad, this was a singular accomplishment. The *Stars and Stripes*, the official newspaper of the American

102

forces in Europe, ran a story about the Statue as did the French newspapers. It was a public relations triumph. A few months later Dad was promoted to brigadier general.

The dedication of the Statue of Liberty was significant for the people of Chaumont. There are only two other Bartholdi Statues of Liberty of the same size in France, both in Paris. The Germans melted down others that had been scattered around France before the War. In 1966, when General De Gaulle ordered all the American forces to leave France, the American commander of Chaumont Air Base obtained official approval to take the statue with him to England, where the 48th Fighter Bomber wing was to relocate.

Dad received a letter from the Mayor of Chaumont reminding him of what he had promised in his dedication speech: "Long after there is no longer a need for American forces to be stationed in France this statue will remain as a witness to the long-standing friendship between France and the United States." Dad succeeded in obtaining orders from the Pentagon rescinding approval to remove the statue. It remains today where it was dedicated, now on a small French military base, outside the town of Chaumont.

The grateful City of Chaumont has invited Dad and other members of the 48th back for a Fourth of July celebration every ten years since. We attended this extravagant event with Dad in 1986 and 1996. In 2006, when Dad could no longer travel, we represented him at the 50th Anniversary celebration. I laid a wreath and delivered a speech in French to several hundred people, most of whom were French. Then we went again in 2016, when I laid wreaths, and presented a plaque in memory of my grandfather and father. It was always a moving experience and I always shed a few tears. The French were overwhelming in their appreciation and affection for Americans and when I am in France, I always feel a little bit like the French-speaking schoolgirl that I once was so long ago.

The Skyblazers roar over the Statue of Liberty at Chaumont, a gift from America to France on July 4, 1956.

Not long after, Dad gets his first star, pinned on by Mom and me.

104

Greece, September 1956. In the fall, when Dad went TDY to North Africa to transition the Wing from F-86s to F-100s, Mom decided to take me with her to visit Uncle Bobby, who was still in Athens. Our trip was planned for September after Pat and Mary went back to school and before classes began at the Sorbonne. I remember this trip as the most enjoyable time I ever spent with Mom. She was happy and we laughed and had fun.

We drove south and east into Switzerland, putting the car on a train that took us through the Simplon Pass, over and through the Alps into Italy. We visited Verona and then drove down to Rome where Mary Wilbourn was living in a roomy apartment and working at the Embassy. We stayed with her for a couple of days before taking the train east to Brindisi, on the heel of Italy. On the way, we passed through bleak terrain, interrupted by stops in small villages where people came in droves begging at the open windows of the train. The terrain looked like Texas, Arizona and New Mexico. I half expected to see a band of cowboys chasing masked bandits beside the train. This was to become Hollywood's land of the "spaghetti westerns."

When we arrived in Brindisi, we boarded an overnight ferry bound for Piraeus, the harbor for Athens that lay across the Ionian Sea. There were a few other passengers and many sheep, cows and crates of chickens. The Captain ushered us into one of just two staterooms. The other passengers slept on deck. We dined with the Captain at a small round table for the first-class travelers.

We enjoyed our stay with Uncle Bobby. He introduced us to a good-looking schoolteacher from New Zealand named Graham Bruce. We learned later that he was the man Mary was in love with. After Bobby and Mary's divorce was final, Graham and Mary married. But the marriage was not happy, and they separated some years later.

In about 1985, I found a phone number for Mary in London and spoke to her several times before she died. When

105

I told her that I loved her, she cried. Ted and I attended her burial, which Bobby arranged, in her family's burial plot behind Monticello where her mother and Thomas Jefferson are buried.

To the Sorbonne, University of Paris: October 1956`
In early October, Mom took me on the train to Paris, where I would live with Madame Baudon de Mony at #1 rue Maréchal Harispe, a couple of blocks from the Eiffel Tower. Madame, as we always addressed her, lived with three of her adult children and four students in a large third-floor apartment. An Algerian woman was her full-time cook and maid. I shared a room with a Belgian girl studying pre-med. The household spoke only French.

Madame had fewer rules than had governed my life in Switzerland, but I was required to eat all three meals with her family. The big meal of the day was at noon. Because the Sorbonne was a 45-minute trip by bus, and I had classes in the morning and the afternoon, I spent three hours every day commuting back and forth across Paris. I left in the morning just before the sun rose, came back at noon, returned to the Sorbonne after lunch and came home after dark.

This was a turbulent time in French history. There were riots almost every day and night near the Sorbonne. Some of the students were communists demanding a bigger role in the government. There was also a bloody war for independence going on in Algeria, long a French colony, and there were demonstrations for and against the war. I was nervous trying to avoid all this as I traveled across Paris every day. Paris is on a latitude north of Maine, with long dark winters but little snow. There was no heat in the Sorbonne, and not much heat anywhere else in Paris. Coal was expensive. I was always cold. I had an almost ankle-length dark grey wool coat, which I wore all the time, even in class.

The classes were lectures, except for the French grammar class, and all were conducted in French. We sat on hard, backless wooden benches writing in notebooks on our knees. Lighting was low, there were no power-point presentations, no handouts. I scrounged for books in second-hand bookstores. The most important book in my possession was a petite Larousse English/French dictionary. It's torn and tattered but I still have it.

There were no other Americans that I could discern in any of my classes. I was surrounded by strangers speaking all the languages of Europe except English. I began to lose my self-confidence and enthusiasm for this venture. To make matters worse, I soon figured out that Madame did not like Americans. She only liked American money. I found a Catholic church about two miles away that had one Mass every Sunday with a homily in English. I walked there and back every Sunday. As time passed, I began to blend in. I looked like any other French schoolgirl.

During the fall of 1956, the people of Hungary revolted against the occupying Russians and the newspapers declared that war was imminent. The Hungarians hoped that the United States would step in to help them. The daughter of an American diplomat lived with us. She told me that war was unavoidable and would occur within a few days. She was going to the American Embassy. I asked her if I could come with her and she said, "Absolutely not. Only diplomats' families can be sheltered in the Embassy."

Terrified and teary-eyed, I called Chuck Billingslea, who was stationed in Paris. I asked him what I should do. I wasn't sure that I could ever find the caravan going to the French coast to evacuate with Mom. Chuck tried to calm me down and told me to sit tight but gave me no other information. Then the United States decided not to help the Hungarians. The papers continued to report on the carnage into November, and I'll never forget seeing the photographs of those young men throwing rocks as they were being run over by Russian tanks.

Sometime in the previous summer, Bud had begun to ask, "When are we going to get married?" I would laugh and tell him that I was going back to the States to college, not getting married. He told me that he had asked two other women, one a show girl in Las Vegas, to marry him and had been turned down by both. Although I asked, he provided no other details, and didn't seem particularly daunted by those rejections.

I really wanted to go to college in the States. And I had misgivings about Bud. He had not graduated from college, was not a Catholic, and his parents were divorced, which meant something in those days. He had come into the Air Force during the Korean War when they needed pilots and would be required to leave the service after a couple more years. He said he'd probably drive a truck. I couldn't imagine being married to a truck driver. But his situation changed when, at my father's urging and with his strong recommendation, Bud took and passed a test. That granted him a regular commission in the Air Force; he could be an Air Force officer for at least 20 years.

On a visit to Chaumont in the fall, Bud again asked when we were going to get married. I laughed and responded that he'd have to ask Dad for my hand. I thought that would shut him up because I never thought he'd ask Dad if he could marry me for two reasons: because Dad had been promoted to brigadier general and because I was so young, just 17. I had clearly underestimated Bud's relationship with my parents.

Before I went back to Paris that Sunday, Bud came over for lunch. While I was in the kitchen, he told my parents that we were going to get married. When I came back into the room Mom jumped up with tears in her eyes and told me how happy they were. I must have looked confused because she quickly responded that she and Dad were delighted that Bud and I were going to get married.

I remember shrugging a bit and putting on a forced smile. "Well," I thought, "this seems to have gotten way out of

108

my hands." But Mom was so happy. I trusted her judgment more than my own. Although she had warned that Bud had a mean streak, she assured me that I could handle him. I didn't know what to do if I couldn't go back to the States to college. Maybe this was the answer to what I often asked myself "What am I going to do now?" Bud was handsome and now had a secure future in the Air Force. Maybe marriage was a way to get my parents' approval and the affection I craved.

December came and the Air Force reassigned Dad from Chaumont to the U.S. Air Force Headquarters in Wiesbaden, Germany, to be Chief of Staff to the three-star general there. At the farewell dinner reception, Dad announced that he was leaving someone very dear to him behind, going on to say that I was to be married to Bud. There were sharp intakes of breath followed by applause. A couple of wives approached me later and tentatively suggested that I should reconsider marriage and go to college. I was polite, but thought to myself, "I'm in too deep. It's too late for that now." I felt that I couldn't get out of it now without embarrassing myself and my parents. Besides, I thought, Bud was a good catch. He was a skilled pilot, respected by everyone on the Base and now had a regular commission in the Air Force. The wedding was set for June 1957.

Achtung! Wiesbaden, Germany: December 1956

The day after our second Christmas in Chaumont, we packed up and left France for Germany. Mom decided to leave Freya in France with a family of several children. It was hard to say good-bye to her, and I hope that she was loved and pampered during her last years. The drive to Wiesbaden was through cold and snow. Dad was assigned quarters on the "gold coast" where all the generals lived. The quarters were spacious and modern. Auckham was the name of the housing area and it looked like it could have been anywhere in the U.S. We greeted the automatic furnace and the luxury of plenty of hot water with hoots of joy.

I took the train back to Paris, stayed for ten more weeks and took the French language exam, passing with decent grades and earning a Certificate in French. I decided not to take exams in the lecture subjects or finish the school year in Paris. In early March I flew from Paris to Wiesbaden in an Air Force cargo plane, a flight arranged by Dad.

I spent the next three months with my parents in Wiesbaden embroidering tablecloths and napkins with the initial "H." Mom bought me some clothes and gave me a choice of three silver flatware patterns. We found a seamstress and bought white Chantilly lace for a wedding dress and lavender lace for Mom's dress.

When I was addressing the wedding invitations to my parents' list of invitees, Dad asked me to enclose a note in the invitation to Dick Park, an artist who had painted Mom's portrait. I was to tell him that the only wedding present I wanted from him was the portrait he had painted of Mom before she married my father.

Bud came to Germany in May for the civil ceremony that was required because Germany did not recognize religious marriages. As time passed and the June 15 date for the formal wedding drew nearer, my relationship with Mom grew tense. She was paying for this extravaganza and she wanted to make all the decisions. We both seethed with quiet resentment. Boxes and boxes of wedding presents arrived, an astonishing amount of loot that filled a room on the first floor of the quarters.

Pat arrived from Washington. All the Lincolns came: Mary, Abe, Clark and Anne from Morocco, and Jim from his freshman year at West Point. Fritzie came and Mary Wilbourn, not yet married to Graham, came from Rome. My sister was to be my Maid of Honor and my bridesmaids would be Anne Lincoln, Liz Thatcher, and Anne Craig, a friend from La Chatelainie.

Bud was expected to drive to Wiesbaden several days before the wedding to attend various pre-wedding events. His mother arrived from California, but he didn't show up. I paced the floor asking myself, "What's happened to him!" We were already legally married, so I didn't think he'd changed his mind. "Maybe he had an accident in that Austin-Healy," I thought.

I imagined my grief, the funeral, and what I would do next. I decided that I'd go to the University of Maryland, the campus only about thirty miles from Wiesbaden. I could start college there and then transfer to a college in the States. Bud finally did show up the day before the wedding, clearly hungover. He confessed that he was late because the bachelor party in Chaumont had gone on for two days and nights.

We had never heard back from the artist who had painted Mom's portrait, now an Army colonel. On the day of the wedding, there was a knock on the door. When I opened the door, Dick Park was standing there holding the portrait. Dad had tried on numerous occasions over the prior 18 years to get that painting, but Dick had steadfastly refused to give it up, keeping it hanging over his fireplace long after he had married someone else. Mom said later that Dick shed the only tears at my wedding.

The painting was my wedding gift, but Dad wouldn't let it go. He decided that it didn't belong in a trailer in the mud of Chaumont. He said he would keep it safe until I had an appropriate place to hang it. When he was assigned to Saudi Arabia the next year, the portrait went with him. It was hanging over their fireplace when the house caught fire and burned down. The painting was damaged but not destroyed. Dad took it to Germany where an artist who was restoring the art in the bombed-out Cologne Cathedral repaired it. Eventually, a bit reluctantly, Dad gave it to me.

Marriage. On June 15, 1957, Bud and I were married by a Catholic priest in a little Air Force chapel on Wiesbaden Air Force Base. Just as the wedding ceremony began, we were startled to hear a bugler loudly announce "Colors" on the parade ground right outside the open door of the chapel. The ceremony came to a halt as "Retreat" rang out, the cannon boomed, the "Star-Spangled Banner" played across the Base and the flag was lowered. We had blithely planned the wedding for 5:00 p.m. without taking into consideration that the Chapel was next to the parade grounds. It was the perfect beginning for my life as a military wife.

The reception was in my parents' quarters. Using Pappy's recipe, they mixed up a batch of Cavalry Punch, rumored to be lethal even for fighter pilots. I confided in Mary Wilbourn that I was afraid, and she looked alarmed. Mom hurried me out of the reception, and we sped off in a shower of rice to a hiding place where Bud's red Austin-Healey sat waiting for us. The party went on without us for most of the night, and later we were re-galed with all the stories of how much of the punch was drunk by the fighter pilots.

I truly believed that I loved Bud and that he loved me. But we had never shared our thoughts or fears. In fact, neither one of us was a very good commun-

June 1957 at Wiesbaden AFB

112

icator. I knew Bud mainly as a celebrated pilot whom both of my parents admired. And despite my outward skill at appearing sophisticated, I didn't know much about myself, either. We were both introverts, although I had learned how to act like I wasn't. He liked to drink and I didn't. I was a devout Catholic and loved books. He loved flying and had no interest in religion or books. I hadn't realized how little we had in common. We were not a good match. The honeymoon couldn't live up to this 18-year-old's fairy-tale fantasies and Bud couldn't hide the fact that he could hardly wait to get back into the air. A bad start.

Mom had provided me with a few facts about married life, but I was still   ignorant. I had impossible expectations of marriage: that it would provide unconditional love, an ecstatic intimate experience, a tried-and-true path for me to follow for the rest of my life, and that Bud would always love, cherish, and care for me. I believed this despite Bud having told me that his career would always come first. "If the Army wanted you to have a wife, they'd have issued you one" was the saying. I thought I could handle that, but I had no idea what that would mean for me and my children.

Home to a Trailer in France: June 1957

When we ran out of money part way through the honeymoon, we sped back to Chaumont and moved into a trailer on Base. Mice, roaches and ants greeted us. Bud soon left to perform in an air show somewhere in Europe. I had no driver's license and stayed alone in the trailer. The priest who had married us had provided us with a brief lecture about the laws of the Church regarding marriage. He told us that birth control was not allowed. Useless information for me because I had no idea how to keep from getting pregnant. Soon I began to feel sick and stayed in bed for days at a time.

When I finally went to the doctor, I heard "Yep, you're pregnant alright." There were murmurs about the Base that I was pregnant before we were married .... tsk, tsk! The only other teen-aged girl at the Base had gotten pregnant before she married her pilot and had delivered a "seven-month" baby. This made me grist for the gossip mill. The doctor told me that my due date was the ninth of March and that I should not gain more than 20 pounds because I would not be able to deliver a baby weighing more than six pounds. I was 5'7" tall and weighed 108 pounds.

Bud returned from TDY only to be placed on alert, and then sent to Germany for a week. Night after night, he didn't come home or, when he was on base, came home late after spending time at the bar. I put on a brave face and tried to act like a good fighter pilot's wife. One night, I accompanied him to the bar but found myself sitting alone with no one to talk to while he was surrounded by other pilots trying to out-do each other's flying tales. When I began to feel queasy, I asked him to take me home. I waited awhile longer before I walked the two miles in high heels back to the trailer in the dark, without my glasses. I was proud of my spunk, but he was livid.

I went back to Germany on the train for a month during one of his trips and pretended that everything was okay. Mom was delighted with my pregnancy and had maternity clothes made for me. She looked forward to being a grandmother and decided she would be called Gam, which meant "leg" in the slang of her time (she had very nice legs).

Mary was attending the American high school located in Wiesbaden after spending the previous two years in different Swiss schools. When Dad was ordered to Saudi Arabia in December of 1957, Mom would take her back to San Antonio to live with my grandparents and Mary would start yet another new school. Her high school experience was more fragmented than mine. But at least she would spend half her junior year and her senior year at an American high school and have the graduation experience that I'd missed. As a bonus, and maybe because she felt guilty about leaving her in San Antonio, Mom gave her a car and a credit card.

Dad was ordered to Saudi Arabia, in part because he was as tall as King Saud and could look him directly in the eyes. That seemed to be an important factor in the decision to send him as a military attaché and diplomatic advisor. With me married off, Pat in boarding school and Mary in San Antonio with our grandparents, Mom would be free to go with him.

While I was in Germany, I came into the kitchen one morning to see headlines on the front page of "The Stars and Stripes." The date was October 4, 1957. Russia had launched Sputnik I, the first man-made earth satellite. Dad was closeted for days and nights. This event did not bode well for the United States and President Eisenhower. We were enmeshed in the Cold War, and now faced the prospect of a costly competition into space. The race to the moon had begun and we were behind. The tiny baby growing inside me had just kicked me for the first time. He would be 11 years old when we won that race.

In late October, Bud received orders to Turner Air Force Base in Albany, Georgia. He sold his Austin Healey and bought a Volkswagen, which we would pick up in New York and drive to Georgia. I wasn't afraid to move so far away from my parents. I thought I knew how to be a good Air Force wife, to help Bud in his career, and to win his love and respect.

We left for the States on a prop aircraft from Paris. We waited for hours before boarding the flight, flying from Paris to Frankfurt, then back to Paris. When the flight took off again, we flew to Ireland to refuel, then refueled at Keflavik in Iceland, and Thule in Labrador, before finally landing in New York. When we fell into bed in the VOQ at Hamilton Army Depot, we had been upright for 48 hours. My legs and feet were so swollen that I could hardly walk. My two-and-a-half years in Europe had ended. Instead of coming back as a college nursing student, I had come back a pregnant teenaged wife of an Air Force lieutenant.

$$\star \: \star \: \star$$

PART II

The Third Generation of Brats

Chapter Four
Moving, Moving, Moving

First stop: The Deep South

We arrived at Turner Air Force Base, in Albany, Ga., in early November, five months after the wedding. Bud deposited me and our luggage in a small apartment just off Base and began the lengthy process of checking in and reporting for duty. When he returned with news that there was no base housing available, we found a partially furnished two-bedroom duplex about two miles from the base. Its previous and current occupants were cockroaches.

Bud must have been feeling apprehensive about fitting in with the pilots in a new squadron. But it was deeper than that. When his mother visited us a few months later, she made a two-minute 8mm movie. When I watched it years later, I saw again his bowed head and unsmiling young face. He looked morose, preoccupied as he bestowed a perfunctory kiss on the baby to please his mother holding the camera.

The wives of Bud's new squadron mates were not friendly to me. I was a teenager. As a schoolgirl in Europe, I had missed more than two years of American television, movies and pop music so I was also a cultural misfit. When Bud was teased as a cradle robber, he would say, "I married her young so I could bring her up right!" He began to attend social functions without me. He didn't say that he was leaving me home because he was ashamed of me, but I felt that he was. Eventually I learned that my nickname was "Junior Miss."

A lieutenant's pay was slim. Bud drew it in cash and hid it under the sheets in the linen closet. I wrote to the Bank of Fort Sam Houston and opened a checking account. We rented some worn furniture and borrowed the money to buy a washing machine and a crib. We couldn't afford a television. What did I do all day alone in that little apartment? I read magazines and the newspaper, knitted a blanket, embroidered a little quilt for the coming baby, cleaned and cried.

I was scared and alone. I spent hours pacing the apartment, sobbing. Sometimes I know that the neighbors could hear me, but no one came and knocked on my door to ask what was wrong. I hoped that Bud might come home and hear me, but I grew too exhausted to keep it up long enough. I was a sorrowful, frightened and lonely young girl. I felt totally abandoned with no one to turn to for consolation.

My spirits rose when Pat came to spend Christmas. He had driven down in Dad's Oldsmobile, which we'd named "The Grey Goose." It was a wonderful reunion with my best friend. He let out a gasp of astonishment when I lifted my maternity blouse to show him my baby bump. We talked our heads off. I was supposed to be happy, and I tried to pretend that I was. I was ashamed to tell him that I was miserable.

Within a few weeks of our arrival, Bud had been selected for the unit's Fighter Weapons Gunnery Team. Training for the ensuing competition took him TDY to Nevada for six weeks in early January. Just before he left, he brought me a little black puppy. He never wrote or called while he was gone. I had no friends except the puppy.

I made a small step toward growing up and taking responsibility for myself when I drove into town for an appointment with the doctor that I'd picked from the phone book to deliver the baby. And I drove onto the base to buy groceries at the commissary and to attend Mass on Sundays. I was careful. I didn't have a drivers' license.

One evening, I answered a knock on the door. There stood a stranger with a sample case. I can't believe that I let the guy in and decided, on the spot, to buy the Encyclopedia Britannica that he was selling. All my children would go to college and the encyclopedias would help them get there. When Bud came home from TDY, he was so preoccupied he didn't even notice them. I paid the bills—ten dollars a month, including interest, for five years.

Only a couple of weeks after I bought the encyclopedias, which included a dictionary, I needed important information. I had begun to have alarming symptoms. "I have worms," I realized with horror. I frantically called my doctor who, by the way, had been a veterinarian in his first foray into the medical field. He checked the sample I brought in and told me that I had liver flukes. He would send the sample to the Centers for Disease Control in Atlanta for definitive diagnosis.

I rushed home and looked up "liver flukes" to learn that they usually appeared in farm animals, killing them within ten to twelve months. I freaked out and made an expensive telephone call to Mom, who had just flown from Germany with Mary to San Antonio to be with my grandparents. When I told her that my doctor said I had liver flukes, she laughed. She didn't believe me.

Ten days later, the doctor called to inform me that I had a tape worm from beef, not nearly as serious as liver flukes. I had brought the worm back from France, where I had eaten steak tartare. By this time, I was very pregnant. Bud returned from Nevada as the doctor was instructing me on the treatment to kill the tape worm: two Atabrine tablets (generic is hydroxychloroquine, usually prescribed for malaria) every 15 minutes for two hours, followed by an entire bottle of Sal Hepatica, similar to the cocktail prescribed today prior to colonoscopies. The worm was done in. Given the current medical advice to pregnant women, I'm astounded that Hal was not born prematurely. Although he was my smallest baby, neither the treatment nor the worm had hurt him.

Hal, My First Baby: March 1958. Mom came from San Antonio a few days before the baby was due. On March 6, my water suddenly broke and I went into labor. We drove to Phoebe Putney Memorial Hospital in Albany. A nurse put me into a bed, sliding the sides up. There were several other such beds in the room occupied by women in labor who were moaning and screaming, their hands tied to the sides of the beds. I was frightened out of my wits. In Chinese there are two symbols for motherhood —one the symbol for love, the other for pain, a pretty good definition. There were no prenatal classes in those days, and I knew nothing about what to expect. I sat up on the bed, horrified, and suddenly felt the baby turn around. He must have felt my fear and decided that he wouldn't be born after all. The nurse came back and stuck a needle in my arm without a word.

I regained consciousness 18 hours later, six hours after the baby was born. My arms were covered with bruises. According to my doctor, I had been quite "active" during the several hours of labor. Mom came in and told me that I'd had a baby boy. She explained that the birth had been a risky frank breech. "What is that?" I asked. The baby was born butt-first, risky because the cord is often wrapped around the baby's neck, causing suffocation or brain damage. Today, doctors automatically perform Cesareans for breech births. The doctor laughingly told me that he had not realized that the baby was breech until he saw a little butt appear instead of a head. He performed a three-inch incision to speed the delivery and avoid complications. I could not sit down for a month.

Breast feeding was discouraged, so I didn't see my baby until the next day when a nurse wordlessly deposited him on the side of my bed and rushed out. I was afraid to pick him up. We looked at each other for a few minutes before he was hastily removed. We gave in to our family tradition and named the baby after his father and decided to call him Hal.

The drug used for labor and delivery in Georgia, and elsewhere in the 1950's, was Scopolamine, or twilight sleep. While it did not alleviate pain, in a large enough dose it deleted memory of the pain. I had asked the doctor whether my husband could be present when I gave birth. I'd read of this new approach to labor and delivery. My doctor told me that he wouldn't allow this because he'd then have two patients to deal with. He said, "men can't handle witnessing childbirth."

Bud left on TDY the morning after, and Mom brought us home from the hospital a week later. Bud came back a few days after that. After a brief glance at his crying son, he took Mom to the airport to catch a flight to join Dad in Saudi Arabia and left on another TDY. Looking back, I don't know how I managed to figure out how to care for a baby. I had no

Hal was born in 1958, my first beautiful baby.

model for child-rearing besides my mother. I was terrified of somehow accidentally hurting him.

A few weeks later, Bud's mother, May, came for a visit. While she and I spent time together, she filled me in on her life and Bud's. She loved caring for the baby but soon became bored and went back to California. There wasn't much to keep anyone occupied in Albany, especially if there was no television set. It wasn't long after her return from that visit that her second husband died suddenly of a heart attack. He was relatively young and left her with nothing but debts and grief. She was to marry twice more but this man was the only one she truly loved.

We had no baby furniture except a crib, and I was afraid to put the baby on the floor for fear of the cockroaches. He was either in my arms, on the sofa or in his crib. I had no friends with babies who could model good mothering for me. I never went out except to church, to the doctor or to buy groceries. Hal went with me. There were no car seats for babies then and he lay on the seat beside me. I went to Mass every Sunday with the baby, earnestly praying for strength, and for Bud's love. In addition to my decision to grow up to be brave and strong like my father, I am certain that my faith in God provided the support I needed.

Although the puppy was adorable, I had no idea how to train her. I stayed inside, afraid to walk her because she pulled me over. Besides, I had no stroller and couldn't leave the baby alone. She grew and grew, chewed on everything and pooped and peed in the apartment. I finally tied her outside and found a big cardboard box for her to sleep in.

My Maid, Ainna. I was back in the south again ten years after I had first noticed signs at service stations indicating different restrooms for "White" and "Colored." Those signs were still everywhere in the 1950s. But I was reading the paper and knew that change was coming.

One day, a black woman timidly knocked on my door and asked if I wanted to hire a maid. I didn't need a maid, but I did need company, so I said yes. Ainna (probably Edna) came once a week to work all day for $1.50. I looked forward to her coming. It was easier to shop for groceries if she was there while the baby slept. I began to feel that she was a friend and I tried to overcome her reticence by chatting her up. One day, something happened that left me confused for a long time.

I had prepared a sandwich for her lunch and put it on the dinette table. She sat down and began to eat. I brought my sandwich in and sat down across from her, upon which she jumped up with a cry of alarm and ran into the kitchen. I went in and asked her what was wrong, but she just stood with both hands up at her face huddled against the back door, shaking her head. I asked her if something was wrong with the sandwich, but she just looked at me with wide eyes, and kept shaking her head.

There is a file deep in our brains where we sometimes store the memories of events we don't understand. Later, something may happen that triggers the memory, the file opens and suddenly we understand. I didn't know that in the south in 1958, blacks and whites did not eat at the table together. I had eaten many times at kitchen tables with black women and men when I was a child. But I was unschooled in the proper behavior of Southern white women toward blacks. We could not eat together now that I was grown. She never explained why she was so upset. But eventually she overcame her fear and continued to come faithfully every week, though she never ate at the table again.

Pat Comes for the Summer. When he graduated from Georgetown Prep in May, Pat came down again, this time on a Greyhound bus, to spend the summer of 1958. He was flat broke when he arrived, and reluctantly told me his nickname at school was "rag picker" because his clothes were so worn out. He had been accepted at Georgetown University and wanted to buy some new clothes for college. When the brother of an acquaintance in construction offered him a job digging ditches with a crew of black men, he began working. It never crossed our minds that the Southerner who offered him the job had never expected him to accept it.

Pat worked in the humid and blistering heat of the southern Georgia summer digging ditches beside a group of black men who were astonished to have a white boy from a prep school up north working with them. He came home every evening with hilarious tales about the jokes the guys told and tricks they played on each other. We laughed together, and I was proud of him. Pat grew to respect the head of the digging team, who was illiterate, but kind and wise.

I began receiving phone calls from some guy who knew Bud was TDY and kept suggesting that he come over and do some unprintable things to me. I was on edge, but Bud had left a loaded handgun in the drawer of the bedside table. One night, Pat and I were sitting together talking. Suddenly I heard someone trying to open the front door. I ran back to the bedroom, grabbed the gun, and pointed it at the door as it opened. In walked Bud, who had not told us that he was coming home.

Home for a few days, he asked Pat to stay with the baby while we went down to Florida for the weekend. Pat, 18 at the time, readily agreed and stayed home from his job, feeding the baby, bathing him, and changing and washing diapers and hanging them on the clothesline. Hal was five months old and eating strained baby food, which he had a habit of suddenly blowing out of his mouth. It would fly into my face, and all over my clothes before I learned how to stop him. When we came home from Florida, my rocking chair and the wall behind it were liberally splattered with strained spinach and remnants of the other baby food Pat had patiently tried to feed Hal. He just laughed and marveled at how "the kid has a good strong mouth for spitting!"

While we were in Florida, Pat received a telephone call from someone, whose name he didn't recognize. "Mrs. Wilbourn has died," the voice said. We were confused. "Was she talking about Granny?" we asked each other. We had no idea Granny was sick. I called my grandparents' number and learned that Granny had indeed died of breast cancer. She was only 65. We cried together but couldn't attend a memorial service so far away. I invited Mary to come live with us, but she declined. Then I began writing to my parents urging Mom to come home for Mary's sake and telling my Dad he shouldn't extend his tour over there.

Apple Valley. When Pat left for college in August, Bud was scheduled to be TDY to George Air Force Base in southern California for three months. Dad sent me money for a ticket to fly out and join Bud for a couple of months. We found a family to take the puppy, and I guiltily said good-bye to another dog. Bud found someone to drive the car out and I flew to California with the baby, changing planes twice. We moved into the Chief Desert Lodge in Apple Valley. Because we couldn't afford to rent a crib, the floor of the closet was Hal's bed. I saw little of Bud, but there was another Air Force wife from Georgia staying at the same motel. We became friends and spent a lot of time together.

When it was time to go back to Georgia, my friend Joanne and I decided to drive and stop in San Antonio, a long way on many two-lane roads. We covered the luggage in the back with blankets and put Hal there with toys. There were few cars as small as our VW on the roads in those days. Joanne and I were a nervous curiosity, especially with a little baby looking out the back window. Trucks would come up behind us, honking, waving and laughing. Hal was a chubby little baby with blond curls and brilliant blue eyes. He rarely cried and adjusted to sleeping on a different motel floor every night, and for many days in the back of the car.

When we arrived in San Antonio, we found Pappy bereft, loudly sobbing every night grieving for Granny. It must have been a difficult visit for Joanne. Danny and Lisbeth came over and hugged and kissed the baby. But I saw little of Mary. She had moved in with Dad's stepmother, Ruth, and her daughter, Anne, who was waiting to marry her fiancé in Mexico City. Anne finally wrote and asked Mom to come back from Saudi Arabia. Mom came back a few months later, they attended Anne's wedding, and Mary graduated from high school.

By the time Joanne and I arrived home in Georgia, I was throwing up and pregnant again. To make matters worse, I came down with a serious asthma attack. Having learned from my parents that I should just sit it out, I sat in bed struggling to breathe. Foolishly, I didn't feel that I could ask anyone for help. I was barely able to get bottles and put them in the crib for the baby. He cried pitifully for two days and nights while I struggled for each breath.

When Bud came home from California, and learned that I was pregnant again, he chuckled and said, "Leave 'em barefoot and pregnant!" I asked him to take me to a doctor to get an inhaler, but the doctor refused to give me one, telling me that if I had another attack to go to the emergency room. There would be many trips to emergency rooms before I was given proper medication and learned how to manage my asthma.

Where the Cockroaches Grow Large

In December Bud was ordered to report to Eglin Air Force Base in the Florida panhandle. He was to transition into the F-105 test squadron there. He rented a cottage on Boggy Bayou in nearby Niceville. We drove down to Florida with the baby. The crib, the washing machine, our clothes and the wedding presents followed in a small moving van. An Air Force couple with three young boys rented a house next door. Our cottage had one bedroom, two sun porches, no central heat or air conditioning, and many trees with Spanish moss hanging down onto the cottage roof. There was some beat-up furniture and a dock out front that extended into the Bayou.

I was pleased with the little cottage until the first night when I got up to use the bathroom, turned on the light, and surprised an army of insects that looked bigger than mice. I screamed in terror. I still get chills thinking about those Palmetto bugs, which infested every inch of the cottage. I called an exterminator the next day. He came every month to spray horrid-smelling poison that stunned but often didn't kill the critters. The brown trails they left behind proved that they crawled on everything all night, hiding during the day. If I saw one, I would throw something at it, usually one of Bud's boots. When I scored a hit, the bug cracked open, emitting a disgusting odor. I was horrified that my babies would be crawling around a cottage with an infestation that required monthly sprays of insecticide.

The gas heater was unfiltered and dirty. The cottage was dusty and moldy. The air was humid and heavy, and sometimes thick with cigarette smoke. Soon Hal had his first asthma attack and the doctor put him in the hospital in an oxygen tent for three days. I slept on a bed next to him. My heart ached as I watched him struggling for breath, uncomplaining, and playing inside plastic walls where I couldn't hold or hug him. No sooner did I get home with him, than I also had an asthma attack. The emergency room staff gave me shots of adrenalin until I could breathe but did not give me an inhaler.

Winter in northern Florida is depressing—grey and dreary. It rained for weeks at a time. But spring came and Bud bought a television set. I began to feel better. After Mary graduated, she and Mom drove to Niceville from San Antonio. They slept in twin beds on a sun porch. The morning after they arrived, Mary announced that she had awakened to find a rat in her hair. We laughed heartily and told her that she'd been dreaming. Fuming the next morning, she insisted that the rat had been back.

That's when I noticed little brown specks on shelves in the bathroom, and in the crib where Hal slept. With a sudden shudder, I thought, "Maybe Mary wasn't dreaming." The next night I was startled awake by the sound of what I momentarily thought had been a book falling from the bed to the floor beside me. But there had not been a book on the bed. The rat had been on the bed while we slept. Although Bud and Mom were still dubious, I realized that we were harboring a curious rat in our midst.

The following night, I went to bed with a flashlight and sat up listening. Sure enough I heard stealthy noises moving around the cottage. A cup was overturned on the bookcase. A bump in the kitchen was followed by a scratching sound. When the noises approached the bedroom, I shone the flashlight in their direction. There were beady red eyes staring at me. I screamed and gave Bud the flashlight. The rat scampered over to the rug by the bed and Bud killed it with the flashlight. As a mean joke, he then put the dead rat outside the front door with a note to Mary to dispose of it, which she did not appreciate one little bit.

Pappy with baby Billy, 1959

Billy was next, in June 1959. I went into labor on the morning of the rat's demise, my contractions just ten minutes apart. When I arrived at the hospital, the doctor on duty was the chief of obstetrics. He listened with some disapproval to my story of Hal's birth, then said he believed that women should be awake and give birth under a local anesthesia. Still, my history of severe asthma put me on the high-risk list, so the doctor took me back to a private room, started an epidural and never left my side. I was wide awake when the baby was born a couple of hours later, a joyful experience. But again, the doctor told me not to consider breast feeding, warning that I'd be pregnant again too soon.

When I got home with the baby four days later, Mary was understandably unhappy, lonely and bored. There was little for her to do except read. The strained atmosphere did not improve when Dad arrived from Saudi Arabia. He had hoped for orders to Nellis to command the Fighter Weapons School and was bitterly disappointed by orders to the Pentagon. He and Mom moved into the VIP Quarters on the Base.

Dad surveyed my living arrangements and decided that the cottage needed work. With the temperature and humidity in the 90's, he installed the window air conditioner I'd bought in Georgia. He put linoleum on the sun porch floor and a folding gate across the entry. Finally, he rigged an ingenious changing table for the babies, hinged across the top of the washing machine, which resided with the babies on their sun porch. When I needed to access the washing machine, I lifted the table up and hung it from a hook in the ceiling. It sure made my life easier.

After Mom, Dad and Mary left in early August, I bought a portable fold-up crib for the new baby, named for his great-grandfather, Arthur Wilbourn, as I had promised. We nicknamed him Billy and moved him from the bassinet next to my bed to the sun porch next to his brother. They quickly became buddies, laughing happily and playing with each other.

I invited Pappy to come for a visit to see his namesake. Pappy came and spent several days holding Billy, talking to him and loving him. Billy was an easy-going baby and was content to sit on his great-grandfather's lap for hours at a time. Those few days may have been the happiest days in the remaining six years of Pappy's life.

I washed diapers every day that the sun was out, hanging them on the line to dry, hoping that they would dry in fewer than three days in the humidity. On Boggy Bayou, the black flies, deer flies and mosquitoes grew large and numerous, so hanging the wash out and bringing it in involved a lot of dancing around, slapping and cursing. My life consisted mainly of feeding the babies and changing their diapers; washing, hanging, folding diapers; and scratching bug bites. When it rained, I went to the laundromat, taking the babies along.

Motorboats, water skiers, and fishermen were often speeding by on Boggy Bayou and the babies loved crawling to the windows and watching all the activity on the water. Although one might not think it based on his later obsession with airplanes, Hal's first word was "boat." That was soon followed by "brokie" as his favorite activity was taking his toys apart and teaching Billy to do the same. I wrote glowing letters to my parents, reporting all the cute things the boys said: when Hal took his first steps, when Billy started crawling, when they said their first words, how well they played together.

I was proud of my two beautiful babies, each with heads full of soft curls. One Saturday morning I left them with Bud and went grocery shopping. When I came back, no one was home. I was shocked when Bud walked in with them, each sporting crew cuts. Hal was not quite two, Billy was barely six months old. They looked like miniature military recruits. Bud said they'd looked like sissies with all those curls.

Another serious asthma attack came while Bud was in Las Vegas during the Navy's Tailhook Convention in the fall of 1959. I was wheezing and Billy was sick with a cold. My neighbor drove us to the doctor, who promptly put me in the hospital in an oxygen tent for the next two days. The doctor called Bud, who declined to come home, believing that my asthma attacks were emotionally based bids for attention. My neighbor took the babies back to her house until the doctor released me. Because she couldn't bring herself to change dirty diapers, she waited until her boys came home from school and directed them to change the diapers. Hal and Billy were fine when I got home, except for diaper rashes, and had loved being around the neighbor's three boys.

A Tough Assignment and No Place to Live

In January of 1960 Bud's F-105 test squadron became an operational unit ordered to Seymour-Johnson Air Force Base in South Carolina. Bud, now a Captain, wanted to go instead to the Fighter Weapons School at Nellis Air Force Base, which is in Las Vegas. Luckily, his squadron commander ordered him to Nellis to help set up fighter weapons training in the F-105. We fixed up the back of the station wagon with blankets on top of the luggage, making it one big playpen for the boys. I carried a plastic bag for the dirty diapers and off we drove, stopping at a laundromat every other day to wash, dry and fold the diapers.

There was no housing available either on Base or on the economy in Las Vegas, so Bud left us with his brother and sister-in-law, Alan and Bev, in San Jose, California. Al was a pilot for Pan American Airways and they lived with their three children in a new house, on a tight budget, with little furniture. The babies and I slept on the carpeted floor of one of the empty bedrooms.

I learned some sign language so I could communicate with Bev's mother, who lived with them and was deaf. Bud's mother was also living with them off and on, looking for a job, but waiting anxiously for us to find a house in Las Vegas so she could come live with us. After a couple of months, life with five little kids and two mothers-in-law became a strain on all of us. Al drove us to Bakersfield, where Bud picked us up.

First Stop: Motel 6. Over the next two years, we would live in a motel and three different homes in "Sin City." Motel 6 was near the Las Vegas strip, one dark room with a little kitchenette opening onto a patio, swimming pool, and six-lane highway. It was hot and noisy, and I was on constant alert lest one of my active, curious babies escape through the screen door and crawl into the pool. We lived there for six weeks before we moved into a cinder-block rental. Because the rent was so high, Bud decided to use his VA loan to buy a house still under construction and move again as soon as it was finished.

Bud was adjusting to a demanding new assignment, and volunteering for every TDY he could. His fellow pilots referred to him as a "time hog." We had only one car and were both under a lot of stress. I was upset when he came home late on our third anniversary and had forgotten the anniversary. I said, "I feel like you just don't love me." He replied that I could take the babies and leave if I didn't like it here, opening the front door and motioning me out into the dark. I stood there speechless looking at the open door. Where could I go?

I called my parents. Mom answered the phone and I tearfully told her what Bud had said. Speaking softly, so as not to wake Dad, she asked to speak to Bud, who took the telephone, listened for a minute, laughed, and gave the phone back to me. She told me that Bud hadn't meant it, and for me to just "buck up." In the letter I wrote to my parents afterwards, I apologized for waking Mom. But, I wrote ". . . Bud threatened to divorce me for incompatibility and told me that he would get custody of the boys." I asked them if that was true.

Bud had started complaining about the baby's thumb-sucking, saying he didn't want his boys to be sissies. He taped the baby's thumb so he couldn't suck it. When I protested, I got a whack in the face. I would sneak in to un-tape the baby's thumb when he cried in the night. I asked Mom if thumb-sucking was dangerous. I remembered that Pat had sucked his thumb when he was a boy and no one had ever made a big deal about it.

Mom's letter back essentially told me to "just get over it." She told me that when she got married her mother had told her that she could never run back to her parents if things weren't going well. Later I heard from Dad that I should stop writing letters that were upsetting to my mother. "Your life is up to you now," he said. As a military Brat, I had learned to be obedient, not only from my parents but also from my church. I stiffened my upper lip and reported only good news in subsequent letters.

Homeowners for Six Months. In October, temperature 110 degrees, we moved nearby to another cinder-block house surrounded by sand and littered with construction debris. When the boys got outside one day, Hal stepped on a rusty nail and Billy found a rusty razor blade, which he promptly put in his mouth. I had no car, so I had to beg a neighbor for a ride to the base hospital for Tetanus shots.

There were no cockroaches, or rats in our homes in Las Vegas. But spiders! Hundreds of them. They seemed to thrive in the dry climate. The most terrifying was the black widow I found spinning a web under the kitchen window. When I saw the little red hourglass on her underside, I called the boys over and showed them, telling them they should always stay away from little black spiders. But they were too young to understand or remember. Something else for me to obsess about.

May came to live with us soon after we moved to the new house and I learned that I was pregnant again. For a while she helped me with the children, watching them when I did the grocery shopping. Then she found a job at a high-end department store, I. Magnin's, on the strip. I felt a little jealous seeing her get all dressed up and tool off to work every morning leaving me to throw up, change diapers, do laundry, cook and clean. Besides, her little grandchildren were adorable, and I thought she'd want to spend more time with them. But she was distracted by her own problems. She was recently widowed in her fifties, with poor credit and plenty of debts. When she was laid off from her job, she went back to live with Al and Bev, and we began to send money every month to help them cover her expenses.

Our financial situation was always strained. I tried to pinch pennies at the commissary and we rarely had steak for dinner. I refused to go to the Class VI store to buy any liquor. I worried about how we would pay to send these children to college, and began to set a little aside each month in a joint savings account that I opened by mail at the Bank of Fort Sam Houston.

Flying Can be Dangerous. One day I was fixing lunch for the boys when another pilot's wife came to the door, acting strangely nervous. In a few minutes the phone rang. It was Bud. I was surprised because he rarely called. He said that he had flown that day and, "I came down the easy way." I did not understand what he was trying to tell me. Finally, my friend interrupted and said that Bud had been forced to eject just before his plane had crashed and burned. She had come at the request of his squadron commander to make sure I didn't have a radio on. He didn't want me to hear anything on the radio before they knew that Bud was okay.

Bud had ejected from the back seat of an F-105 at 300 feet. The parachute had swung once before he hit the ground. Although he was not hurt, the accident was a tragedy. The pilot, named Hoganmiller, had ridden the plane into the ground after telling Bud to get out. He was killed.

I wondered whether the wives living on the Base might have seen the dreaded black plume of smoke and known that a plane had gone down. If so, they'd have wondered whether someone's husband had just "bought the farm," as the saying went. The plane went down close enough to the base that they could have seen Bud's parachute.

The Hoganmiller family lived on base. His wife gave birth to their fourth child the very next day and the family was soon flying back to her parents. There was an unwritten rule that families should be moved away as soon as possible after a death. I'm not sure that was such a good rule. It must be hard to make important decisions when in shock. There is a street on the base now named Hoganmiller Street. Pat lived on that street for several months when he was stationed at Nellis a few years later.

This was Bud's third ejection. His first had occurred during flight training. He had been a student in a T-6 trainer when the plane stalled. Though he and the instructor got out, Bud broke his ankle and washed back a class in flight school. His second ejection was from an F-86 in France sometime in 1956. I don't know much about that one except that he parachuted onto a farm field and had a heck of a time explaining himself to the French farmer.

Whenever I asked Bud how his day had been or what was going on, he'd reply, "None of your business," or "I can't tell you because it's classified," or "If I told you, I'd have to kill you." But I learned some of the details of what went on from other pilots or their wives. Bud was to experience more emergencies in the F-105, including three in as many days. In one, he had a problem that left him with twelve minutes to land. On another flight, his canopy blew off at 400 MPH and an altitude of 300 feet because he had failed to lock it. And once a compressor stall prompted an emergency landing on the nearby Indian Springs runway, blowing two tires and going into the barrier. I wrote all these details to my mother in a letter in December 1960.

Then There Were Three: Carrie is born, March 1961.
The baby was due on April 6 but the Base doctor decided to

135

induce on March 31, Good Friday and Passover. When I walked into the Quonset hut that served as the hospital at Nellis, I passed through a ward of new mothers and heard, "She can't be full term. She's too small. There must be something wrong." That scared me right down to my worry-warting soul.

The nurse put me on a bed and drew the curtain around it. The doctor started the drip to induce the birth, saying he'd be right outside. Labor pains began slowly and steadily, but not fast enough for the doctor, who was in a hurry to get downtown. He increased the drip. I calmly listened through earphones to Straus Waltzes. When the contractions began coming frequently and hard, I called the doctor. No one answered. I tried to get up but the baby was coming out and I couldn't stand up. I screamed, and the doctor finally came into the room, immediately called for a stretcher and told a nurse to hold my legs together. There was no time for any pain medication. They rushed me into the delivery room, and I heard my baby screaming as her head emerged.

The next thing I knew, I was no longer in my body. I was hovering above the delivery table near the ceiling, still attached to my body by a wispy, white cord similar to an umbilical cord. The excruciating pain was suddenly gone, and I felt free of the heavy burden my body had been. I must have died, I thought, which didn't bother me at all. I could hear the baby wailing, saw the tops of the doctors' heads, and my body lying on the table. One of the doctors was shouting instructions to the others. I watched, quite unconcerned. Then everything went black.

I woke up with a doctor slapping his hands together and calling my name. The table was tipped with my head down toward the floor. I was covered with blood. "You have a girl," a nurse said, and showed her to me, still screaming inconsolably. My poor little baby girl was terrified of the world into which she had just been so rudely thrust. Mom flew

136

in on the next morning to care for the boys. I was kept in the hospital for five more days.

I tried to talk to Mom, to the doctor, and to friends about my out-of-body experience, but they were perplexed by it or uninterested. I obsessed over it

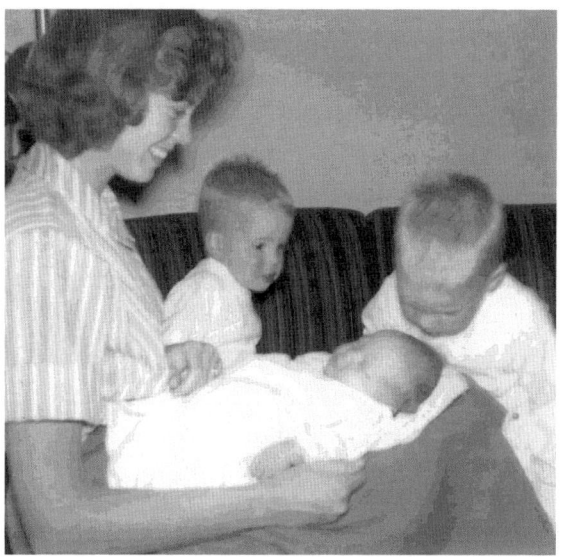

The boys welcome Carrie, their baby sister.

for months and could make no sense out of what had happened to me. Sometime later, I heard about Elizabeth Kubler-Ross and read her book about near-death experiences and understood. I had hemorrhaged and my blood pressure had suddenly dropped. But unlike the description in the book, there had been no white light, only peace.

A New Home on the Base. As Mom expected, the baby girl was named Carolyn Pierpont. I decided to call her Carrie. (Nowadays, it seems vain to name a baby after yourself!) A few weeks earlier, the Base Housing Office had called to tell us that there would be a set of quarters available for us. Bud decided to sell our house and move on base as soon as the baby was born. Carrie was ten days old when the moving van showed up. We moved to a two-bedroom house with no air conditioning and only a moldy swamp-cooler on the roof to deal with the 100+ degree days. The windows were etched from years of wind-blown sand, allowing light in but no clear view out, typical military housing for lower-ranking officers.

Mom stayed for a few more days to help me get organized. I rose twice a night to feed the baby, and early in the morning to feed the boys. She and Bud stayed up late drinking, smoking and laughing. I felt that she found him much more interesting than she found me and I wished that she had the same warm relationship with me and with Pat.

Going from two children to three involved an exponential increase in stress, diapers, and sleeplessness. I only had two arms, and three babies were much harder to manage than two. I had no time alone even in the bathroom. I showered at night when they were asleep. Billy was still in diapers, as was Hal at night. I put a lock on the outside of the boys' bedroom door to keep them in there, taking naps or playing, while I fed the baby. I had never propped up a bottle for the boys at feeding time and didn't want to prop bottles for Carrie either.

In the busy chaos caring for three babies and toddlers, I was hardly aware of the miracle that was the birth of each. Out of all the billions of possible combinations of DNA, chromosomes and genes, each one of us is statistically unlikely, each of us a miracle. Although I felt overwhelmed and inadequate to properly care for three babies, I believed that I was following God's path for me and doing the right thing. I loved them with all my heart but hadn't the energy to joyfully celebrate them. Sometimes, as I've grown old, I miss my babies so much that it feels like a sharp pain in my heart.

Crazed and Sleepless. We had a small black-and-white television that didn't hold the boys' attention for long. They were active and rambunctious, with endless energy. One day as I was feeding Carrie, I suddenly noticed no sounds coming from their room. "Maybe they're asleep," I thought, and carefully unlocked the door hoping not to wake them. The room was empty and the window wide open. I couldn't imagine how a two and a three-year old could have climbed out the window and down to the ground, but they were nowhere to be seen.

I went outside and started calling their names. As the minutes passed with no sign of them, I became increasingly frantic, running all over the neighborhood asking if anyone had seen them. Then I noticed that their tricycles were also gone, and I heard noises coming from inside the neighbor's house. I knocked on their kitchen door, but no one answered. They were not home. The door was unlocked so I opened it a crack and there were my two ruffians riding their muddy tricycles on the neighbor's living room carpet. I whisked them out of there, praying that no one would see us leaving their house. The commander of the Air Police Squadron and his family lived there. I never told his wife that my children had been in their home and were responsible for the dirty carpet.

I nagged and pleaded until Bud put a wire fence around the grassless back yard. Adventurous and determined, the boys quickly learned how to unlock the gate and take off when I was busy in the house. One neighbor testily informed me that, "We all cringe when we see those two kids coming our way," and implied that they'd probably be in prison by the time they were grown. I found a rope and double knotted the gate closed. Hal climbed the fence and taught Billy to do the same. I was a nervous wreck trying to care for a newborn, do the laundry, cook, clean and keep up with the two boys.

One day, thinking she needed a little sun, I put Carrie out in the yard strapped in a baby seat where she enjoyed watching the antics of her brothers. When I heard Billy giggling hysterically, an ominous sound, I went outside. He was putting pebbles into Carrie's mouth and laughing at the quizzical look on her face as she spit them out, one by one.

On another occasion, I awoke to hear the boys in the bathroom involved in something that sounded questionable. I pulled myself wearily out of bed and found Hal feeding Billy a bottle of baby aspirin. The bottle was almost empty, and Billy was happily gobbling them down, one after another.

Fortunately, I had the car that day because Bud was TDY. I threw on some clothes, grabbed the babies, jumped in the car, and headed for the hospital. The doctor put both boys on an examination table and fed them big doses of ipecac. I held Carrie and watched while the boys threw up for the next half hour until both little tummies had been emptied. It was apparent that Hal had been quite generous, giving most of the aspirin to Billy.

Then one day, Hal came in and told me that something was in his nose. I looked in his nose and saw a screw stuck up there. There was no way I could get it out. If I pushed on it, he could choke. No car that day, but a doctor lived behind us. I carefully walked Hal over and knocked on the doctor's door. He was home! He found medical tweezers and, closing them and placing them carefully into the groove in the screw, gingerly opened them enough to apply the necessary pressure to remove the screw. Hal was only three. What did he know about such things? Relieved, I trudged home, hoping Billy was still in his room with the door locked, and Carrie still in her crib.

When Carrie was about eight months old, for some reason I moved her crib into the room with the boys. She was delighted to have such an excellent vantage point for watching her two mischievous brothers. One morning I came in to find them patiently teaching her how to climb out of her crib. She caught on quickly, and then there were three little rascals scurrying around the tiny house amidst a shamble of toys.

All these little adventures—the children's first words, first steps, the cute things they said and did—I reported to my parents in frequent and voluminous letters. In retrospect, I told them more than I told their father, who usually came home after they were in bed, if he wasn't TDY. There were only rare phone calls to my parents. Long-distance phone calls were too expensive.

My sense of duty was my anchor. Keep the house and the clothes clean. Buy the groceries and cook thrifty and nutritious meals, save as much money as possible so the kids could go to college, pay the bills on time, and keep our credit good. The women's magazines emphasized that keeping a clean home was a big deal. I worked hard and felt great satisfaction when the floors shone, the laundry hung on the line, or was folded and put away. I was a "neatnik," like my Dad. Maybe that's genetic or maybe it comes from a need to control one's environment when there is precious little else under one's control.

The Russians Again. The newspaper and the television were my primary connections to the outside world. I read the paper every night and watched the TV news. The Cold War was growing colder, and the Russians were getting bolder. I knew that we were storing and testing atomic bombs nearby. Nevada hosted the primary atomic test sites and I was worried. I have since read that the U.S. carried out a total of 1,032 nuclear tests in Nevada, 96 of which were in 1962.

One day a neighbor came over and asked whether Bud had been flying that day. He told me that a pilot had inadvertently flown through a radiation cloud from a nuclear test and would have to be de-contaminated. Bud was not the unlucky pilot, but when I asked him about it, he was furious that the guy had revealed classified information. This incident confirmed my worst fears. I reasoned that if the Russians were finally going to bomb us, as the papers suggested daily, they'd certainly be bombing Nevada and my babies and I would all be radioactive toast.

I read everything I could about how to survive an atomic blast. I called Dad and asked him what I should do. He tried to calm my fears. I told him that I'd put all four of us in the hall closet with food and water and pray that the babies would die before I did. I was overwhelmed with anxiety. When

I tried to talk to Bud about it, he would just laugh and say that he'd be long gone on his way to bomb them back.

Home to Mom and Dad, March 1962. I began to get upsetting letters from Mom about what was going on back in Washington. Some months earlier Pat had allowed his friend Mike Mooney to drive their car. As they crossed a bridge over Rock Creek on a winter night, they hit black ice, spun and went over into the creek upside down. Pat climbed out, losing his shoes, and pulled out an unconscious Mike, who was submerged head-first. When Pat went up to the road to get help, cars whizzed by until he stood in the middle of the road and finally got someone to stop. They both ended up in Georgetown Hospital, Pat with badly frost-bitten feet and in worse shape than Mike.

Then the last straw. Pat had been with a group of friends at some establishment when a fight broke out between the "townies" and the college kids. The cops were called and took all the boys to the police station. Dad let Pat stew in jail for a while before picking him up and giving him a choice of following new house rules or moving out. Pat decided he couldn't live with the new rules. He moved out and Mom didn't know where he was, or whether he was still at Georgetown

I was worried about Pat, and I was at my wit's end. The children were often sick, maybe due to the dirty swamp cooler, and Bud was seldom home. He was expecting orders anytime to Japan. I was not sleeping, worrying about the Russians bombing Nevada. Mom was bemoaning the fact that she never got to see her grandchildren. I decided to fly back to Washington with the kids for a visit. I told myself that I was going to give Mom the pleasure of seeing her grandchildren, and to try to help Pat. But I was also fleeing a life I couldn't bear any longer.

With Bud gone on yet another TDY, I bought tickets on a flight leaving Las Vegas in the middle of the night, arriving in Washington mid-morning the next day. I put the children to bed dressed in their clothes, and a friend helped me carry them, still half-asleep, to the car and onto the airplane. Carrie would celebrate her first birthday at my parents' home in Washington and take her first steps there.

The next ten weeks were full of turmoil. Dad was in bed with Hepatitis from drinking dirty creek water on a fishing trip. Mary was living at home, working at the State Department. Pat was still attending classes at Georgetown University but sleeping in a sleeping bag stashed in a friend's dorm room. Mom decided that Hal and Billy would sleep up in the attic in Pat's room, which would result in many tumbles down the steep attic stairs. Carrie slept in a rented crib beside me on the second floor.

We had been there only a few hours before I realized that this was not a house meant for toddlers. As they eagerly explored their new surroundings, their energy and curiosity overwhelmed my parents. Mom scolded me for not properly disciplining them. They were expected to finish all their food, display proper table manners, not touch anything but their toys, and go to their room in the attic if they cried. I was relieved when, a week later, Mom went back to her retail job at Lord & Taylor. Dad eventually recovered and went back to work as chief of Air Force personnel at the Pentagon.

With Dad back at work, Pat came over during the day and we discussed his troubles. His tuition had been paid for the rest of his junior year, but he was depressed and had little money for food. He had failed a couple of courses and decided to change his major to philosophy, the subject in which he excelled.

I typed his papers, fixed him meals, and sent him back to school with his pockets full of food filched from the kitchen. He was always hungry. He told me that he got much of his food at sorority open houses and parties he crashed. But one night he was so hungry that he'd gone into the White Tower on M Street and ordered ten hamburgers. When he had them

143

in hand, he'd turned and raced out the door and around the corner, leaving the clerk out on the sidewalk yelling after him.

When Pat completed that semester, Dad gave him a one-way ticket to Parris Island, South Carolina, the Marine Corps training facility. Maybe partly due to all the bullying he'd experienced, Pat went through Marine boot camp successfully and graduated as the top recruit in his platoon. Dad went down for his graduation and his attitude softened. He let Pat come home and finish college after six months in the Marine Corps Reserve.

While I was in Washington, I went to see the family doctor to seek advice about my marriage. I couldn't bring the issue up with my parents, and I never told anyone else. I was ashamed and felt that somehow Bud's treatment of me was my fault. The doctor told me to pray. He said I had no alternative if I wanted to keep my children fed and clothed and go to heaven. I had to continue trying to make the marriage work. Dad had told me once that the ten most important two-letter words in the English language are: "If it is to be, it is up to me." Sadly, I realized Dad was right. The doctor was a devout Catholic and gave me a prayer book, which I still have.

I began to pray every day and tried to lean on God as an ever-present source of strength. Spring came and there is no more glorious season than spring in Washington. After the barren desert of Nevada, the green trees, the flowers, and the birds gave my spirits tremendous lift. I began to feel ready to carry on.

Bud called and said that he had orders to report to Hickam Air Force Base in Hawaii. He was to serve on the ORI (Operational Readiness Inspection) Team. This was a plum assignment. I relaxed my concern about Russian bombs, believing they would never bother to bomb Hawaii.

Sometime in late May or early June, I flew with the children from Washington to Denver, a seven-hour flight. Bud met us there and we visited with his father, Harold, and his stepmother, Isabel, before driving to San Jose, California, to stay with Al and Bev. A few days later, Al drove us to Travis Air Force Base, and we climbed on board a plane for the ten-hour flight to Honolulu.

Hawaii, the Land of Flowers and Beaches

We landed in the middle of a June night in 1962. As we stepped off the plane, we were enveloped in the fragrance of tropical flowers. I fell instantly in love with Hawaii. We lived the next several weeks in a room on the top floor of a hotel in Waikiki with a view of the ocean. We spent a lot of time with coloring books and an assortment of toys before we walked down to the beach every day.

No Base housing was available so, on the weekends, we scoured the area for a rental. On a drive up to Aiea Heights, we came across a couple in a car with a Hickam Air Force Base sticker. We asked whether they knew of any rentals. They told us they were moving out of a rental up the road in a couple of weeks. Although the rent was a stretch for us at $185 per month, we were lucky to get it. We moved in July and requisitioned quartermaster furniture and carpets to furnish it.

The House on Aiea Heights sat on a half-acre with a large orchid plantation behind it overlooking Pearl Harbor. A state park, the Keawa Heiau, was 100 yards up the hill. There were groves of two different kinds of banana trees, Apple and Chinese. We always had a bunch of bananas hanging from a hook on the lanai. If the children were hungry, they could pull off a ripe banana any time and have a snack. I made banana bread, banana pudding, and banana ice cream and still we had plenty of the ubiquitous fruit to give away.

There were trees laden with mangoes, papayas and avocados. A fence covered with wood roses and passion fruit formed one side of the property. Several stands of Anthuriums bloomed across the yard, Plumeria (also called Frangipani)

145

trees hung with flowers, and hibiscus shrubs grew along the fence line. It was lush, colorful, and fragrant. When I close my eyes, I can still smell the Plumeria blooms that fell in soft pink and yellow piles onto the grass, and the sweet and spicy fragrance of the tropical fruit that filled the yard. A large Samoan man often came by asking if he could have a papaya or a mango or two. We would watch him climb up the trees barefoot and bring the fruit down wrapped in the sarong he wore around his hips.

Soon after we moved in, Bud went TDY on his first inspection. He would be gone for six to eight weeks at a time, then home for about the same period, for the next four years. The team's destinations were secret to ensure that the inspections were surprises. There was no communication with home during these trips. The wives of the other officers on the ORI team helped me learn my way around the base. There were no other young families living near us up in Aiea, but the three children entertained each other.

When there was a tsunami alert, loud sirens echoed across the Island and cars streamed up to the higher ground in the Heiau. The forest behind the Heiau was deep and dark, and held the remains of a Japanese Zero that had crashed twenty years earlier as it came over the mountains to bomb Pearl Harbor.

We didn't venture far when we went for a walk because the forest was full of wild pigs. Hunters often came up in noisy caravans, with excited, barking dogs, to hunt the pigs. Sometimes, the hunters couldn't round up all the dogs. We adopted one such pig dog for a few weeks until his owner came back up, saw him in our yard and took him home. The children loved him, and we were sad to see him go. But he left us a good-bye present—fleas. When I came down to the kitchen the next morning, they covered my bare legs. They were impossible to see on the brown carpets.

Life in Hawaii: Billy picks a banana in front of the house; the kids at Christmas in 1962

We were covered with flea bites for weeks. That pig dog was also the cause of Carrie losing her first tooth. About 18 months old, she was playing with him in sock-feet on the tile floor and fell right on one of her front teeth. It clinked onto the floor intact in a flood of blood. I rushed her to the dental clinic sobbing all the way. They shrugged and said there was nothing they could do, and it was a baby tooth, anyway, which would be replaced in time. My baby girl was already sporting a snaggle-toothed smile!

Our days were mostly peaceful. But the boys were naturally curious and adventurous, and wanted to explore farther away than I was comfortable with. Carrie toddled after them wherever they ventured. The yard was not fenced, and I was concerned about their safety because of traffic on the way to the park. The children weren't supposed to go out of the yard or climb up on the carport or storage shed roof. But they were always trying to get away with a quick exploratory adventure.

I finally resorted to spanking them, as my parents had done—the accepted way to discipline children in those days. I didn't know any other way to keep them out of harm's way. I was outnumbered and they knew it. As they grew older, I would usually say, "I'm going to count to ten," or "You can go to your room and write 100 times, 'I must not...'" whatever it was that they should not have done.

I went to Mass at a small mission church in Aiea when Bud was home, and occasionally took one or more of the children with me. I prayed with them every night before kissing them good night. And I talked to them about God. I wrote the following in a letter to my parents in January 1963. "Billy asked the other night where God lives. I tried to explain that He lives in heaven and that no one really knows just where heaven is but that God was everywhere anyway so it didn't matter, and that He was even inside each one of us." Billy gulped, wide eyes looking slightly worried, and finally said, 'Well, Mommy, I didn't swallow Him. He just climbed down there by Himself.'"

I gained a bit more freedom when I learned that a teen-aged girl, Mary Helen Walker, lived down the street and was available to baby-sit during the summer and on weekends. Mary Helen and her parents were wonderful to me. Her parents sometimes even took care of the children in their home when Mary Helen was in school. Mrs. Walker missed her grandchildren and was especially fond of Carrie.

I also found a Japanese American woman, who lived down the hill in Pearl City. Matsuyo came for several hours once a week and cared for the children. One day she asked me if she could take Carrie down to visit her family in Pearl City. Matsuyo told me later that Carrie, noting all the Asian eyes around her, had pulled her own eyes out at the corners, to uproarious laughter.

Matsuyo made it possible for me to join the Red Cross Grey Ladies and to volunteer half a day a week in the dispensary. And I started singing with the Skylarks, an Air Force Wives' chorus at Hickam. I heard a lot of the other wives complaining about "rock fever," meaning a sense of isolation from being on a "rock" in the middle of the Pacific. I never felt isolated. I loved the climate, the people, taking the children to the beach, and my growing outside interests.

For a long weekend, we took the boys to The Big Island to see the Kilauea Volcano while the Walkers took care of Carrie. We stayed at a military camp that provided tour service along with interesting and humorous commentary. The volcano was a sight that amazed all of us and I found the Big Island to be the most interesting of the Islands I've visited.

All year round, I took the kids several mornings a week to a small military beach on Keehi Lagoon where the water was calm and shallow. They loved playing in the sand and the sea, hunting for treasures, trying to avoid being stung by the

"pork 'n cheese" (Portuguese) men-of-war, and I relaxed knowing that they were safe, running and jumping to their hearts' content. These were lovely, happy times and I had hopes of at least one or two of them napping after lunch.

Within a couple of months of our move, Bud's mother came to live with us again.

The kids enjoyed their life on the beach.

149

We rented a piano for her and she decided to try her hand at teaching. But we had only one car. When Bud wasn't TDY, I had to drive him to Hickam and then drive May where she wanted to go because she didn't know how to drive a stick shift. Then I had to pick Bud up at Hickam at the end of the day. Her attempt to teach piano fizzled. I liked May and was determined at the outset to try hard to make the arrangement work this time. But we all began to tire of it and she decided to go back to California.

In the fall of 1963, Hal started kindergarten in Aiea. I found a little pre-school in the neighborhood for Billy. If I had only known about the pre-school, I'd have entered Hal the previous year. He started out behind the other kindergartners who had all been in pre-school for a couple of years. He was one of few Caucasians in the class. His Japanese-born teacher was not helpful, and I hadn't learned yet how to help him.

Sometimes I have thought that the first child should be entitled to a "do over." The oldest is often expected to grow up too fast and too much expected of them when they are still too young. Their parents are new at the job. They tend to be blamed when the others act up, and responsibility placed on them when it shouldn't be. As the oldest child, my way of dealing with this was to scrupulously follow the rules. But the good ones don't tend to get much attention. It's a "hard row to hoe" that can make children stronger, more resilient, and more determined, but also, sometimes, insecure and angry.

Historical Events. Many events of historical significance occurred while we were in Hawaii. In 1962, a few months after our move there, the Cuban Missile Crisis caused alarm throughout the military community and the world. Bud was ready to go at a moment's notice as I nervously watched news of the Russians sending ICBMs to Cuba. Still, I wasn't as concerned as I had been in Nevada because I figured that the Russians wouldn't bother with Hawaii. It was too remote and, as far as I knew, there weren't any nuclear bombs around. But Washington would be within range. We let out sighs of relief when Khrushchev sent the missiles back. The fear of Russian bombs, which had been hanging over me for ten years, receded.

One day in November 1963, I was in the dispensary getting a prescription filled. I must have appeared too calm, because the corpsman asked me, "Didn't you hear? They've shot President Kennedy!" That's when I noticed people around me white-faced and in shock; some had tears running down their cheeks. I went home and turned on the television. There was the picture of Lyndon Johnson taking the oath to become President, with Jackie standing beside him in a blood-splattered suit.

A dark cloud of grief hung over everyone. While the previous generation could tell you exactly where they were when they heard that the Japanese had bombed Pearl Harbor, my generation would remember where they were when they heard that President Kennedy had been shot. A few days later, I watched on TV, dumbfounded, when Lee Harvey Oswald, the President's assassin, was murdered by Jack Ruby as he walked, handcuffed, down a hall to a court hearing in Texas.

Some months later, in 1964, Martin Luther King came to speak at the University of Hawaii. I went with two friends to hear him. It was an exciting event, history in the making. Hawaii was a melting pot of many races. I believed strongly in civil rights and had been following King's growing political influence with great interest.

Meanwhile, the State of Hawaii decided to grant voting rights to the dependents of military personnel over the age of 21 who were living in the State but were not permanent tax-paying residents. I wrote a letter, which was published in the paper, thanking the Hawaiian legislature. And then I voted for the first time in a presidential election. I don't remember whom I voted for!

Christmas on Okinawa. In 1963, Dad had been promoted to Major General and reassigned from the Pentagon to take over as commander of the Air Forces on the island of Okinawa, Japan. My parents joyfully moved into quarters with a full-time maid, a cook and a driver. They invited us to fly to Okinawa on a military flight, space-available, for Christmas. In mid-December, we all boarded a jet passenger plane filled with uniformed military and dependents. Before take-off, we watched through the cabin windows as one of the engines on our side of the aircraft suddenly burst into flames, a "flame-out." We watched fire trucks cover the engine with foam and extinguish the blaze. Then we were evacuated from the aircraft, boarded another and flew to Okinawa.

Mom was happy being the Commander's wife. The other wives were friendly and there was much partying. At the time, Uncle Abe was the Army commander on Okinawa, and we saw him and Aunt Mary numerous times. Santa Claus and his elves came to the house for a Christmas party, and it was a memorable Christmas. Mom doted on Carrie and was patient with the boys for short periods of time until I took over. The children were warned not to venture outside alone as there were Habus around, deadly poisonous snakes also called "two-steppers" because after being bitten, a victim takes two steps and falls dead. The boys were impressed by this scenario and stayed inside unless accompanied by an adult.

We left Okinawa on a KC-130 to fly back to Hawaii, sitting in "bucket" seats and landing on Guam to refuel. An 18-hour flight, it was uncomfortable, particularly for me as I was six months pregnant.

Then There Were Four: Timmy Is Born, April 1964. I found a Chinese obstetrician and a Japanese pediatrician and decided to give birth in St. Francis Catholic Hospital in Honolulu. On April 15, all five of us went down to the docks to wave good-bye to friends leaving for the mainland on an ocean liner. As we approached the top of a long set of stairs, I began to have the first labor pains. When we stopped at the commissary on the way home, I shopped and surreptitiously timed the contractions as Bud watched the children in the car. After we arrived home, I called a friend who had agreed to come watch the children, and Bud drove me to the hospital.

I was left alone in the labor room and when they checked me a short time later, it was too late for anesthesia. Timmy was quickly born just before midnight. In sharp contrast to Carrie's loud protests at her traumatic entrance into the world, Timmy arrived mewing like a kitten. I had expected another girl, and I knew Carrie was going to be disappointed.

The first thing Bud said to me, as I was being wheeled out of the delivery room, was, "The next one will be a girl!" With tears in my eyes, I just shook my head. I decided that four was enough. I requested the birth control pill from my doctor and went on it for brief periods over the next ten years, always feeling guilty about it, and admitting my mortal sin in the confessional to be chastised by the priest. I hadn't yet begun to question the Catholic Church's teaching on birth control, which I now see as absurd. But I knew that I could not handle any more children. Our children were already at a disadvantage being so close together in age, especially given the frequent moves and the fact that I was a single parent most of the time with no family or support network.

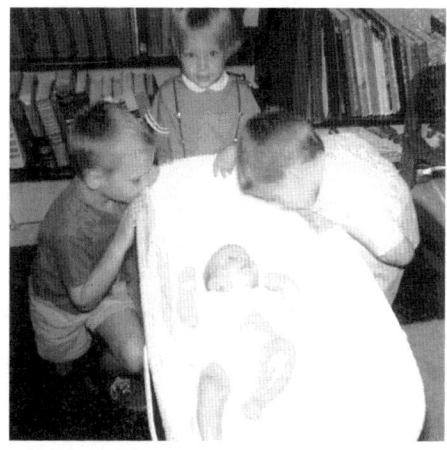
Timmy meets his sister and brothers.

The Asian doctors and nurses encouraged breast-feeding and I decided to give it a try, since Timmy was the last baby. In the hospital nursery, surrounded by smooth, brown-skinned

Animals always liked Timmy.

babies, Timmy stood out like a speckled albino monkey. But he was a good baby and I soon found nursing to be much easier than washing and sterilizing all the bottles. The children were delighted with their baby brother and spent many hours trying to make him smile. Timmy gazed with interest at those who came his way, bestowing his smiling blessings indiscriminately on all worshippers at the side of his crib. His skin gradually cleared of the speckles and the birth marks faded.

I'd been hanging diapers to dry on clotheslines for almost six years, a daily, time-consuming chore. After a short visit, Dad quietly decided that I needed a dryer. He arranged with Sears Roebuck in Honolulu to call and say that I had "won" a dryer as a result of my name having been entered in a contest. One day a truck arrived. The driver confirmed my name, and two men brought a dryer in and installed it. When I asked them for details about the contest, they wouldn't say anything more. I don't remember how I finally learned that it was a gift from Dad, but my new dryer became my most cherished possession.

To a New Home on Hickham

After two years in the rental, the landlord told us we had to move because he planned to move his own family into the house. Luckily, we were able to qualify for small quarters on base. Timmy was about six weeks old. Suddenly we were surrounded by hordes of noisy children. There were a couple

154

of playgrounds and a treehouse nearby. I bought a whistle and told the children that they must stay close enough to hear the whistle when I blew it—two short blasts followed by a long one meant "come home." Otherwise they were free to roam. We all felt that children were safe on a military base.

The boys were overjoyed with their playmates and new-found freedom, but it was a difficult transition for Carrie. She was three and had just been replaced as the baby of the family when she suddenly had to compete with all these strange children for her brothers' attention. She was bereft.

My beloved dryer was installed next to the kitchen sink. One day, I pulled out the lint filter and was surprised to see what I thought was thick, dark lint. I grabbed the lint and discovered that I had grabbed a dead rat. I screamed and a neighbor ran over to remove the rat, laughing all the way to the dumpster. OMG, the roaches and rats were after me!

My parents came to visit soon after we moved onto the base. Dad had to attend a conference at Hickam and brought Mom along. They sent Mary a ticket to meet them in Hawaii, and she brought a friend. I was not ready for all this company. Nursing mothers were a rarity in those days, and I couldn't deal with nursing my baby in front of my parents and my sister. Sounds crazy today, but I decided to stop nursing and put Timmy on the bottle. I hadn't reckoned on the difficulties of stopping cold turkey. My bed was often wet in the morning, as my milk leaked as it dried up.

As a perk of my Dad's rank, we were able to

The Walkers at Timmy's baptism

155

stay for a week in the vacation house assigned to the Commander in Chief of the Pacific Air Command (CINCPAC). A sleek, modern house with walls of glass, it sat on a bluff overlooking the Pacific Ocean with a wide expanse of beach below, a lovely place! I spent most of our time there shopping for groceries, planning meals, cooking, doing laundry and taking care of the children. Mom played with Carrie and the baby, Dad was mostly conferencing, and Mary and her friend enjoyed the beach and some Honolulu night life.

After the crowd left, the children and I spent the rest of the summer either at Keehi Lagoon or at the Officers' Club swimming pool. In the fall, the children entered Mokulele Elementary School, a block away. Hal began first grade and Billy started kindergarten. I enrolled Carrie in pre-school on the base three days a week. My neighbor and I took turns caring for each other's babies and I went back to volunteering for the Red Cross and singing with the Skylarks except when the children were sick, which was frequently.

With three children now in school and so many germy children in the neighborhood, I shouldn't have been surprised that the kids were often sick. In addition to chicken pox and the mumps, we all caught the German measles and were quarantined. My neighbor, who was pregnant with her fourth in six years, was desperate. She tried to come into the house to get exposed in hopes the doctors would perform an abortion. There was no vaccine yet for German measles, which was known to cause serious damage to fetuses. I locked her out and begged her to stay away. She had a healthy baby girl seven months later.

After repeated strep infections, the doctor decided that both Hal and Billy needed their tonsils removed. The surgeries were scheduled at Tripler Army Hospital and repeatedly rescheduled when they both continued to test positive for strep. When Hal tested clear, I took him for the surgery. Parents were required to leave their children overnight, picking them up late the next day. Hal weathered this experience without much difficulty. But when Billy finally tested clear, he had a much tougher time.

My children's illnesses were extremely painful for me. I felt that my parents had not taken my asthma seriously enough, leaving me with a weakened pulmonary system. I was determined to do better. I would take my children's illnesses seriously. Consequently, I spent a great deal of time with them in military dispensaries and hospitals. They were rarely seen by the same doctor twice. Military doctors were often fresh from medical school or residencies, eager to pay back their commitments and get out to a more lucrative private practice.

Life on the Base was much more interesting than life on the economy. My position as a volunteer in the dispensary allowed me inside information about some of the things that went on, including tragedies that were never made public. The military hushed up events that would have been in the newspapers if they'd occurred off Base. I learned from a nurse at the dispensary that a baby down the street died when he choked on a baby aspirin after his mother left him alone. In another tragedy, a child was stabbed while the parents were nearby at a party. There was gossip that an intruder had climbed through a window, but then it was rumored that an older sibling had done the stabbing.

One day, an officer sat down at home and shot himself in the head. That incident was hushed up and his wife left the Base within 36 hours. Days later I heard whispers that his wife had been having an affair, but others said that the officer had been found to be a "homo."

There were numerous whispered reports of beatings that sent wives and children to the hospital. These were hushed up or explained away to avoid ruining the husbands' careers. A squadron commander beat his wife, breaking her nose, blackening her eyes and putting her in the hospital when he thought that she was having an affair. He was never reprimanded. As it later turned out, his suspicions, if not his actions, were correct: they were divorced, and she married her best friend's husband. There were always rumors about wives going out with other men while their husbands were TDY. It seemed to go with the territory. In fact, when Bud came home from a trip, he would often accuse me of going out on him, which I never did.

One of the wonderful benefits of being in the military was the recreation areas with cabins, and Hawaii had one of the best, Bellows Beach. I took the children to Bellows several times. I have always loved the beach and have many happy memories from the times we spent there, watching my children laughing and playing together. Cabins were in demand and it was hard to get reservations. Telephones didn't have answering machines yet, so I set my alarm for 2 AM and dialed the number. I would put the receiver down on my bedside table and go back to sleep until about 7:45. The phone would ring until the staff came to work and I would get first choice of the cabins.

Granny May Comes to Visit. We continued to provide financial support to Al to help with their mother's expenses, hoping that she would marry again. After a close friend of hers died of cancer, she and the widowed husband married, and we stopped sending money. Unfortunately, the marriage did not go well. Still grieving, he finally asked her for a divorce. But they decided to go on a round-the-world cruise together first. They left on their cruise and stopped in Hawaii for a couple of days on their way to the Far East.

Nothing would do but that we have dinner with them in the cruise ship's glittering formal dining room, surrounded by extravagantly dressed elderly voyagers, and a bemedaled Captain. I was reluctant to bring my four active children to such an event, but May was insistent. I wondered what I would do if one of them threw a tantrum, or spilled tomato soup all over the white tablecloth. They were generally well-behaved kids, but who knew what could happen on such a stage? We dressed in our Sunday best and headed for Honolulu Harbor where the ship lay at anchor. We were seated in the middle of the dining room. My fears heightened when I realized that there was not another child in sight.

The children were initially pre-occupied looking around at all the diners who were eyeing them, some with distaste and others with indulgent smiles. There was a bowl of fruit in the middle of the table. Timmy noticed that his brothers' eyes were clearly focused elsewhere and not on him. Suddenly he grabbed an apple from the center of the table and lobbed it right into Hal's face. Hearing the gasps and laughter from nearby tables, he grabbed an orange with his left hand, signaling the ambidexterity that would serve him well playing ball years later. The orange flew toward Bill, missed him by a hair and landed in the middle of the Captain's table.

I was on my feet instantly, stopping the three boys from grabbing pears, bananas, and mangoes and launching into a full-fledged food fight. Carrie sat nervously watching her ruffian brothers. I heard "good shot" from across the room, and "that's my boy" from his father. We had the riveted attention of the entire dining room.

Embarrassing and Frightening. Timmy seemed to have decided early on that laughter was the best reward. He was egged on by everyone, kids and parents alike. I put him in his playpen outside so he could watch the other children playing. His life, caged inside a playpen in the crowded yard on Ilima Lane, became a contest: get their attention and make them laugh! Eventually, he decided that he wanted to participate in all the activity. He would get a little help from one child or another to climb out of the playpen. When he was free there was no stopping him. He especially liked to play in the small barbeque grills that the neighbors kept on their front porches. He would sneak out when my attention was momentarily diverted, and I'd soon find him covered in black soot.

159

By now, the children had become interested in Saturday morning cartoons and the afternoon TV programs. One evening I was fixing dinner while the children watched TV. There was no lock on the front screen door, and the front door was always open to the soft Hawaiian air. Before long, there was a knock at the door and an AP was standing there holding Timmy. He asked, "Is this your baby?" Mortified, I acknowledged that it was. He warned me to take better care of my children and relinquished the smiling Timmy.

He had crawled across the street and into a neighbor's back yard before starting to whimper. The neighbor brought him inside, changed his diaper, and called the cops, knowing full well whose baby it was. I scolded the children for letting him crawl out the door without saying a word. But I knew it was my fault and I felt like a terrible mother, ashamed before all the neighbors.

When Timmy was about 20 months old, he suffered a horrifying accident. Billy and a friend were in the living room and Timmy climbed up on the coffee table and began to do a little dance. We all laughed, and Timmy was enjoying himself. Then something jiggled the table and Timmy fell headfirst on the thin quartermaster carpet that covered the concrete slab foundation. I watched him carefully all day. He never lost consciousness but woke several times crying during the night. The next day his head was so swollen that we took him to the dispensary. An X-ray revealed a fractured skull. The doctors questioned me suspiciously, asking me how it had happened. I was delirious with worry. I bought a little football helmet and hovered over him for six weeks while it healed.

Pat Comes for Christmas. Pat came to spend Christmas with us in Hawaii while he was in pilot training. I've never seen him so happy. He joked and played with the children. We found him a "mess dress" and a date and he came with us to a black-tie holiday party at the club. After he had graduated from Georgetown with a major in Philosophy, he had applied to the Air Force Academy but was turned down due to a history of hay fever. He worked for a time in a mail room, on an early punch-card computer, and tended bar at a local jazz club, Blues Alley. Mom and Dad were worried. He was struggling and had few prospects for a career.

One day an Air Force recruiter called and invited him to apply for pilot training, saying that his ROTC classes at Georgetown qualified him for a commission. Pat was thrilled to learn that he still had a chance to fulfill his dream. For the rest of his life he believed this had been a happy coincidence, or an especially industrious recruiter. After Dad died, we found letters in his files that proved that Dad had set up the happy coincidence, arranging for the recruiter to call on the condition that Pat never learn that Dad was behind it. I think Dad saved the letters, hoping that Pat would learn this after he died, never dreaming that he would outlive Pat.

Where to Next? About this time, what had been reported for a couple of years as "incidents" in Vietnam began to sound like war. Sometime in 1965, the situation deteriorated, and a decision was made to evacuate all the military dependents living in Vietnam back to the States through Hawaii. As a Red Cross volunteer, I was scheduled to meet the aircraft, talk to the dependents and provide them with whatever they needed.

The Army set up a camp to replicate the Southeast Asian jungle where the Army was fighting the Viet Cong and I was invited to take a tour. I brought Hal and Billy. We ate roasted mongoose meat, or maybe it was rat or snake meat. Katherine Westmoreland, the wife of General Westmoreland, Dad's West Point classmate, happened to be along on the tour and complimented me on my two sons' exemplary behavior.

As Bud was coming up for a reassignment, there was a good chance that he would be sent to Vietnam and I'd have to find a place to live on the economy, expensive even then. But he was promoted "below the zone," a good sign for his future career, and was ordered to attend the Air Command and Staff College, part of the Air University, at Maxwell Air Force Base near Montgomery, Alabama.

In May 1966, we began moving out of base housing at Hickam, a major chore because I had to pass a "white glove" inspection before we could clear quarters. For a couple of weeks, I furiously scrubbed and cleaned every inch of our quarters, including the furniture. The packers came, packed our belongings, and I passed the inspection. We moved into guest quarters in Honolulu about six weeks before leaving the Island in order to allow enough time for our hold baggage to make its way to our next station, and our car to arrive in San Francisco.

The ORI Team gave a going away party for us at the Officers Club, a formal sit-down affair. I wore a long dress and had my hair done in a fancy up-do for the occasion. The affair was marked by heavy drinking, a few short speeches, and bawdy songs. Dessert was pie-a-la mode, with three little scoops of sherbet—lime, pineapple and mango. Bud apparently harbored a strong dislike for one of his fellow pilots and chose to take this occasion to express his opinion. He grabbed a scoop of sherbet and hurled it at the guy, who quickly hurled a scoop back at Bud. In seconds, multi-colored globs of sherbet were sailing around the room. The men laughed uproariously while the ladies screamed, as sherbet landed in upswept hair and on formal gowns. Mortified, I jumped up and ran to the ladies' room to hide.

A few weeks later, Mr. and Mrs. Walker arrived to say good-bye as we were walking out to board our flight. I gasped when I saw that Mrs. Walker had brought a large rectangular ironing board as a going-away gift. The baggage handlers shrugged and put it on board with our luggage. It turned out to be useful in the back of the car as a table on which to make sandwiches on our way to Alabama. For many years afterwards, whenever I ironed, I thought of Mrs. Walker and her kindness to me. I would miss Hawaii and the Walkers.

On the Road Again: Heading East, June 1966. Al met us when we landed in California. We stayed with him and Bev and visited Bud's sister's family. We had planned that I would fly with Carrie and Timmy to the east coast and spend time with my parents. Dad had been reassigned to Langley Air Force Base in Virginia as chief of staff of the Tactical Air Command. Bud was going to wait for our car to arrive and drive across country with Hal and Billy, stopping in Wisconsin to visit his father, who had retired from his job as a supervisor for the Carnation Milk Company.

There was one big problem—a widespread strike in the airline industry. All flights from California to the east coast were cancelled. We hung around with Al and Bev, certain that the strike would end any day. When it didn't end, Bud decided that I should stay in California. I adamantly refused. I'd imposed on Al and Bev before and I wasn't about to do it again. Bud reluctantly agreed that we would all drive to Wisconsin. It was the right decision because the strike lasted most of the summer of 1966.

We drove through Wyoming and South Dakota, stopping in the Black Hills and at Mt. Rushmore to see the sights along the way. We spent several days in Wisconsin with Bud's father and his wife, Isabel, at their small house on the banks of the Fox River. Carrie, Timmy and I were able to get a flight from Milwaukee to Washington. By then, Uncle Abe was a three-star general living on the Post at Fort Myer. Aunt Mary met us and took us to their quarters. Mom drove up the next day from Langley and took us back to their spacious quarters on Langley's "gold coast," where all the generals lived.

Time for the Southern Accent Again

A few days later, Bud arrived with the boys. Mom begged us to leave Hal with them for a couple of weeks while the rest of us drove down to Maxwell. Bud had rented a house vacated by another pilot who had attended Air University the previous year. About a week after we moved in, Mom brought Hal down on a train. When they drove up in a taxi, Hal jumped out of the car and ran into my arms in tears. He had missed us and had not had a happy time with his grandparents, who must have decided that he needed more discipline.

I had enrolled the boys in a Catholic school while we were still in Hawaii. I did not realize what was happening in southern schools. Desegregation had resulted in white flight into private schools. The Catholic schools were overrun with non-Catholic white kids whose parents wouldn't hear of their children attending the public schools with blacks. I was shocked to discover that classes in the Catholic school had fifty or more children. I had paid non-refundable tuition up-front to guarantee their places.

The boys began second and third grades, wearing dress pants and white shirts and walking two blocks to school every day. I put Carrie into a Catholic kindergarten and car-pooled with four other mothers. I was trying to be an obedient Catholic mother. Hal was particularly unhappy and felt that his teacher had it in for him. I talked to her repeatedly and worked hard helping him with homework. I remember drilling him on the three types of rock, which I learned right along with him: igneous, metamorphic, and sedimentary.

Bud was not happy in school, either, and his temper was short. He had never been home with us for such an extended period and the children got on his nerves. I helped him with his assignments, editing and typing his papers.

Christmases were always a big deal for our family. I began making gift lists and buying and wrapping presents in October. I did all the shopping and wrapping. I didn't want to mark all the presents from "Mom" so I labeled some from their Dad and made up names that hinted at what might be inside. The children were not allowed downstairs on

Christmas morning until we were all up and ready to enjoy the happy show.

Until Christmas Eve, gifts were hidden under the bed in the master bedroom, where Bud's guns, ensconced in leather cases, were also stored. I am amazed that I never asked whether any of the guns were loaded, and that I never worried that the children might try to play with them. They were absolutely forbidden to go under that bed and, for the most part, they were obedient and well-behaved. As they got older, they got braver and managed to unwrap and rewrap presents from time to time. If they ever touched any of the guns, I hope never to be told.

We drove up to spend Christmas 1966 with Gam and Grandfather at Langley. Sgt. Whitaker, their black cook, told the children he would do the "snow dance" for them. He must have known that snow was forecast. When the children woke up and saw snow for the first time on Christmas morning, they were ecstatic! Santa brought Timmy a little lawn mower and he spent hours pushing it around in the snow. Billy found a Batman mask under the tree and Grandfather wore it around to everyone's amusement while Carrie wore her little nurse uniform. Sgt. Whitaker cooked a roast suckling pig for Christmas dinner. Bobby and Lily came down from Washington and joined the party. On a dare that cold afternoon, Bobby and Dad bundled up and went sailing on Dad's boat, the Windhover, named for a Gerard Manley Hopkins poem.

I hadn't played the piano for more than seven years and I was hardly aware of how much I missed music. Even listening to the music I loved was no longer a part of my life. I had thought that the piano and dancing were long lost joys that I'd never experience again. But one day I came across a beat-up piano and bought it. I still had a few pieces of my old piano music and I gingerly tried to begin playing again and decided

165

that the children would take piano lessons when they were older.

Our new car began giving us trouble, stalling out often and sometimes dangerously. One day it stalled on the Southern Bypass, the major freeway around Montgomery, when I was driving home from the Base with Timmy. I left the car by the side of the road and walked a couple of miles to a service station carrying him. They gave me a ride home, but Carrie had already been dropped off from Kindergarten, and was sitting forlornly in tears on the front steps. That day is clear in my mind because it was the day I learned that I was not pregnant again.

It was understood that after Bud's graduation in June, his entire class would be sent to Southeast Asia. I know that preyed on Bud's mind and he told me that he didn't expect to survive. Numerous friends and acquaintances had already been killed or were missing in action. As expected, Bud was assigned to fly F-105s in Thailand. He was ordered to attend six months of training at Nellis and then to report to Tahkli Air Base for one year and 100 missions. The mission, new and

The official family portrait at Maxwell Air Force Base, 1967

dangerous, was to identify, evade and jam surface-to-air missiles over North Vietnam. These pilots were called "Wild Weasels."

Back to Virginia: Our Life in Hampton

I decided to leave Montgomery and take the children to Hampton, Virginia, where Dad was still assigned at Langley, Tactical Air Command Headquarters. We packed, drove up to Hampton, and began looking for a rental. No rentals were to be had but we found a house for sale two miles from Mom and Dad. A four-bedroom, two-story house with two-and-a-half baths, it was only a couple of years old and was being sold by an Army officer for $18,000 on a loan assumption. We bought it. It was by far the nicest house I'd lived in during the ten years since our marriage. I was thrilled!

Bud left for Nellis Air Force Base in Nevada for training and I moved in with help from Dad's driver, Sgt. Kelly, and Sgt. Whitaker. The children were delighted to find a mother cat and her several kittens living in the garage. The Army wife who was selling the house gave a coffee in my honor and I met Sue Broadway, who lived in the house behind us. Sue and I were to become lifelong friends.

I was happy to be making friends on my own, not just neighbors or acquaintances that I met because our husbands worked together. We spent much of the summer at the Officers Club swimming pool with my new friends and their children. The humid Virginia summer drifted along, punctuated by wet bathing suits, mountains of damp towels, and ring worm. When school started, Hal was in fourth grade, Bill was in third, and Carrie was in first. Sue and I watched each other's three-year-olds, Timmy and Barry, and I began singing with the Skylarks.

The Base hospital needed volunteers. I loved my Red Cross work helping the doctors and patients. I soaked up all the medical knowledge I could, listening carefully as the doctors and nurses counseled the patients. When I had the uniform on, adjusted my cap, put on my white stockings and white nurses' shoes, I felt competent and appreciated.

Our new house had rose bushes all around the backyard fence, and Shasta daisies growing in the front yard. I began to take an interest in flowers and gardening. Carrie was my little helper and we spent hours weeding and planting flowers together. She loved helping me and was a sweet and serious gardener.

My parents were busy with the social activities required of high-ranking officers. Neither was happy at Langley. Dad would have preferred a command. He traveled frequently, including to Vietnam and Thailand. Mom spent her days reading and knitting. When we were invited for a meal on a weekend, Dad worked with the boys in his shop and taught them how to use and care for tools. Mom entertained Carrie.

While at Langley, Mom and Dad decided that they would eventually retire in Virginia, so they bought Springdale, an historic house in Mathews County about 50 miles away. The original wing of Springdale was built in the late 1700s by a tobacco farmer. It was located on Put-In Creek, which flowed into Mobjack Bay and the Chesapeake, the perfect transportation route for tobacco in Colonial days.

Dad still had his boat and took us sailing from time to time. When we sailed from Langley to Springdale, he would anchor in the creek and row us ashore in the dingy. Mom never liked to sail, and during these trips she often could be heard calling loudly or muttering under her breath in a voice dripping with sarcasm, "Yes, Captain." On a couple of occasions, we ran aground. All the adults except Mom got in the water and, huffing and puffing, rocked and pushed the boat until it drifted off the shoal. With sighs of relief, we'd continue our sail to Springdale or back to the boathouse on the Back River behind Langley.

Springdale was full of antiques and we spent several happy visits there. In the spring the house was surrounded by fields of yellow daffodils, flowering fruit trees and blooming azaleas. When they were reassigned to the Air Force Academy, Mom and Dad took a few items of furniture out of it and decided to rent it. But not long afterwards, they changed their plans and sold it, antiques and all. Springdale is still there with an historic marker at the entrance.

Pat came and stayed with us for the Christmas of 1967, and Bobby and Lily came down from Washington. To everyone's delight, it was yet another white Christmas. Her grandfather gave Carrie a special gift that year. Using the wooden crate that his new Mercedes had been shipped in from Germany, he quietly set about building a play-house that was modeled on Springdale, complete with a hip roof, shuttered windows, a real kitchen, and curtains made by Mom. Dad and Sgt. Whitaker brought it over and set it up on our back patio, and Carrie spent many happy hours inside.

One afternoon I heard some noise out back and discovered a small African American boy in Carrie's playhouse. He told me that his parents had left him alone and he had nowhere to go. He politely asked whether he could stay in Carrie's playhouse. I was puzzled as to what to do about this strange request. I asked him where he lived but he wouldn't say. Carrie and I talked about it and she agreed to let him stay. I brought him out some bedding, some food, and let him sleep there overnight. We looked for

Carrie loved her playhouse.

169

his return after school the next day, but never saw him again.

Off to The Vietnam War. Over the next six months. Bud came back from Nellis twice on weekend cross-countries; the second visit came just before he left for Thailand in November of 1967. I drove him to the base to catch his flight to Thailand, and a month later I drove Pat to catch his flight as he also left for a tour in Southeast Asia. I hugged both of them good-bye filled with hope and dread, and a sudden loathing for the Vietnam War.

By this time, the husbands of three of the women in my circle of friends were missing in action (MIA) or known to be prisoners of war (POWs) of the North Vietnamese. North Vietnam was not a signatory to the Geneva Conventions and the prisoners were tortured and used for propaganda. In a vain effort to combat the mistreatment, my friends and I spent many days on the sidewalks of shopping centers and speaking in local schools—any place we could get a foot in the door or attract a listening ear, seeking signatures on petitions requesting that the North Vietnamese permit the International Red Cross to visit the prisoners, and allow exchanges of letters between U.S. prisoners of war and their families.

The boys salute their dad, who was serving as a fighter pilot in Vietnam.

Of course the United States did not have any diplomatic relations with North Vietnam at that time, so the petitions and letters were sent instead to the North Vietnamese embassy in Paris. Newspapers published photographs of trucks filled with letters and petitions being dumped outside the gates, which would not open to accept the mail. All this was to no avail. The North Vietnamese released a propaganda video, in which a POW surreptitiously blinked the word "torture" in Morse Code. It wasn't until shortly before America's hasty departure from Vietnam that the POWs were finally allowed to come home. Even today, many pilots are still officially listed as MIA in Southeast Asia.

My good friend Billie Hartney's husband was at Tahkli with Bud. Jim finished his 100 missions and was preparing to return home when he decided that he was "golden" and would fly a few more missions. He was shot down by a Russian MIG on his 103rd mission and declared MIA. The staff car arrived to give Billie the news at a neighbor's house where she was playing bridge. When she heard the officers asking for Mrs. Hartney, she ran out the back door. She was chased down by a friend and brought back to hear the devastating report. Her husband's remains were never found, and when Billie died of cancer a few years later, the Air Force declared Jim KIA to allow her children to collect his death benefits.

Just before Christmas 1967 my friend Audrey Craner was told that her husband had been shot down and was MIA. She told no one and took the children away for a month. We were mystified. Why would she suddenly disappear without saying a word to her friends? When she returned, she told us that she hadn't wanted to ruin our Christmas. Her husband, Bob, was taken prisoner and shared a cell with John McCain, who credited Bob with saving his life while they were in the "Hanoi Hilton." Bob came home when the POWs were freed in 1973, only to die suddenly while playing squash a few years later.

I wondered how I would act, what I would say, if the chaplain came to inform me that we, too, were the family of an MIA. Every day, I snatched the newspaper from the doorstep as it was delivered and hid the headlines from the children. Remembering the ever-present radio of my childhood war years, I wouldn't let the children watch television when the news came on. I'd race from the kitchen at 6:00 and shoo the children outside so I could watch the progress of the war alone. Every day there were grisly reports of aircraft shot down and soldiers killed. One morning I retrieved the newspaper from the front porch and the headlines read, "Five F-105s shot down by the North in one day." I expected the doorbell to ring later that day. I agonized over my growing doubts about the war. I didn't want to be disloyal but couldn't understand why we were fighting such a terrible war so far away and for such ill-defined reasons.

One late afternoon, a group of us were sharing a bottle of wine in my living room. Billie and Audrey were there. Suddenly, our conversation stopped abruptly as we all looked out the window and saw a blue Air Force staff car pulling into our cul-de-sac. A uniformed officer sat in the front seat next to the driver. The car stopped, looking for house numbers, continued driving around the circle, and then slowly drove away. We let out a collective sigh of relief. Each of us had thought we were about to learn that another husband had been shot down.

I no longer thought about our unhappy marriage. Bud was a hero just like all my friends' husbands. We were a small, close-knit group as we shared letters from our husbands, wrote to them frequently, and tried to keep our spirits up and our children happy. The children and I prayed for his safety, and I imagined that all would be well when he returned.

In the spring of 1968, Bud was slated for R&R (rest and relaxation) at the mid-point of his tour. The children moved in with Gam and Grandfather and I flew from Virginia to Hawaii. Sgt. Whitaker and Mamie, Mom's maid, helped care for the children. Mom told me that Sgt. Whitaker put his foot down when she asked him to drive the children to school. "Don't you know what would happen to me if anyone saw me,

Bedtime was story time, 1968

a large black man, driving a car with a little white girl?" So
Dad's driver, Sgt. Kelly, took them to school. Carrie celebrated
her seventh birthday while I was gone.

On the last night in Hawaii, we had dinner with our
old neighbors, the Walkers, up in Aiea Heights. Bud left in the
middle of the night to return to Thailand and the Walkers
drove me to the airport the next morning. As we neared the
airport, their car radio reported that Martin Luther King, Jr.
had been assassinated. I boarded the airplane feeling sick at
heart. I couldn't believe such a terrible thing could happen
again in the United States. I feared that there would be a great
uproar and calls for vengeance despite King's philosophy of
nonviolence.

Sure enough, our cities began to burn with hatred and
fire. Many square blocks of Washington, D.C. were burned,
and buildings would remain boarded-up for the next thirty
years. Today, when I think that times are hard, I remind
myself of the violence of the sixties, the anti-war protests, and

the hatred unleashed during the fight for civil rights for our African American citizens. And yet, we survived it.

Mom Memories. I was busy waiting patiently for the war to end. I wrote to Bud faithfully every week. We had a little tape recorder, and the children and I recorded tapes for him, which I mailed with my letters. What I would give to have those tapes today! They were full of the details of the children's lives, sweet little voices, funny and loving. I took photos of the children with my little Brownie camera and sent them with the tapes.

Memories of beautiful moments with my children have stayed with me: Bill asking, "What's for dinner, Mom?" And when I said, "Chicken," excitedly telling me how much he loved my chicken. Carrie saying, with an angelic face, how much she loves getting presents for people at Christmastime. Hal excited and proud to be made a School Patrol and given the task of raising the flags at school every day. Tim jumping into my arms, leaning way back toward the ground, knowing I'd never let him fall.

One day I heard Hal use the "F word" and decided that it was time to have "the talk." I steeled myself and took him into my bedroom and began by telling him that was a terrible word for something sacred and he must never use it again. As I began to struggle for the words to explain what it meant, I realized that he had no interest in knowing what it meant when he finally asked, impatiently, "Can I leave now?" I don't remember bringing up the subject of the birds and bees again. I guess they learned the same way I did, word of mouth from the other kids.

The Hampton school board decided to balance school enrollments by requiring the children in Tide Mill Farms, mostly military kids, to change schools each of the three years we lived there. In the fall of 1969, a school was built down the block from us, Luther Machen Elementary. The children could walk to that school. This is where Hal was on the school patrol and was responsible for raising and lowering the flags.

That year, Bill and Carrie began weekly piano lessons. Hal wanted to play the guitar, so I bought a guitar and hired a teacher to come to the house to give him lessons. Bill and Carrie joined the Children's Chorus of the Skylarks and sang with us in the Christmas Concert at the Officers Club.

Susie Broadway and I enrolled our daughters in the Hampton School of Ballet and took turns taking them for lessons. They danced in the Nutcracker Ballet and I saw right away that Carrie had exceptional talent. At seven years old, she already lifted her arms as gracefully as a swan, tilted her head exactly as her teacher did, and kept perfect time with the music. Eventually she chose ballet over the piano.

We always had four birthday parties a year, sometimes a fifth if Bud was home for his birthday. If we were too new in the neighborhood, they were family parties. If we'd been there awhile and the kids had made friends, they were invited. Hal's and Bill's parties sometimes included contests with the cross bows that Grandfather had brought back from Southeast Asia, gifts of the Montagnards. Whoever shot an arrow closest to the bull's eye got a prize. Our birthday cakes went round and round on a musical cake platter that played "Happy Birthday."

While we were living in Tide Mill Farms, we witnessed a total eclipse of the sun. I'll never forget the awesome power of that experience as the sun, high in the sky, slowly turned black in the middle of the day, and was finally outlined by a bright corona of light. The world around us gradually darkened, the streetlights suddenly blinked on, an eerie greenish light surrounded us. Houses were emptied as everyone streamed outside to watch the spectacle through periscopes that allowed us to see what was happening without endangering our eyes. We watched while the sun gradually reappeared, growing bright again. We stayed and talked in our backyards in the late afternoon shadows, marveling at this

175

mysterious event. I can only imagine how terrifying this phenomenon must have been to our prehistoric ancestors.

The Warrior Returns, November 1968. Bud arrived home just before Thanksgiving 1968, having completed 100 missions over North Vietnam. With Bud's agreement, Dad had arranged an assignment at Langley. We all believed that a couple more years of stability would be good for the children, although Dad knew he and Mom would leave before Bud returned home. Dad had orders to take over as the Commandant of the Air University at Maxwell Air Force Base. Bud reported to his new assignment at Langley's Tactical Air Command Headquarters two weeks later. He had been gone for a year and a half, having briefly seen the children twice.

      The war had taken a toll on Bud and his readjustment was hard. My friends welcomed him into our social circle, but he was morose, unhappy. He would often walk around the house in a daze with a drink in his hand or sit on the floor listening to tapes of his combat missions. I began to feel that he missed his fellow pilots more than he'd missed us. I tried to pretend that all was well and that we were a perfectly happy family. I put on that stiff upper lip. The only time my anger surfaced was when I felt that he was mistreating the children. But I was overwhelmed with disappointment and struggling with depression. I fear that those feelings were a dark presence in my children's lives.

Summers. In the summer of 1968, while Bud was still in Thailand, a friend had encouraged me to send Hal and Bill to a YMCA Camp near Hopewell, where they sent their son every summer. I decided that would be a good experience for the boys. I prepared them carefully according to the Camp instructions and sewed their names in all their clothes. They were both good swimmers and I was promised that they would be together. They would swim, fish, learn to sail and participate in arts-and-crafts activities. It sounded like a wonderful adventure for them. When they reported that they'd had a good time, I decided to send them again the following summer. This would also be an opportunity to separate Hal, who was the subject of frequent harsh discipline, from his father for a couple of weeks.

When I dropped them off at Camp, Bud was TDY, so I decided to drive up with Carrie and Timmy and visit my cousin Anne for a couple of days. Bud came back the Saturday we were to pick the boys up at Camp. He had told me not to go to Maryland to visit Anne and I had disobeyed him. He was angry and delayed leaving to pick up the boys until I was frantic. The camp counselors had emphasized the importance of picking them up on time.

By the time we got there, all the other campers had left, and the boys were standing alone in front of a cabin in the woods, teary-eyed. My heart overflowed with guilt and relief when I saw them. Hal had suffered an accident to his eye, which was black and blue and nearly swollen shut. He told me that they had taken him to the doctor, who had said that he'd be fine, so they hadn't bothered to call me. I decided there would be no more summer camps.

On July 20, 1969, we were transfixed by man's first walk on the moon. Friends gathered in front of our black and white television. We sat up into the wee hours as our astronauts landed on the moon and Neil Armstrong took his "...one small step for man, one giant leap for mankind." We were breathless and incredulous as we watched this momentous event, but also proud of our country and our astronauts.

That summer, we made our first of several summer trips up to Nantucket to stay in the Martin Box, the cottage across the island in Siasconset (S'conset) that my parents had bought several years earlier. They had not been to Nantucket for a number of years. The real estate agent complained that he couldn't rent it because it was so damp and dark.

The Martin Box, Mom's and Dad's cottage on Nantucket

We found the back door open and the kitchen full of leaves. It was a mess. We quickly set to work sprucing it up: new lamp shades, a new cover and colorful cushions for the sofa, and bright new mats for the beautiful Audubon prints. We aired out the mildewed mattresses and bought mattress covers. Bud built bunk beds in the dory shed. When we moved the mattresses that had been under the trundle beds to the dory shed, the cottage could comfortably sleep six. We went to the dump, a trove of abandoned treasures, and found a grill and a bicycle that were in usable condition. We painted the picket fence white and began to feel that the Martin Box was ours.

There was no television, so I read to the children every night. Bambi was a favorite. The children played around the village and we spent many happy hours on the beach. One of those summers, the three boys wandered far down the beach and ended up at what was called Tern Beach looking for birds' eggs. Coming around a sand dune, they surprised a naked young couple. Hal and Bill turned and walked quickly away, embarrassed, while Timmy (age six or seven) called after them excitedly, "Hey guys. Look. Streakers!" This was the wild sixties and Tim had seen naked college kids on television running the streets, "streaking."

Our summer visits to the Martin Box were usually in June before the renters took it over. The children loved Nantucket and played happily all day entertaining each other. Those were among our happiest times together as a family. Pat came with us on one of those trips and helped with the clean-up and painting.

One day I opened a letter from friends of my parents whom we had visited on their farm in West Virginia when I was a child. Their farm, Walnut Grove, was near Union. They invited us to bring the children for a long weekend. They had baby animals, including an adorable colt that Carrie was allowed to bottle feed. Later we went on an old-fashioned hayride sitting on top of a wagon filled with fragrant newly mown hay. It was an unforgettable visit.

During the summers while we were at Langley, I took the kids to the sand pool at Fort Eustis, about 20 miles away. We all enjoyed swimming and picnicking there on the humid days of Tidewater summers. We rented a tent from the Base Quartermaster Office and went camping on Lake Gaston with the Caffery family. In the fall of 1969, I reserved a tent again and we camped for a weekend in the George Washington National Forest in the Blue Ridge Mountains. It had rained and the forest was a kaleidoscope of falling leaves burnished in red and gold.

Maxwell Air Force Base: Alabama Redux

In the spring of 1970 Bud's name came out on the list to spend the next year attending the Air War College at Maxwell. Dad had just been reassigned from the position as commander of the Air University at Maxwell to take over the Air Force Academy in Colorado Springs. I don't remember the children ever complaining when Bud received orders. They seemed to realize that moving was their lot in life as military Brats. But they were unhappy to hear that we might go back to Alabama and begged me not to send them to that Catholic school again.

I considered not going to Alabama. I remembered how unhappy Bud had been during his last assignment there. Staying in our home in Tide Mill Farms where the children could all walk down the block to school seemed like a good idea. But Bud was so adamant that we all go that he threatened divorce. I caved but insisted that we not sell the house. The Vietnam War showed no signs of ending anytime soon and Bud could be sent back. I had made many friends and become attached to the house that had been my home for the longest I'd ever lived anyplace. We put it up for rent.

When we finally decided to sell that house three years later, all of us went to Hampton to fix it up. We stayed with neighbors and set to work, cleaning, painting, mowing the lawn, and trimming bushes. I was so proud of our four kids, who worked hard without complaints or bickering. We couldn't have done it over one weekend without help from all of them.

On our way to Montgomery, we drove through Niceville, Florida to see the cottage where we'd lived when Billy was born. It looked abandoned except for a large rowboat sitting in the middle of the living room. I wondered how I could ever have lived in that shack for a year with two babies, rats and Palmetto bugs. Boggy Bayou, where Hal had first gone swimming with Gam, and I had water-skied for the first time, was opaque and brown, filled with sticks and fallen trees. How could it ever have been safe for swimming or skiing?

Our household goods would not get to Alabama for at least a week, so we went over to a military recreation area in southern Alabama, Pippin Lake, and rented a cabin. It was a fun week of boating and swimming. Bud was relaxed and seemed happy. It was a peaceful break before I set about making a new home for us in Montgomery.

Bud had rented a house, sight unseen again, from another Air Force officer. It was in an old established neighborhood where Spanish moss and mistletoe hung on large trees in front yards. The previous renters had had a dog, which left several piles of poop, now dried up on carpets in the bedrooms. The yard was overgrown. I looked around wearily. The house was dirty, but I could make it do.

No sooner had we arrived at our new home and begun cleaning and unpacking than we were treated to a real, honest-to-goodness southern thunderstorm. The wind sprang up, thunder shook the house, and buckets of rain pelted the windows. Suddenly a tremendous blast of thunder unleashed a surprise. The children called me over with shouts of, "Mom, come look at the little white frogs jumping all over the back yard!" Hail stones the size of half-dollars bounced up and down all over the yard. A wide, concrete lined drainage ditch behind the house filled with hail stones followed by rushing water. What a welcome to Alabama!

There was a busy social agenda and I was soon glad that I'd come back to Alabama. I met a fellow Brat, Anne, who suggested that we work together on a craft project. She showed me how to make clay and form it into fruits and vegetables. We painted our creations, mounted them on pieces of weathered wood, and began selling them at craft fairs as "Rustics by Anne and Caro." Bouncing ideas off each other, we developed a portfolio of several dozen designs. We found an old abandoned shack and slowly tore it down, piece by piece, selecting the most worn, knotty, worm-eaten pieces of wood on which to mount our creations. And we paid the kids to bring us interesting pieces of wood that they found in the parks and wooded areas nearby.

All four of the children entered fully integrated public schools, with African American teachers half of each day, and African American kids bussed in to fill half of each classroom. The Virginia schools had been excellent, and the children were ahead of their classmates in Alabama, making good grades. I found a Scout Troop for the boys and scouting activities kept them busy.

I had failed at two things my mother had hoped I would do well: play the piano and dance ballet. Those failures were probably behind my continuing to encourage Bill to play the piano, and Carrie to dance. In Montgomery, I found a piano teacher for Bill and ballet lessons for Carrie. They both showed talent and their teachers were sad when we left a year later. Bill's piano teacher had tears in her eyes when we went to say good-bye. I hoped that one day my mother would see Carrie and Bill perform.

Although Bud had completed his tour, the Vietnam War was still filling the news. While we were in Alabama, the Montgomery Advertiser broke the story of the My Lai Massacre, which had taken place more than a year earlier. Lt. William Calley was ultimately held responsible. There was an outpouring of sympathy for Calley, who was stridently defended in the newspapers. I was horrified and wrote to the newspaper that their defense of him suggested that they expected this kind of behavior from all American soldiers fighting the war. I said that what Lt. Calley had done was wrong, immoral and an insult to all those in uniform. I discussed this with the children, and I remember that Bill made the same argument in school but didn't think that he had changed any minds.

Pat's Visits in Alabama: Pat visited us during both our assignments in Alabama. From his first visit, we have photos of Carrie and Bill standing next to two-year-old Timmy, who is wearing Pat's helmet. His second visit three years later was particularly significant. He was about to complete his second tour and described in detail the mission he was flying out of Ubon in Thailand as a "Wolf FAC." As a FAC (forward air controller) flying an F-4 Phantom jet, the mission was to fly in

182

Pat visits in Alabama (left) and Timmy gets to wear his helmet.

low and slow over certain areas in Laos and North Vietnam to draw anti-aircraft fire so that our bombers could target the guns and disrupt the flow of arms moving south along the Ho Chi Minh Trail. It was dangerous, and the loss rate was high. At the end of his second tour, with about 400 combat missions under his belt, he revealed that he had extended for a third tour. Mentioning the "statistical law of averages," he muttered that, "This time my number might come up." When he left, I hugged him good-bye with tears in my eyes and wondered if I'd ever see him again.

Not long after he left, a friend called me on her way through Montgomery. Her husband was a general at Air Force Headquarters in Saigon. Their oldest son had been killed in Vietnam flying an F-4 a year earlier and I had attended his funeral and burial at Langley. She asked about Pat and I told her that he was extending for a third tour. She was astounded and said that only sons should not be allowed to serve three tours. Then she asked me how my parents felt. I told her that I didn't think they were happy about it. Suddenly Pat was reassigned to Saigon. Pat was furious and asked Dad to reverse the orders and help him get back to the Wolf FACs. Dad tried but I don't think the general thought his heart was in it. He refused to send Pat back to Ubon except for a few missions a month to allow him to stay proficient in the aircraft.

Pat used his position as the generals' briefer in Saigon to point out both the tactical and strategic errors in current policies that he believed were responsible for losing the air war in Southeast Asia. Gen. Clay, in command at the time, agreed with Pat. Policies were changed. But as soon as Gen. Clay was reassigned, his decisions were reversed. Pat was livid and probably verbally insubordinate. The Air Force continued to lose pilots, many of them Pat's friends. Pat believed they had been betrayed by their superior officers in Headquarters and this preyed on his mind for the rest of his life. I am grateful that Pat didn't blame me when he heard of my indirect role in his reassignment, but I caught plenty of flak from other family members.

Years later, during a visit with us in Virginia, I took Pat to the Vietnam War Memorial Wall in Washington. I stood with Kathleen and Edward while he slowly went down the length of the wall, gently touching all the names of his friends who were KIA. He had tears in his eyes when we finally headed for home.

Again, Bud was not happy at Maxwell. He was allowed to fly TDY cross-county less than one weekend a month, just enough to stay proficient in an aircraft and continue to collect flight pay. As a Lt. Col., he was likely to be flying a desk for most, if not all, the rest of his career. He was drinking even more heavily by now and alcohol seemed to be his primary comfort. He was angry and morose most of the time.

Then it got worse: he was ordered to the Pentagon, an assignment dreaded by all Air Force pilots. He was assigned to work as an action officer for the Joint Chiefs of Staff, a prestigious position. But Bud was unhappy about the prospect of a desk job, although few high-ranking Air Force officers manage to avoid a tour at the Pentagon during their careers.

He complained that the Washington area was the most expensive tour for military families.

While we were still at Maxwell, he rented a house in Alexandria from a classmate. He was planning to get out of the Pentagon as fast as he could, and he didn't want to be saddled with a house to sell. He didn't believe people who told him that houses in the Washington area were good investments and cheaper over a three or four-year assignment than renting.

Snakes and Pigeons and All the Animals We Loved

As soon as school was out, we drove up from Maxwell and stayed with Bobby and Lily in their Capital Hill townhouse, waiting for our household goods to arrive. Our visit must have been a significant disruption to their daily working lives, but they were happy to have us there. They took us sailing and were delighted that we'd be living close by. Hal and Bill spent many happy hours during that week, trapping pigeons on their patio.

Our four brave children faced the challenge of yet another new school (their sixth in six years), of figuring out how to fit in, of making new friends. Hal and Bill were good buddies and always had each other, and Tim attracted friends without even trying. Carrie, as the only girl, had a harder time and her brothers weren't much help.

I had another house to turn into a home, curtains to alter to fit new windows. I found new dentists and optometrists, located the nearest Commissary and Base Exchange, and found the nearest military medical facility. I didn't have the Skylarks or the Grey Ladies anymore. The dependents of military personnel assigned to the Pentagon live in the community as civilians. There is no ready-made social life and no military installation to anchor the families.

I decided to teach religion at the nearby Catholic Church. The children all attended religion classes and we went together to Mass every Sunday. We set up the playhouse and a couple of neighborhood girls found Carrie. We put the boys' pigeons in a coop in the backyard. I found an orthodontist who put braces on Bill and Carrie. Hal wanted to join the Boy Scouts. I found a Boy Scout troop nearby and he began going to weekly meetings there. We were soon a very busy crew.

Bill had shown such promise at the piano that I wasted no time in finding him a teacher, the organist at the church around the corner. It wasn't long before he was playing Debussy's "Claire de Lune" and Beethoven's sonatas. I loved hearing him play and was disappointed when he decided that he'd had enough.

I found a ballet studio and enrolled Carrie. She immediately drew the attention of the teachers, a Russian couple who had danced with The Ballets Russes. Watching her dance brought me such joy that I would leave home early to pick her up and watch her through the one-way glass. She seemed to especially glow when dancing to the Straus Waltzes Mrs. Tupine favored.

That December, she danced in the "Nutcracker" for the first time. Attending her performances became a family Christmas tradition for the next five years, the boys often helping to sell drinks and cookies. We all think of our graceful ballerina whenever we hear the Nutcracker playing at Christmastime. Carrie would go on to earn scholarships, three summers in a row, to George Balanchine's School of American Ballet in New York City.

Timmy began playing soccer and was soon "scouted" by a select soccer team while he was still in second grade. During the game that got the coach's attention, he fell to the ground after grabbing the ball between his feet, rolled away from the opposing player, and jumped up to continue running with the ball.

I was always attentive to report cards. Bill seemed to weather all the new schools without having any academic problems and I was very proud of him when he was placed in the GT (gifted and talented) program. Carrie had always been a straight-A student. But the fourth grade in Alabama was practically a repeat of her third grade in Virginia. Soon after she started school in Alexandria, I realized how far behind she was. Fifth grade was a struggle for her while she caught up.

Hal was getting mediocre grades. When I met with his teacher, she told me that not all kids were college material. I just stared at her for a minute and coldly told her that all my children would go to college. Then I took him for testing at George Washington University. They told me that he was fine, just a little behind due to all the school changes. When summer came, I took him and Tim to a reading tutor every week.

As we were settling in, Pat came back from Thailand. He was agonizing over whether to marry Aree, a beautiful Thai girl whom he had met at the officers' club at Ubon. She had lost two fiancés, both pilots who had been killed in combat, and Pat felt deep compassion for her. While he was visiting, Bobby strongly advised Pat not to marry Aree, stressing their cultural differences. "She'll never know who Winnie the Pooh is!" Bobby told him.

Although Bobby and Lily had been deeply in love, they had grown up in different parts of the world and did not share the cultural background that became increasingly important to him as the years passed. But Pat decided to marry Aree anyway. Soon after that visit, he brought her to Alexandria to meet us and they planned a wedding. I flew out to Colorado Springs for the ceremony, which was held in Mom's and Dad's quarters at the Air Force Academy.

Bill went for a month-long visit with his grandparents at the Air Force Academy in the summer of 1971 and had a great time. Mom came through Virginia the next summer and took Tim back to the Academy for a visit. Later that summer we drove out to Colorado to spend a couple of weeks and to bring

Tim back. Both boys had wonderful visits, riding horseback on the Academy trails with their grandparents and spending a lot of time with Sergeants Whitaker and Kelly. Tim loved to ride around the property on the riding mower with the gardener.

Carrie was fortunately able to visit with her grandparents on Nantucket after her classes in New York City at the School for American Ballet. These were lovely visits for her with her Gam all to herself. Hal always had a job in the summers and we counted his visit with them at Langley, when he was seven, as his grandparent visit.

Shopping for food at the Commissary was a family affair. I only shopped every two weeks and the Commissary was always jammed. So one of the older children would come with me as I filled two carts to the brim. They would wait in line as I continued to find items to add to the carts. When our groceries were bagged, we'd get in line to pick them up at a carousel outside the building. Tim's job was to fold the bags when we got home, and there were often as many as twenty. "Oh, Mom. Do I have to?!" Someone would usually pitch in and help.

I wasn't a very inspired cook, partly because I always tried hard to save money. I had bought some mutual funds that I hoped would put the children through college. We had a lot of spaghetti, hamburgers, chili, fish sticks, hot dogs and oven-fried chicken. Alas, the vegetables were always a challenge. They didn't like any of them. But I didn't give up cooking them and begging the kids to eat them because I believed they were important for their health. I did give up on liver, bacon and onions. The bacon always disappeared and I think what liver was not scraped into the garbage had gone into a dog's hungry mouth. But there was almost always banana bread or bread pudding available for after-school snacks, and ice cream for dessert.

The Animals. We had lots of pets over the years. Sometimes they startled us into fright or laughter, but always they were objects of deep curiosity and sometimes love. There were the geckos in Hawaii, the "lizards in space" in Alabama, the black mollies that the angel fish took great bites out of, the gerbils and the snakes; but also a rabbit, a cat, a squirrel, and one very special dog.

Our first pet, a Guinea Pig, was a parting gift from the Kemps when we lived in Hawaii. He was comfortably caged in the back yard except when the children sneaked him into their beds on weekend mornings. His leavings among their rumpled sheets gave them away. There were tropical fish for a time, and wandering kittens and dogs often found their way through our open doors.

Thumper, Carrie's pet white rabbit, joined our household at about the same time we acquired a part-Siamese cat named Tiger. Thumper lived in the garage and Carrie walked her on a leash. We had to find her another home when we began to spend time in the summers on Nantucket. Hal's cat, Tiger, ruled the household, chewing holes in our wool sweaters and blankets, and traveling in the car with us on vacations and several changes of station. I had to find Tiger another home when my asthma kicked up and the doctor warned of serious lung problems if we continued to own a cat.

After Hal and Bill had figured out how to trap preoccupied pigeons on Bobby's and Lily's back patio on Capitol Hill, we set up a pigeon house in our backyard. Bobby was so intrigued by these new pets that he bought a pair of tumbler pigeons for the boys. They were mottled shades of brown and white. They would fly to great heights and tumble slowly down to earth before righting themselves just before they hit the ground, gracefully landing on their feet. Eventually the tumblers mated with one of the original grays and hatched a beautiful baby.

For a while, there were terrariums filled with snakes in Hal and Bill's bedroom. Garter snakes of various markings, they sometimes wriggled out through the wire screen coverings and disappeared. I always knew when such an incident had occurred. The boys would arrive home from school and quickly close their door. I would hear hushed voices and furniture being pushed around until they found the escapee.

One day, their school principal called to tell me that Hal had found a snake and wanted to take it home. "He says it's okay because he has lots of snakes at home." "Yes," I proudly replied. "Hal says he wants to be a herpetologist when he grows up." There was a short silence before the principal replied with obvious skepticism, "Okay, ma'am, I'll tell him he can take it home." I gasped when Hal came into view with a huge black rat snake wrapped across his shoulders and hanging off both arms, longer than he was tall. He and Bill bought mice at the pet shop with their own money and watched, fascinated, as the snake swallowed the mice. The snake was an alarming sight hanging from the apple tree in the back yard and the boys finally got tired of spending their money on mice and set it free in the woods nearby.

One afternoon, Uncle Abe surprised us with a call to report that he had an injured baby squirrel and wondered whether we could save it. Bill performed surgery, removing the bone from the lower half of the little guy's tail, which had been left bloody and furless, presumably by some cat who'd planned on a squirrel dinner. Nibbles enjoyed free reign throughout the house, riding around on Bill's shoulder and sometimes on the kids' heads. After his tail healed, Bill decided that Nibbles should be set free. But Nibbles did not want to be set free. Bill would climb up a tree, carefully setting the squirrel on a branch, and Nibbles would simply jump back down on Bill's head. But one day Bill returned and dejectedly reported that Nibbles had finally decided to stay in the woods. There were sightings over the next few months of a squirrel with a short tail, and we hoped that Nibbles survived to live a long and happy life.

Our great gerbil adventure began when Tim found a cage with a gerbil in it under the Christmas tree. The poor guy seemed bored and lonely, so we bought him a mate. The next morning, Tim tearfully reported that there had been a bloody brawl during the night. The new gerbil was dead. Maybe it was another male. We ensured that we introduced the next newbie, identified by the pet store as a female, slowly into the life of the lonely bachelor. Preoccupied with other things, I didn't notice until the two gerbils had multiplied into 27. Housed in the garage in four separate cages with signs identifying them by age, they escaped regularly and romped around with Tim in hot pursuit. I had finally had enough.

Tim was tearful as I waited outside the pet shop and told him to take them in and give them away—all of them.

Then there was the day Hal called me upstairs to see what he had bought. A gigantic iguana was lounging in the bathtub, so big that its tail hung over the edge. At this, I put my foot down! I said a stern "No" to accepting that one into the family. "Aw, Mom!" he said. But I think this one was for shock value. He took it back to the pet shop and brought

Land of the animals, from top: Adam, who loved to climb onto the roof and bark at confused passersby; Tim plays with Nibbles, the squirrel; and Carrie tends to her kittens.

191

home a smaller one, which we continued to feed long after he left for college. I think we finally returned it to the pet shop. But some years later, Jason brought us another one when his Mom decided that we'd be better caretakers than she.

Adam, Part of the Family for 16 years. A little black puppy named Adam by his birth family came as a gift to Carrie on the Christmas of 1974. He wriggled his way into all our hearts, a foot-long squirmy wail of loneliness as he slowly adjusted to leaving his mother and accepted his new role in life. The kids played with him endlessly, stuffed him up their shirts, into their book bags, into their clothes and under their covers. His proper training was neglected in the busy household and it was a couple of years before he could be considered somewhat house broken. I'm sure the faint odor of his puppyhood lingers still in the pantry of the house on Larstan Drive. He arrived back from a stay out west with "Wild dog, pisses on everything" scribbled on the crate. He was so intelligent that he was able to convince selected people in certain circumstances that he was not. This allowed him to get away with peeing on people and things he didn't like.

He must have been barely a year old when Tim began his formal soccer training. They spent hours dribbling soccer balls around the yard. In fact, it was during one such training session that he ran into the street after the ball and ended up under a neighbor's moving car. It was a frightened and hurting pup that Tim brought back to the house after hurling all the invective that a 12-year old boy could muster. But Adam was back at it in short order, the only apparent after-effect being a tender butt. It wasn't until 14 years later, when the vet did an X-ray, that we learned his back had been broken.

He learned to say please for his supper, sitting motionless for long, silent disciplinary sessions, while the pungent fragrance of his supper set his salivary glands into overdrive. When he finally heard "Okay," he'd pounce on his supper with barks of thanks and grumbled epithets for the one who kept him waiting. Although we have each said rotten things about him from time to time, we took good care of him and he did what dogs are supposed to do. He loved us, played with us, protected us (or tried to), was always there to greet us, and happily accepted every scrap of affection that came his way, returning it with all that was in him.

Rocks! How he loved to chase, dig for, and chew on rocks, a habit that left him with teeth ground to the gum, little threat to all the mail carriers he viciously insulted. He would take hilarious plunges into the creek to gales of laughter. With the heart of a lion and just a touch of ham, he thoroughly enjoyed entertaining us. When discussing his lineage, the kids usually forgot his champagne-colored poodle mother and were certain that his father had been a championship mixture of German Shepherd, Irish Setter and Labrador. Whoever he was, this sire passed on a love of water and a penchant for suddenly going into a pointing stance as he waited for a ball or rock to land. He had rough-hewn, ragtag, ungroomed good looks, although we sometimes told him that he was the ugliest little black mongrel anyone had ever laid eyes on. He would respond with a wagging tail and smiling face as if his ugliness were a badge of honor.

Being a roof dog was one of his special attributes. He would climb up on the roof of the garage where it dipped close to the ground in back, walk over the peak and survey the activity going on in the neighborhood from the top of a two-story brick colonial. He was unfailingly generous and openhearted to all the other creatures who came to share his hearth for a while. Bill's squirrel would chatter at him menacingly and Adam would wag his tail and give a couple of barks. He showed little concern about the 27 gerbils that scurried around the garage. He welcomed Bobby and Lily's dog for several visits, though he learned from her the habit of biting the mail when it was dropped through the door slot.

I'll always remember Adam's uncanny ability to recognize the vulnerable, and an unwavering sense of responsibility to protect them. He was drawn by instinct to sleep by those who were sleeping and to leap to attack stance when approached. When one-month old Danny was in the house, we always found Adam sleeping by him. And for the next three years, Danny replaced Tim as Adam's best friend. And we'll never know how many burglars he scared away with his occasional bursts of midnight barking. On a few occasions, certain family members, returning home late at night, slept in the car rather than wake Adam and thus the rest of us.

Adam accepted his growing frailty as naturally as he accepted all the other conditions of his life, without complaint. He simply went on enjoying what he could in each new day. It was as if he knew that one of the benefits of growing old is that one grows wiser, sometimes painfully, but with occasional glimpses of a deeper understanding. That not one sparrow falls without God's knowledge and caring is true. And love is the key to it all—not the grasping and clutching that is sometimes called love, but the free surrender to love that sometimes feels like jumping off the high dive.

We knew he had become hard of hearing when he let the mailman come and go without a bark. He continued to follow us up and down the stairs, painfully but with determination. One of the last times I saw him wag his tail was when a small boy of about ten came walking through the yard headed in his direction. He paused, wagged his tail and lifted his head in expectation of a pat and maybe a ball to be thrown his way. The wagging tail slowed and drooped between his legs as the boy moved away.

Ambulance Rides and Hospitals. Bill and Hal were in seventh and eighth grades, old enough to be responsible for each other and Timmy. One evening when I arrived home with Carrie from her ballet class, Bill met me at the door with the news that Timmy had fallen and couldn't move. Bill had carried him into the house and laid him on his back in the living room. Timmy confirmed that he couldn't move. I feared his back was broken and called an ambulance.

All the neighborhood kids came over to watch as they carried Timmy on a stretcher into the ambulance. Carrie sobbed piteously as I told them I'd be back but didn't know when. Then I got into the back of the ambulance and we were off, siren blaring in the middle of rush hour, to the Fort Myer dispensary. Timmy was shoeless, dirty face and dirty clothes. I'll never forget the fear that filled me, as I looked down at him and tried to assure him that he'd be okay.

When we arrived in the emergency room, the doctor began touching him in various places, asking him if he could feel the touch. He said he could, so the doctor asked him to move his feet. He moved his feet and the doctor told him to sit up. Up he sat! We frantically lifted his dirty shirt and looked at his back. There was nothing there but dirt, no blood and no evidence of a broken back. The doctor laughed and said she wished all emergencies could be resolved so easily. Embarrassed, I wanted to get out of there as fast as possible but had no way to get home. Finally, I called the only person I could think of, Genie Lincoln. She chuckled and I blushed all the way to our doorstep.

There were more medical challenges. Bud's doctors told him that he had to go to San Antonio for surgery to fix a problem that had plagued him for years. Just before he was to leave, the landlord, his classmate and friend, raised the rent substantially. I was hurt and furious that he did this when he knew Bud was about to leave for major surgery. The children and I knelt and prayed for their father while he was in San Antonio, and I began preparing for another move.

May 31, 1973 was the day I picked Bud up at Andrews Air Force Base after his surgery. While I was picking him up, Lily and Ellie, her sister, came over to wait for me to return because Ellie needed me to go to court to testify regarding custody of her two children. She temporarily surrendered custody until she could find a job, by which time their father disappeared with the kids. Eight years would pass before she saw them again.

As soon I arrived home with Bud, I received a call telling me that Carrie had had a bicycle accident and was bleeding. I quickly drove a couple of blocks to get her. She was bleeding heavily from her mouth, which she was unable to close. She was pale and in shock and her teeth were hanging loose in her braces. I raced home with her. Bud got in the car, I climbed in the back seat and put my arms around her. We headed back to the Andrews Hospital in rush hour traffic.

I was heartbroken when the doctor told us that her jaw was broken in four places, her condyles shattered, and all her front teeth loose. Two doctors wired her jaw closed and admitted her into the hospital, where she stayed for eight days. She was extraordinarily brave and comforted me as the tears flowed silently down my face. Bud stayed home convalescing, and I visited Carrie in the hospital every day.

The night Bud and I had arrived home from taking Carrie to the hospital, exhausted and scared, a message from Mom told us that Pat's baby, Kathleen, had been born that day, some happy news to close out a horrendous day.

Downsizing to Larstan Drive

Shortly after Carrie was released from Andrews Hospital, and a month after Bud had returned from surgery, we moved a few blocks away. The landlord had put our rental up for sale, so people were trooping through the house while Bud was convalescing, and we were dealing with Carrie's accident. We hastily purchased a house nearby and Dad sent Sgt. Kelly to Virginia to help us move. Most of our household goods were transported down the hill in our two cars.

We borrowed a blender from friends and Carrie sucked her meals through a straw for the next eight weeks. I pureed everything we had for dinner in separate batches. She never complained, but she lost almost ten pounds. At thirteen, she was tiny and small-boned.

The house on Crestwood Drive had been on a large lot. We had a pen for the pigeons, and plenty of room for Carrie's playhouse. Hal and Bill had a large room downstairs with their own bathroom, and plenty of room for several terrariums filled with their snakes. In the new house, all four children shared a bathroom, and Hal and Bill shared a smaller bedroom, requiring bunk beds. The yard was much smaller and consisted primarily of a steep hill up to the houses behind us. The boys decided to free the pigeons and the snakes, and we reluctantly sold Carrie's playhouse to the neighbors.

School started, finding us all a bit shell-shocked. The neighborhood kids hadn't liked the previous owners and took their hostility out on us, bullying the kids and filling my gas tank with sand. Bill started high school at Jefferson without any of his friends from middle school because the school boundaries had changed. Hal continued delivering newspapers and tried out for the high school football team. Carrie gingerly began taking ballet classes again. I wasn't sleeping and was probably suffering from post-traumatic stress myself. Bud's health problem seemed to have improved following the surgery in San Antonio, but his morale was still in the dumps.

Chapter Five
An End and a Beginning

At times our own light goes out and is rekindled by another.
                                                                -Albert Schweitzer

A Life-Changing Experience
In November of 1973, Hal's scoutmaster asked me if I'd like to attend a religious retreat. After the spring and summer we had endured, I was emotionally exhausted. I said, "Yes. I'd like to do that." Bud agreed to come home early from the Pentagon to be with the children after school on Friday, and for the weekend. On Thursday evening, I was picked up and driven 25 miles to a Benedictine convent in Bristow, Virginia.

The retreat was a Cursillo, a four-day course in Christianity developed by a Spanish Jesuit priest. I was one of the twelve women "students" to be instructed in the course by a team of eight, which included two priests and a nun. We were all a little nervous the first night. But by the middle of the next day we were praying, laughing, singing, dancing and having fun. It was not the quiet and solemn event I had expected. People were listening to each other, laughing and before I knew it was happening, all these strangers were becoming friends.

The women on the team talked openly from their hearts about the struggles and difficulties they'd encountered and how their faith and God's love had saved them. I had never heard such honest and heartfelt discussions. They were deeply authentic, and warmly responsive to my questions. Although I had always believed in God as a distant and strict deity, I now felt the presence of a kind and compassionate God who loved me just as I was, flawed and sad. I felt seen, understood and respected as I had never felt before, covered and overwhelmed by affirmation and kindness. It felt like a miracle. All the unhappiness and anxiety that had darkened my life were gone and I was filled with an indescribable joy.

I returned home on Sunday with powerful feelings of hope and love for my family. I promised God that I would begin anew to love my husband and my children with all the strength and courage my heart could muster. I had become used to feeling half alive but now I heard a voice calling me to new life, sparking renewed energy, erasing sadness. My life was on a new path. I hoped that Bud would attend a Cursillo, and that he would also change and be filled with love for me and our children.

But Bud was not impressed by my enthusiastic response to the Cursillo. He was suspicious. A colleague of his who had made a Cursillo tried to persuade him to attend the next retreat for men. Bud told me he said, "It would be good for your marriage." But Bud remained uninterested. I began attending daily mass, and prayed with increasing fervor for him, and for our children. In March, I gave a birthday party for him and invited his colleagues from the Pentagon and my new Cursillo friends. Bill served as the bartender. Everyone was friendly and kind, but Bud didn't trust my new friends and remained unrelentingly wary of the Cursillo.

Then he received orders to Korea for a one-year unaccompanied tour. As the time grew near, he became angrier at me, and began drinking even more heavily and exercising harsher discipline on the children, especially on Hal. Aunt Mary had taken both Hal and Bill for numerous driving lessons. But Bud refused to allow Hal to drive either of the cars despite his getting excellent grades in driver's education and having passed the test and obtained his drivers' license. He told Hal that if he ever drove one of his cars, he'd kick him out of the house when he came home. I quietly told Hal to be patient and promised him that I would let him drive as soon as Bud left.

Korea: August 1974

Bud was due to leave for Korea in the summer. Dad was retiring on July 31 after 38 years. There would be a parade, a change-of-command ceremony and a celebration at the Air Force Academy in Colorado Springs. We decided to fly out for that, after which Bud would leave for Korea from Denver. Bobby and Lily moved into our house to care for the children until I came home.

The festivities surrounding Dad's retirement went by in a blur. There was a great deal of handshaking, a full-dress parade on the parade grounds at the Academy, a fly-by, and a lot of cocktails. Bud remained grim and unsmiling throughout the festivities. After the ceremonies, Pat drove us to the Denver airport. I found an earlier flight and flew home to my children. I cried most of the way back as I realized I was glad he was gone.

I can never forget the luxury of waking up in the morning alone in my bed and feeling the first soft edges of peace, so long forgotten that I thought I was dreaming. As the children and I sat together at dinner, I felt a moment of such pure grace that tears filled my eyes. We were looking each other in the eyes, talking and laughing. I gazed around at each of my dear children's faces. Seeing them smiling, relaxed and happy was a profoundly moving experience. The sweet chuckles—had ever such laughter sounded in this room! Tears sting my eyes as I write this. No more at the dinner table with eyes on our plates, not daring to say a word. The cloud of fear and anger lifted. I came to the stark realization that I had been living in a kind of hell with sadness, fear, and dread so deep that they had become myself.

I gave Hal the keys to the station wagon, and watched as he smiled widely, got in the car and drove away. He was back in a few minutes with joy on his face. I'm not sure that he had believed me when I told him that I would let him drive as soon as Bud left. His confidence in himself took a giant leap.

200

He began to help me with errands, driving Carrie to ballet lessons and Tim to soccer practice.

I decided to seek marriage counseling. A priest at our nearby church gave me the name of a licensed Catholic psychotherapist and I made an appointment. I was nervous as I drove to his office. But I remember hearing Cat Stevens singing "Morning Has Broken" on my car radio. Maybe it was

The kids in 1975

a sign that there was a way to make our lives better.

At our first meeting, I told the therapist, Dr. Whyte, "I feel hopeless, helpless and trapped. But I'm a Catholic and can never get divorced. I need help figuring out how to love him like I promised that I would." I wrote to Bud and told him that I was in counseling because I felt that our marriage was in trouble. Although I had begged Bud to accompany me to counseling many times before, he had always refused, saying that it would ruin his career.

The therapist told me, "If you had options, then Bud might change his behavior in order to save the marriage." He encouraged me to go to school, get a college degree, and a job. His confidence in me gave me courage and I checked out the nearby community college. "Maybe I can do this," I thought. After a couple of months, I wrote Bud that I planned to go to college. In his next letter, he warned that if I went to college, I'd be neglecting our children, which was grounds for divorce. I replied that I would never neglect the children, and I know he knew that.

Bobby and Lily and Aunt Mary and Uncle Abe strongly supported my decision to go to college. They believed in me and were proud of me. We spent Thanksgiving 1974 with Bobby and Lily in their town house in Washington. Then they all came over on Christmas Day. They were always there for us during my years in Virginia and I am filled with gratitude for all of them. They gave me the unconditional love and support that made it possible for me to survive the next few years.

A couple of days after Christmas 1974, as Carrie was excited about dancing "Dewdrop," her first solo in the Nutcracker, Tim fell hard against the curb and was badly hurt. He had allowed a friend to handcuff his hands behind his back and was jumping over trash bags lined along the street for the next day's pickup.

I arranged a ride to the performance for Carrie and drove Tim out to the hospital at Ft. Belvoir. An X-ray revealed a fracture down the side of his skull, his second skull fracture! We were put into an ambulance and sent to Walter Reed Hospital, siren blaring. After much discussion and further X-rays, the doctors sent us back to Ft. Belvoir in the ambulance. It was 2:00 a.m. The doctor told me to wake Tim every couple of hours for the rest of the night, and the next two, to make sure he hadn't lost consciousness. I was also instructed to watch him carefully for listlessness or other changes in behavior for the next several weeks. Tim was told to take it easy and we were assured that it would heal.

I was a basket case. How could this have happened to Tim twice? This was my children's third serious accident. My anxiety level went through the roof. I blamed myself. "What can I do to keep my children safe?" I asked myself. Though I try not to remember them, the memories of my children's accidents still haunt me.

Although he was supposed to be gone for a year, Bud suddenly called to say that he was flying home from Korea in early January. When he arrived, he again warned me not to go to college. I decided that I would go to college anyway.

It was not until four months after he had flown back to Korea that I discovered the reason he had come home. Fairfax County required that cars be brought for inspection annually by the owners to renew registration, and ours were due in April. The cars were both in Bud's name and I needed the Power of Attorney that he had left for me when the cars came due for inspection. I searched everywhere. The POA was gone. I took the cars to be inspected without the POA. I tearfully explained that I had four children, had to have a car, my husband was in the military overseas, and I couldn't find the POA. They relented. The cars passed inspection and I got the necessary stickers.

In my next letter I asked why he'd taken the POA when he knew that I needed it to register the cars. His letter back told me that his lawyer (he had a lawyer?) had warned him to get that POA out of my hands ASAP or I would rob him blind. My heart sank. He didn't know me at all. Could he honestly believe that I would do such a thing? Then I found the joint checking and savings accounts had been closed. I began to feel that I was in a fight for survival and for my children's future. His letters were angry, threatening and accusatory. I tried, sometimes unsuccessfully, to stay kind but firm in my letters. I began to throw his letters away. I didn't want any of our children to ever read them.

The Oldest Freshman: January 1975

After Bud went back to Korea, I screwed up my courage and went a few blocks away to Northern Virginia Community College to register. I was worried about my application being accepted because I did not have a high school diploma. I was shaking as I walked into the school and was assigned a counselor, Dr. Fred Hecklinger. "I'm 36 years old, have no high school diploma, no SAT scores, and four children, and I need to get a college degree as soon as possible so I can get a job," I said in one breath.

The counselor told me I wouldn't need SAT scores or a high school diploma and suggested that I take three classes. One was a typing class. We both felt that a secretarial job was my best bet. I had little self-confidence and, in the mid-1970s, few women of my age were attending college, especially as freshmen. The women's movement was just getting underway but not much had changed yet. When I told the therapist I was taking typing, he said, "Good. You'll need to be able to type your research papers when you go for your master's degree." I sighed. Was he serious, or was this a joke? I tried to smile.

I loved being in school. I made A's the first quarter. The other students, primarily recent high school graduates, discussed assignments with me and asked for my help. My morale soared. When the counselor saw my grades, he suggested the College Level Equivalency Program (CLEP), which grants college credit to students who pass the tests even if they did not take the courses. The tests were normed on tests given to college students a year after they had taken the courses as freshmen. Certain minimum grades were required. The counselor told me, "Buy the *Barrons Study Guide for the CLEP Tests*, study it and then take the five general tests. If you pass, you will be given credit for a freshman year of college." Then he told me to consider taking a subject test as well.

I bought the book and began studying freshman math, English, science, history and humanities. The next quarter, I registered for a full load of courses including biology because it looked like the CLEP science test was mostly biology. I studied every night for my classes, and for the CLEP tests. In May, I paid $40 and took all five general CLEP tests at George Mason University, and a subject test in European History, which I'd reviewed in my old high school textbook. I passed all six tests. With the credits I'd earned in two quarters at the community college, added to those acquired from the CLEP tests, I had more than two years' worth of college credits. Wham, Bang! Six months after entering college, I had enough credits to transfer to a four-year school.

I wondered if I could get some credit for my knowledge of French, so I brought in my certificate from the Sorbonne. The counselor investigated and found that the University of Paris, of which the Sorbonne is a part, was not accredited in the United States until sometime in the '70s, long after I had earned my certificate. This surprised us both because it is the second oldest university in the Western world! My hope for credits in French faded. But he suggested that I go upstairs and talk to the French teacher, who immediately began a conversation with me in French. We chatted in French for about 10 minutes and I apologized for my grammatical errors.

The counselor told me a few weeks later that I had been granted twelve credits in French and would be awarded a two-year degree from the college at the end of the summer of

1975. Furthermore, he had spoken to staff at The American University and they would accept all my credits, putting me several credits into my junior year. In September, I entered AU and was given a small scholarship and a part-time job. I had wanted to be a nurse, but it became clear that I simply didn't have time to take all the pre-requisites and apply to nursing school. I chose the fastest way to a paying job and sacrificed my dream.

My Cursillo friends began to drift away. But I had a lot of other support. One night each week, Aunt Mary brought dinner over in a basket while I took a night class. She and Uncle Abe, and Bobby and Lily, urged me on and showered us with evidence of their love and concern. Sue Broadway was a steadfast friend and confidant throughout all those difficult months and years.

The children were interested in my college career, and I think they were proud of me. When I was rushing to write a paper, Bill went to the library and brought home reference material to help me get it finished on time. As I studied for the math CLEP test, Carrie tutored me in the "new" math, explaining the meaning of "set" and other terms I'd never heard.

When I began classes at AU in the fall of 1975, I found the commute to be long and congested. I had always been home when the children returned from school. Although I tried to schedule my classes while they were in school, I often didn't get home in time. I was always half in class and half at home, wondering if they were all okay and trying not to remember the accidents they'd had. The guilt and worry were almost overwhelming. I registered for a double load of courses. Every morning I woke up and wondered if I could continue. "Stiff upper lip," I told myself. "Just do it." It would take me one stressful year until I'd have a college degree.

Return from Korea
When Bud came home in August 1975, I fully expected him to move back into the house. Although I gave him keys and made

no attempt to stop him, he moved into an apartment and hired a lawyer. I never took any steps to keep him out of the house and he came for dinner on Sunday nights.

I finally wrote and told my parents that we had been unhappy for a long time and were probably going to be divorced. I didn't hear back from them. I learned that he had told them that I was having an affair and that he was grief-stricken. He'd always been on his best behavior around my parents, and they believed him. I was still dependent on their approval of me and my children. But now I recognize that some emotional separation from them was necessary for me to become my own person, to grow up and overcome the ties that kept me so insecure and dependent on them for approval. In time, they learned the truth from the children and Dad wrote me a letter of apology.

Insecurity Disrupts our Lives. It would be another two years before Bud finally sued for divorce. In the meantime, I went to see a lawyer. He was sympathetic and said that he had heard my story before, of heavy drinking and abuse, from military wives. He told me that a wife in Virginia could not get a divorce unless her husband agreed or left her. "If you moved out or refused to let your husband back in the home," he told me, "He would have grounds to charge you with desertion, and to get full custody of the minor children."

Frightened by that information, I frantically focused on getting a college degree as fast as possible so I could find a job. I had faith that God was with me and that somehow it would all be okay in the end, whatever the end was to be. But my extreme anxiety and their father's anger were dark clouds over our children's days. I rarely took time to talk to them about their feelings, to assuage their fears, or ask them what was in their hearts. In that way, I failed them in this way, which I deeply regret.

When Bud cancelled his life insurance, he learned that the policy was in my name, entitling me to its cash value. Despite his demands, I refused to sign it over to him and eventually I received a check for $1,500. I had barely enough money to pay the mortgage and buy food and gas. We went without any extras unless the children could talk Bud into providing them. When my cherished clothes dryer broke down, I put up clotheslines in the garage and on the patio. My shower began leaking, resulting in a hole in the ceiling below, so I used the children's shower.

Those years were punctuated by constant car problems. I called the American Automobile Association (AAA) for jump-starts or tows so many times in one year they cancelled my membership. I was driving a bilious green Chevrolet Vega that burned as much oil as it did gas. I sold it for $300. When I had accumulated $1,800, Uncle Abe went with me to buy a used Toyota Corolla that served us well for many years.

I desperately needed a credit card in my own name. I applied and was turned down. However, I had read in the paper that a law had been passed prohibiting companies from denying credit to married women based solely on their lack of income. The Equal Credit Opportunity Act of 1974 banned discrimination in lending. I wrote the bank a letter, citing the law, pointing out that I had been paying bills on time for 18 years and had never bounced a check. I noted that my lawyer was copied on this correspondence. I made up a name that sounded lawyerly and followed it with Esq. I received a credit card within a week.

A College Degree and a Job: August 1976

The Washington Post got wind of my story, probably from my counselor. They published a story about my experience. I went on to earn my degree from American University in 22 months

Carolyn Homan...
107 Credits in 7 months

By Linda Page

Carolyn Homan, homemaker and mother of four children, entered NVCC in January, 1975 as a Freshman. In August, she graduated summa cum laude with an Associate Degree in Liberal Arts. Within a period of seven months, she had accumulated 107 credits.

Carolyn is now a fulltime student at American University, "straddling the line between her junior and senior years." She plans to receive her Bachelor's Degree in psychology in the summer, which means she will have received a four-year college degree in less than two years.

By taking advantage of CLEP (College Level Examination Pro-

grams), Carolyn was able to accrue 57 credits by examination while attending her other classes at NVCC.

"I attended classes in the daytime and studied for the CLEP tests at night," she said. The CLEP tests are separated into general and specialized categories. She studied from Barron's How To Prepare for CLEP, then for the more specialized subjects, she "studied algebra, enrolled in a Biology 101 course and read a World History Book from cover to cover."

Carolyn had been out of school for a long time. The only other college she'd had was one semester at the University of Paris nineteen years ago. Her four children, now aged 11 to 17 have been as she says, "very good

about pitching in and helping."

"My daughter has tutored me in math and my son has gone to the library with a list of questions to look up when I've been working on a paper."

Although Carolyn realizes her degree in psychology will not be worth much in the job market, she decided to go after it because, "that's what I'm most interested in. I could have gotten my degree in business, but that's now where my interests lie."

Whatever her future holds, Carolyn is interested in encouraging other women to go back to school. "A lot of women want to go back to school but are scared stiff that they won't be able to keep up the pace. I feel that because of my experiences, I could help them."

from a standing start with straight A's. Although my degree cost me only $5,000, an amount I had earned selling Rustics, we all paid a heavy emotional price for my education. It had been a hard struggle. I was more determined than ever to help all my children graduate from college. Although their father didn't feel they needed to go to college, I hoped they realized the importance of a college education when they saw what I had gone through to get one.

I decided not to participate in the graduation ceremony. I quit my part-time $3.00 per hour job at AU and began sending out resumes in response to want ads in the paper. There was no internet yet, but I still had my trusty electric typewriter. I sent hundreds of letters and resumes and was turned down for every job I applied for. I exaggerated my experience, describing my part-time secretarial job at AU as professional. Still, not even a request for an interview.

One day, I ran into a man I had known in the Cursillo and I told him of my predicament. He gave me the name and address of The Urban Institute, a D.C. think tank, and told me to send a resume with a cover letter mentioning his name. In a couple of days, I received a call requesting that I come for an interview. I was hired on the spot.

I didn't know then that my friend was the contracting officer on a big job awarded to the Institute. I imagine that I was hired in hopes he'd award them another contract. I began full-time work in August 1976 as a Research Assistant assigned to work in the Child Welfare section of the Social Services Department. My annual salary was a little over $10,000. I worked hard. After six months they gave me an $800 bonus. I joined a van pool to free up the car for the boys to drive Carrie to ballet and Tim to soccer.

I was the only single mother at the Institute, a major potential negative. But I told all the secretaries that if one of my children called, I would take the call even if I was in a meeting. When Carrie landed the "Snow Queen" solo in December, I took leave and left work in the middle of the day. There were disapproving looks. I might have jeopardized my job, but my heart was still where my children were. I was worrying about them constantly, always wondering where they were and what they were doing.

A Subpoena

Sometime in early Spring 1977, Bud told me he would agree to go to marriage counseling with a psychiatrist that he chose. After meeting with the psychiatrist alone for a few weeks, I asked when Bud and I would begin meeting together. The doctor reluctantly informed me that Bud wasn't participating because he felt that I was the one in need of therapy because of a mental breakdown due to the Cursillo. When I learned this, I quit.

As soon as I left therapy, Bud sued for divorce. I learned of that decision when one of the boys called me at work to tell me that they had arrived home from school and found a subpoena tacked to the front door. Bill read the subpoena to me over the phone. Bud was suing me for desertion, for the house and all the property, and for custody of the children. This was sometime in March or early April.

I felt like we'd climbed to the top of a high dive and I had just been waiting to be pushed off. Splash! I'd been pushed off. I sat among the shambles of pain, anger and fear that engulfed my family, shadowed our children's days and kept each of us teetering on the edge. How had it come to this? When I gave up my dream of nursing school, I had exchanged it for a dream of a happy marriage. That dream had become a nightmare. I knew soon after we were married that I was in over my head. Bud was not the loving husband I had imagined. I thought that if I tried hard enough, I could win his love. At 18, I believed in miracles.

All military marriages face the challenges of frequent household moves and long absences of the military member, whether he is off serving TDY or fighting our wars. Growing up as a Brat, I was accustomed to moving. But I was not prepared, as a teenaged wife and mother, to be so often isolated and alone, and thrust into the role of a single parent before it even had a name. I was scared and lonely much of the time and totally dependent. I felt unloved, trapped and abandoned. I felt like a failure, and I was afraid of my husband.

But maybe this wasn't all my fault. I learned about Bud's childhood from him but also from his mother and sister. He told me he'd felt abandoned by his mother when she left him with his father at age nine and moved to California. His father was tough on him. When he traveled by bus to live with his mother, his sister told me, he did not get along with his siblings, and was often sent back to Iowa. He bounced back and forth by bus (five lonely trips between California and Iowa), to live temporarily with each parent. Maybe he never learned how to feel or show empathy and loving kindness because it was never shown to him.

As the years went by, our marriage relationship had gotten harder. When Bud was home, I felt he drank too much and when I asked him to stop to save our marriage, he refused, saying that his drinking was my fault. He was often unkind and abusive to me and to the children. We never modeled for our children the loving kindness and tenderness toward each other that children deserve to see.

I thought back to the girl I'd been when we met: a naïve and devoutly religious teenager, insecure and unsure of myself. The question uppermost in my mind at the time had been, "If I can't go to nursing school, what should I do with my life?" Marriage was the easy answer, the path my parents wanted for me. I couldn't remember a particular moment in time when hope had withered away. I had learned a hard lesson: you can't make someone love you. And it's hard to pretend to love someone when you don't, someone you're afraid of. Maybe I wasn't wholly to blame for this tragedy.

While the pain of the broken marriage can never be blotted out, I have come to understanding, compassion and forgiveness. Each life is filled with a multitude of mitigating factors—physiological, psychological, social and environ-mental—factors known only to God. None of us has enough facts to judge another. We are all flawed.

The guilt over the shadows that passed through our children's lives haunted me. But the day came when I let go of that burden. Our children would grow into mature adults, responsible for their own lives and happiness and for compassionately putting their childhood issues behind, just as I had done.

We Carry on Bravely

The legal process against me dragged slowly on until December 1977. By this time, Hal was halfway through his second year at Northern Virginia Community College, Bill was a freshman at Virginia Tech in Blacksburg, and Carrie was in North Carolina School of the Arts. I was summoned to a court hearing before a judge. I asked my friend Sue to go with me for moral support.

Bud's lawyer subpoenaed Hal to testify in support of Bud's charge of desertion. I refused my lawyer's request to ask the children to testify for me. The judge asked Hal what was going on at home during the months before Bud left for Korea and Hal told the truth.

Then the judge asked Bud for the full names and birthdays of each of the children. He couldn't remember their middle names or their birthdays. His case for desertion and custody of the children was dismissed and the judge made a finding of "no fault" divorce based on our having lived apart for more than a year. After years of an increasingly painful relationship, it was over. The kids were teenagers, one of them older than I was when I got married.

It would be two more years before Congress passed legislation giving long-married military wives a portion of their husband's retirement pay in a divorce settlement—too late for me. Consequently, I received no alimony and no portion of his retirement pay.

The divorce was granted in the spring of 1978, shortly after surgery to remove what turned out to be a benign tumor in my breast. Two heavy burdens were lifted from my stressed and exhausted heart. For the first time in my life, I was no longer a military dependent. Bud decided to sell the house. I could save both of us money if I bought it from him. Pat loaned me exactly what I needed, and I bought the house at Bud's appraiser's value.

Finally, Bud told me that if I didn't sign over to him everything else we jointly owned, he would appeal the judge's decision to the Virginia State Supreme Court. My lawyer told me that would take a minimum of two more years. I wanted it to be over and signed everything over to him except for a Colorado lot. I refused to sign that over and required that it be sold, and the proceeds sent directly to Hal, who was planning to transfer to the University of Arizona where he would pay out-of-state tuition. This issue dragged on for many months. It finally sold for $9,000 and I signed my half over to Hal.

213

I didn't know that Bud already had orders to Tacoma, Washington. When I learned this, I knew that he would not have sacrificed that assignment to appeal the "no fault" ruling. It had been a bluff. The day before he left, he came by the house. I told him, "Someday you'll be glad we're divorced. You'll be much happier than you've ever been with me. Go with God and find happiness." I sincerely hoped that this would be true for the children's sakes.

He Served His Country Well. His Family Also Served. The marriage that joined us for twenty years is only a small piece of Bud's story. The larger story of his life is told in all the medals, citations and photographs that attest to his outstanding career in the military, and in the eagles on his shoulders when he retired after 30 years of service to his country. He demonstrated grit, courage and determination in his military career and derived a huge amount of satisfaction and pride from his accomplishments. He was successful in the endeavor that mattered most to him. In that way, he lived a long and rewarding life, dying at the age of 91.

While my story may be only a small part of his, his story is a larger part of mine. I devoted seventeen years of my young life to helping him in his career, to enhancing his image as a professional military officer. I stood by him as he was promoted from lieutenant to full colonel. The life of a military officer's wife was hard for me. I traveled to each new assignment and settled us in 13 homes in 16 years. I managed our finances and kept his credit rating spotless, and our savings account healthy. I bore four beautiful children, loved and cared for them to the best of my ability, often as a single parent. My children and I sacrificed a great deal in the service of our country and his career. We gave up stability for the insecurity of continuous moves and the experience of always being the new kids in new schools.

I do not regret one minute of the love and care I gave to my family. I loved them with all my heart and did the best I could under challenging circumstances. Those years are an important part of my story, certainly less illustrious than his. But I, too, served our country, as did our children.

A New Beginning

After Bud sued for divorce in the spring of 1977, I began to think hard about what the future might hold for me when all the children were grown. I foresaw that I could end up lonely, with my children feeling sorry for me as I grew old alone. I didn't want that for me or for them. I decided to join Parents without Partners (PWP), an organization that provided social and educational opportunities for single parents. At my first meeting, I met a woman who lived nearby, and we decided to check out some of the scheduled events.

On a Saturday night in July 1977, we went to what was listed as a wine and cheese party. We were met by a motley assortment of older men, who surrounded us and began asking us to dance. I was polite and danced with a couple of them, one of whom I clearly remember. He had a prosthetic leg and said that his wife had been a dancer and had divorced him because he couldn't dance well. I told him that he was a fine dancer, considering, and I meant it.

Then I escaped to the dining room looking for a glass of wine. There, I saw a table upon which sat a bottle of wine, a jar of cheese whiz and a box of crackers. I began planning to escape the whole disappointing scene when a man across the room saw me looking at the meager refreshments and made a wise crack. We both started laughing, introduced ourselves and began to chat. He made me laugh again. That caught my interest. I sure needed some laughs!

I was preparing to go home with my friend when we were interrupted by some of the guys I had danced with, asking for my name and phone number. I explained that I never gave out my number. The man I had been talking to finally pulled a couple of them aside and quietly told them he had my name and number. "Her name is Donna," he said, and then he made up a phone number. They carefully wrote the name and number on napkins and scrap papers, smirking slyly at me while I tried to ignore what was going on. I was a little disappointed when I realized that this guy had not asked me or my friend for my phone number. I'd have given him my work number. I was pretty sure that he probably wouldn't remember my name. But I remembered his name. Ted.

Imagine my surprise when a guy named Ted called me at work a few days later and invited me to lunch. I accepted and we met for lunch down the street. I asked him how he had found me. He had remembered that my first name was either Carol or Carolyn and that I worked at either The Urban Institute or The Urban Land Institute. He had called The Urban Institute first and asked for someone named Carol or Carolyn. I was the only one.

Neither of us had finalized divorces yet. Our lives were busy and complicated. He had a young son, Jason, whom he saw on weekends. I had four teenagers. I'm surprised that he didn't run away as fast as he could. But he didn't. We talked often on the phone, saw each other for lunch and occasional dinners. He was kind, gentle, and funny. He thought I was attractive and intelligent and made me feel like it. He listened to me and seemed to value and care about my opinions, a new and surprising experience. We talked about life, religion, relationships, children and love. By the time our divorces were final we were in love. But it would be more than another year before we could even think about marriage. I introduced him to Bobby and Lily, and Mary and Abe. They liked him.

The Children Grow up and Go Forth. I had medical benefits with my job and put Carrie and Tim on my medical insurance. I was making a little more than $10,000 a year and $600 a month in child support, half of which stopped when Carrie turned 18 in March 1979. With Hal at the University of

Arizona, Bill at Virginia Tech, and Carrie home from North Carolina attending community college to get her high school diploma, my financial situation was extremely tight. But at least the dark cloud of anger that had hovered over our heads for so long was fading.

Bud was putting pressure on Tim, age 15, to come out to Tacoma and live with him. They had long telephone conversations during which Tim would say little. Bud promised him a car and a boat. Tim was painfully conflicted. He felt that he was being forced to choose between us. I found him in tears on more than one occasion. With a heavy heart, I finally told him that if he decided to live with his father, I would be okay, that I would always love him, no matter what.

I wasn't surprised when he insisted on taking Adam with him in the summer of 1979 when he and Carrie went out to visit Bud. I had bought return tickets for them, but I knew in my heart that Tim and Adam would probably not be coming back. And I wasn't sure Carrie would, either, as she had also been getting a lot of pressure from her father. I had an empty nest for the summer and maybe for good.

Carrie did come back and registered for classes at the community college but she was unhappy and moved out of the house, with encouragement and promises of financial support from Bud. Then Tim called to say he wasn't coming back. After all I had been through, had I lost my two youngest children? Ted's constant love and support pulled me through this crisis.

We had decided that we would not get married until our marriage was accepted by all of the children. Jason and I were getting along well. Hal had been non-committal and was in Arizona, and Carrie and Bill liked Ted and seeing me happy. Tim had seemed resentful of both Ted and Jason, and we knew that situation could explode and hurt all of us. We had been through too much to risk getting married until we were sure it could work. But when Tim decided to stay in

Tacoma, we decided that there was no reason for us to wait any longer.

We were married by a Methodist minister the end of October 1979 in a small ceremony in the chapel at American University. Bill, Carrie and Jason were there, as were Bobby and Lily, Mary and Abe, my father, Pat and his five-year old daughter, Kathleen, Ted's mother and most of Ted's family. Carrie and Bill read passages we had selected, and Jason carried the rings. Aunt Mary made my bouquet and hosted a small reception for us after the ceremony. We went to the Kiplinger resort in Florida for a week. Our honeymoon had the distinct advantage of being free. In December 1979, Bobby and Lily came down from Maine for Christmas and all five children joined us. It snowed and was a memorable and happy Christmas.

The Years Go By
Soon after our marriage, Ted and I welcomed Pat's children, Kathleen and Edward, into our lives, and they began spending their summers with us. In about 1984, we rented an RV and took a summer jaunt with them and Jason, a memorable trip. We camped at the Grand Canyon, toured the southwest and swam at a California beach, Kathleen's and Edward's first view of the ocean. I moved to part-time for a couple of summers in order to be able to spend more time with them. We were with them as we all grieved their father's early death in 2005, and as they struggled courageously to go on with their journeys.

After several years of weekend college, I graduated in 1981 from the Washington Public Affairs Center of the University of Southern California with a master's degree in public administration, most of it paid for by The Urban Institute. Upon graduation, I was selected by the Presidential Management Intern (PMI) Program. I took the oath for all federal

Ted and I get married, October 1979. From left: The minister, Ted with Jason, Bill, me, Carrie, Ted's mom, Lydia, and my dad.

employees and swore to ". . . support and defend the Constitution of the United States against all enemies, foreign and domestic . . ." I felt humbled and honored to begin a career in public service.

My three years as a PMI were exciting and rewarding. My 22 years of paid employment, from 1975 until I retired in 1997, were a mixed bag of achievements and disappointments. Many of my work environments were unfriendly to women. Sexual harassment was everywhere. I let the dirty jokes and lewd remarks slide by, and I knew how to politely and firmly say "No." I didn't complain. I had learned that women who complained did not get promoted and often sat idle with no work until they finally left in despair.

After 22 years of full-time employment, I welcomed early retirement. No more hot-roller hair, hastily pulled-up pantyhose and rushing off in heels to catch the van pool at 8:10, five days a week. My goal had been met—my children

219

had graduated from college and we would be able to help the grandchildren do the same.

Ted and I celebrated as all four of my children graduated from college, and two graduated with advanced degrees. We proudly watched as Hal was commissioned an officer in the Marine Corps. We saw Jason follow his dream to be a professional singer and songwriter, perform on big stages at home and abroad and find a beautiful and devoted life partner in Diana. When Kathleen graduated from college, she came to live with us, worked at Borders for a while, and then applied for a job that launched her on a professional career. Edward has since earned a master's degree in engineering and, as I write this, is closing in on his Doctorate. We've attended four joyous weddings, watched sadly as two marriages failed, and saw our children bravely pick up the pieces and move on.

The kids at Christmas, 1979.

Six beloved grandchildren have joined the family. Memories of welcoming each of them into the family bring us joy and laughter. Carrie's son Danny was the first: funny and smart, adoring Adam, carrying the baby Jesus around in his pocket at Christmastime, singing in my arms in our church choir. Then came Emily, a baby granddaughter! Reading her stories before she went to sleep was a special joy in our lives. We often cared for them when their parents went out or went away on vacations.

We held each of them, including the next four, Connor, Tucker, Kiley, and Colby, as newborns, were trusted to care for them, and especially remember attending the boys' ball games and watching my little granddaughter's eyes slowly close as I sang her to sleep. We took each grandchild on a 13th birthday trip. We were there for their birthday parties, Christmases, summer vacations, graduations and family reunions. We are overwhelmed with love as we continue to see them graduate from college and move into adulthood. They are all talented and intelligent and filled with kindness, integrity, and courage. None of them has chosen a career in the military.

Absolution for Military Families. Anger is the bodyguard of fear, someone said, and fear is an unacknowledged and enduring presence in the military. Successful, intimate relationships require fearless trust, compassion, mutual vulnerability and selfless love. The military life does not encourage these feelings. Those with roots in the military tend to repress feelings, especially vulnerability. Military families are often stoically trying to keep up to the pace of those marching in front, following orders, leading from one place to the next, prepared for separation and military action at a moment's notice. Relationships suffer in this environment. Could the warrior mentality seep into the entire family, nurturing a simmering fear and anxiety that morphs into anger, often fueled by alcohol? This was my experience among the military families I saw around me as I grew up and stayed in the military as a wife and mother.

In my experience, heavy drinking was always part of the military culture. Even during prohibition, they made alcohol on Post, and it was always cheap in the Class VI Stores on military installations. Five o'clock meant time for a cocktail, or two or three. An analysis of CDC data by the Delphi Behavioral Group in 2018 found that the military is the heaviest drinking profession, leading all occupations studied.

Depression and physical abuse often result from too much drinking. And there was plenty of abuse of wives and children in the military. Perhaps what is considered abuse in the military today was not always considered abuse years ago, when strict discipline and obedience were often the rules for wives and children as well as the troops. Misbehavior could hurt husbands' and fathers' career prospects, which discouraged reporting it, as did commanders' decisions to protect their men rather than families. Officers' efficiency reports often mentioned wives' conduct. Wives were expected to entertain well, participate in the Officers' Wives Club activities and behave and dress with the utmost propriety in all observable situations.

Heavy drinking certainly interferes with honest communication and sets a poor example for children. Families who don't communicate well hold grudges. We rebuff apologies when we don't want to forgive. We don't say, "I'm upset about something else and didn't mean to take it out on you." We play the blame game, "It's not my fault, it's your fault," or "it's my boss's fault." The norm in the military service is to keep a stiff upper lip and "suck it up." But anger that simmers constantly beneath the surface can become as addictive as alcohol, and as difficult to escape.

Perhaps one of the most significant deficits in the lives of service Brats is the lack of support from extended family. Grandparents and others who might provide the wisdom and patience that come with age and experience are too far away. Good friends can provide the caring support that helps us survive tough times, but the transience of military life makes it hard to make good friends. It takes time to form close friendships. The orders arrive announcing another change of station long before strong bonds are formed. There are plenty of acquaintances, ultimately too many to stay in touch with except through annual Christmas cards. Time goes by and we shorten the list.

In my extended military family, there have been numerous divorces. In my generation of Brats, counting first cousins, there have been eight divorces, and only three long-term marriages. Among the eight children of the three Clark kids, (my siblings and me), there have been four divorces, and three have remained unmarried into middle age. In all three generations, there have been brothers and sisters who stopped communicating with each other and shut out their parents. The tensions and dramas from our childhood are subconsciously carried forward into adult families.

Was it the experience of war and the uncertainty that we all lived with? Or was it something about the men who chose to make the military a career, or about the women who chose to marry them? War, long absences, the need to keep information secret, the constant moving, and the separation from the support of extended families all contribute to the failure of relationships and to enduring memories of childhood difficulties. Rumi reminds us, "Each of us must enter a nest made by other imperfect birds." And so, each of us must find our own path to resolving the emotional fallout from growing up in imperfect nests.

The View from Near the Journey's End
As Kierkegaard said, "Life must be lived forward, but can only be understood backward." As the future shrinks, one gains a clearer view of the past, and a greater appreciation of the

present moment. The process of writing about my life has helped me to better understand my journey and given me the chance to tell my stories. Although my children have heard some of them, there is much that was left unsaid.

I will leave behind no medals, no citations for bravery, no commendations—only the family stories, stories of struggle and joy, laughter and tears. I cannot say, as Edith Piaff does in her joyful song, "Non, Je Ne Regrettes Rien," that I have no regrets. I have many, but I don't regret any of the big decisions in my life because they taught me what I had to learn. As the Zen proverb reminds us: "There are no obstacles; the obstacles are the path."

When young people haven't developed the protective defenses of mature adulthood, their memories—happy as well as painful—may be more vivid. This is certainly how I experience the memories from my young adulthood, my children's childhoods. As I look back, I am amazed by my grit and determination, and my ability to just "keep on keeping on." At the time, I truly believed that I was following the path God had chosen for me. But I wish I could have been less anxious and worried along the way.

I loved my beautiful children with all my heart. I can still feel the softness of cuddles; see the earnest questioning in their eyes; hear their laughter and squeals of delight, and their sobs of pain and confusion. But I can also still feel the enormous weight of responsibility sitting squarely on my shoulders. Anxiety, fear, anger and loneliness were sometimes the feelings overwhelming me.

If I had been more mature, I would have spent more time playing with my children, and less time worrying, cleaning my house, and preparing for the next move. In my early morning dreams, my children are laughing with joy in a home filled with strollers, swings and toys. I breastfeed every one of them, a happy father races home each night just to be with us, and we are surrounded by loving grandparents, aunts, uncles, and cousins

Living with the questions. James Baldwin wrote that life often teaches us to ask questions of the universe, but then we must learn to live with those questions. Questions about God have been a consistent thread in the tapestry of my life. I laughed when three-year-old Colby, sitting in "God's house" waiting for Dad's funeral Mass to begin, loudly asked, "When's God going to show up?" How often I've asked myself the same question!

When Connor was five, he asked me whether I had ever seen God. "I've never seen God with my eyes," I slowly replied. "Well, what do you think God looks like?" As I pondered how to respond, four-year old Tucker tried to help me out. "Maybe God is just a big head! Or maybe he's a very old man, with long hair and a real long beard!" I told them that even though I'd never actually seen God, I had felt God in my heart and am certain that God is here and loves all of us.

When I was a child, I was given complicated answers to my questions, confusing stuff for an inquisitive young mind to digest. When I was taught the Ten Commandments, I pondered their meanings on my own and concluded that pretending to be an adult constituted the mortal sin of adultery. When I wished Mom were more like my friends' mothers, I feared I was committing the sin of "coveting my neighbor's wife." I thought God a rather puzzling deity but tried hard to obey all the rules.

It was a long time before I doubted the religion that I inherited. I had learned a lot about obedience and God's justice, and not much about God's love. Fear of God's punishment was a powerful force that kept us in line. But I found consolation in the belief that conscientiously following the rules would result in God, my parents, and my husband loving me, and God would make my life wonderful. But the day came when I had to face it: not true.

When my broken marriage caused pain and havoc in my life and the lives of my children, I was angry at God, at the

Catholic Church, at my children's father and at my parents but, more than anyone, at myself. I stopped attending Mass every Sunday. I started forming my own answers to spiritual and religious questions.

My concept of God has certainly changed. I now see God as compassion, mercy, loving kindness, beauty, truth, and joy. I think when we love God, we love all that is best in ourselves, each other, and in the world. But our lives and the future of our world are in our hands. As Anne Lamott said, the opposite of faith is not doubt, it is certainty. In my old age, I like Richard Rohr's definition: "Faith is the emptiness of not knowing, and the fullness of not needing to know."

Despite the hardships, I have experienced great blessings and many joys. My memory files are filled with more laughter than tears. And all are seasoned with the fierce love that I have always had for my head-strong children. I hope they will forgive my mistakes and flaws, come to a deeper understanding of their parents' struggles, and remember anew the happy times. To paraphrase Chaucer and Father Michael Himes, I would gladly have been the perfect mother I aspired to be if I had had sufficient knowledge and ability.

I have faith in my children's capacity to achieve peace and happiness. I am fortunate to have seen them turn out to be good people. I am abundantly grateful for love, given and received, inscribed in my heart forever. Of my many blessings, I count my marriage to Ted as one of the greatest. Now that we are both retired and moving into old age, my heart is full of faith and hope, and love for all that is good, true and beautiful on this earth.

Be like the bird that, pausing on her flight awhile on boughs too slight, feels them give way beneath her, and yet sings, knowing that she hath wings.

– Victor Hugo

★ ★ ★

PART III
Those Who Marched Before

Chapter Six
My Mother's Stories: Life in the Cavalry

Our three generations of military service began with my grandfathers. My maternal grandparents, Granny and Pappy, were very important to us during World War II when we were toddlers and Mom was a frightened single mother. I have come to know them better as I've recorded their stories, and to better understand them, and my mother, as they all struggled to meet the challenges of life in the military service.

Arthur Earl Wilbourn: Southern Stock
Pappy was born on February 9, 1884, in Brownsburg, near Lexington, Virginia to a saddle and bridle-maker, Emory Rice Wilbourn, and his wife, Hester Jane Beeton. Arthur was the oldest of several children. His parents were both born in Rockbridge County, Virginia.

We know little more about Pappy's family except cryptic information unearthed from forays on the internet. His brother, Ashford, was an Army officer who fought in the First World War, was gassed and suffered health problems the rest of his life. Ashford died in Roanoke on June 11, 1953. His obituary reports that their father, Emory, died ten years earlier on June 29, 1943.

A newspaper clipping reports that Pappy's paternal grandfather, my great-great grandfather, was William R. Wilbourn. He came to Virginia from North Carolina in 1848, learned the saddle and harness business, and patented a new saddle design. Another newspaper clipping shows a copy of an Internal Revenue License dated 1865 for the manufacture of the "Wilbourn Saddle." It's not clear exactly how this saddle differed from other saddles, but it was adopted by the Cavalry. William's wife was named Edna Chittum. His parents, Pappy's great-grandparents, were Thomas Wingfield Wilbourn and Phoebe Moore. They lived in North Carolina where their son, William, was born.

William enlisted as a volunteer in the Mexican War but never saw active duty, having been detained with other soldiers at Old Point, Virginia. He later fought in the Civil War as a member of Company I, 4th Virginia Infantry (College Company), Stonewall Brigade. He was captured at Petersburg, March 25, 1865 and imprisoned by the Union Army at Point Lookout, Maryland, where he remained until the end of the War. He died in 1905.

Although neither the Wilbourns nor the Beetons were land or slave owners, they were Southerners, and they went to war for the South and, in their view, states' rights, in solidarity with their friends and neighbors.

Pappy was a handsome, dark-haired boy with enormous brown eyes. Although he was not tall, he was slim and muscular with big feet and a large, generous mouth. He was both a good student and a skilled horseman. He learned to break and train horses at a young age. Probably inspired by his grandfather's war stories, he decided on a military career and won an appointment to the Virginia Military Institute in Lexington. There he studied with George Marshall and George Patton, both VMI graduates and classmates. Here is the write-up for Arthur from the VMI yearbook when he graduated in 1904.

> *"Arthur", from the backwoods of Lexington, . . . came to the Institute to learn the ways of moderns by contact. Like some of the rest of us exhibits traces of*

*having aspired to shine in the military firmament –
that is, if we may judge from the threads of former
chevrons. Is deliriously fond of milk chocolate and, in
citizen's clothes, wears a white carnation habitually."*

In the Army Now. Upon graduating from VMI, Arthur
decided to immediately seek an appointment to the Military
Academy at West Point. He graduated in the class ahead of
George Patton (who had been put back a year), and whom he
knew well. Pappy was older than many of the other cadets and
a more experienced horseman. He somehow earned the
nickname "Nuts." We have always thought that he earned
that nickname due to aggressive behavior on the polo field.
When he graduated in 1908, he was a cadet sergeant, a
marksman and a polo player.

Second Lt. Wilbourn's first assignment in the Army
was to Camp McGrath, Batangas, on the Philippine Islands,
where he served with the 9th Cavalry from June 1908 to July
1909. He arrived there a scant ten years after the U.S. victory
in the Battle of Manila Bay in the Philippine-American War.
Travel from Virginia to the Philippines was long, begun on a
train across the country, and then a ship across the Pacific. I
wish that I'd asked him about this adventure when I had the
opportunity. I know little about his time in the Philippines
except for the following story.

The Camp was large, so large that the guard posts were
remote and required a   quarter to half an hour to reach by
horseback. Early one morning, a riderless horse came gal-
loping into the main area of the Post near the stables, reins
dragging. A small party of soldiers was immediately dis-
patched on horseback to the guard post to see what had
happened to the guard who had been on the previous night's
guard duty. Arriving at the guard post, they came upon a
gruesome sight. A huge Anaconda lay dead, its throat having
been slit by a spur on the guard's boot. The guard had been
swallowed whole by the snake, whether alive or dead when

swallowed was not clear, but he was clearly dead upon the arrival of the search party.

Upon his return to the ZI (zone of the interior, military lingo for the United States), 2nd Lt. Wilbourn was assigned to Fort D. A. Russell, in Wyoming, from July 1909 until March 1911, still serving with the 9th Cavalry. The 9th included three regiments of black soldiers including the famous 24th, known as the buffalo soldiers. Pappy served under Gen. Pershing, who was the commander of Fort Russell, one of the largest cavalry forts in the U.S. In September 1911 he was sent to the Mounted Service School at Fort Riley, Kansas, from which he graduated in September 1912. Robert Cantwell reported the following in an article entitled "They Led the Life of Riley," which I found in my grandfather's papers after he died:

> *"By 1911, a student officer spent 1,320 hours in the saddle during a school year. It was around then that the Fort Riley horse-show team ventured out of Kansas for the first time to the National Horse Show in Madison Square Garden and came back with first prize in military jumping."*

Young Lt. Wilbourn was a winner for the Army at that National Horse Show in Madison Square Garden.

Elizabeth Dallam Cobb: Blue-Blooded New Englander
My grandmother Elizabeth was born in Chicago in 1892. She was descended from well-educated New Englanders who traced their ancestors' arrival in the New World back to 1630. They came on the good ship Arbella, which brought Puritan colonists and the Dudley family to the Massachusetts Bay Colony from the tiny borough of Boston, on the east coast of England. Mom told us when we were still young that "blue blood" ran in Granny's veins, and thus in ours as well. Both Harvard and Yale had originally been started by her forebears.

A full scholarship to Harvard is still available to any Dudley descendent who can get in.

Pappy, a history buff, was so impressed by Granny's lineage that he spent three years after he retired from the Army researching her family and preparing a wheel-shaped ancestral chart that is a marvel of details about the family and the early history of America. This amazing task was accomplished without benefit of a computer or the internet.

The Pierponts. Pappy traced one branch of Granny's family, the Pierponts (Anglicized from *Pierrepont*), back to the year 980 in Normandy, France. The stone bridge after which the family was named was purportedly built by Charlemagne. Sir Hugh de Pierrepont went off with William the Conqueror in 1066, helping him fight and vanquish King Harold. In return, Sir Hugh was granted a Saxon castle in Sussex in southern England. The Pierreponts renamed the castle Hurst Pierrepont. Alas, it burned to the ground centuries ago. But the family gained a manor house when an only surviving heir and daughter of the Manvers family married Henry Pierrepont of Sussex in 1279. Her ancestral home thus became Holme Pierrepont, which still stands today, six miles east of Nottingham in Lincolnshire, and half-a-mile north of A52. Holme Pierrepont is open to the public during the summer. As Sherwood Forest is nearby, I wonder whether the wicked and feckless Normans, whom Robin Hood outwitted in the interests of the poor, were our ancestors.

Our Pierpont line descends from a third son, David Pierrepont, who immigrated in the late seventeenth century to the Massachusetts Bay Colony. Since only eldest surviving sons inherited titles or property, younger sons had to come up with something else to do. David's courageous decision to immigrate to the New World was fortuitous for us, his descendants.

America's First Poet. Of Granny's many illustrious ancestors, she was particularly proud to be descended from Anne Dudley Bradstreet. *Mistress Bradstreet: The Untold Story of America's First Poet,* by Charlotte Gordon, is a wonderful biography of Anne. She came to the New World at the age of 18, after surviving smallpox and marrying Simon Bradstreet. Her father, Thomas Dudley, was the second governor of the Massachusetts Bay Colony, and her husband was the third. Her father, wealthy and educated, was quite progressive for his day and believed in educating women. Both his daughters were educated in England before they emigrated.

In their New England home, Anne lived in primitive conditions, fearing the natives and suffering through brutally cold winters. She bore eight children, all of whom survived. While raising her children, she wrote great quantities of poetry, demonstrating her familiarity with history and classical literature. Her first manuscript was secretly taken to England by her brother-in-law, where it was published to rave reviews and became a best-seller. Critics were amazed that a mere woman could have such an intellect. We are descended from her youngest son, John Bradstreet, who was still a teenager when his mother died. He became a gentleman farmer on land near Boston.

She Who Shall Remain Nameless. I have always been intrigued by another of my grandmother's ancestors, Augusta Adams Cobb, who was married to Henry Cobb, a Harvard-educated businessman, before she left him and he divorced her. It took some delving into historical records for Pappy to discover who she was. Her Boston family considered her to be a "black sheep" and had stricken her name from the family records.

Henry and Augusta lived in Boston, the parents of seven children. At some point during the marriage, Augusta met Brigham Young and converted to the Mormon faith. She left Henry and married Brigham Young in 1843 on the trek to Nauvoo, Illinois. She took her two youngest children, Charlotte and an infant named Brigham, with her in a covered wagon. Baby Brigham died on a canal boat on the journey west, was placed in a little coffin and carried to Nauvoo. This information was recorded by Brigham Young in his diary of the journey. He does not say where baby Brigham was buried.

Augusta and Charlotte went on to Utah with Brigham, where Augusta lived the rest of her life. Charlotte ultimately rejected the Mormon faith and returned to New England after at least two plural marriages. We are descended from Augusta's second son, Albert Adams Cobb, who had remained in Boston with his father. Henry divorced Augusta on the grounds of adultery, although Augusta insisted that she was only bound spiritually to Brigham. After the divorce, Henry Cobb married a younger woman who was ultimately accepted by the children who were still living at home.

There are many letters from Augusta to Brigham Young in the University of Wisconsin archives. Carol Cobb Schooley, Mom's cousin, borrowed microfiche containing most of the letters and transcribed them at her home in Staunton, Virginia. They reveal a long love affair between Augusta and Brigham, and the contents strongly suggest that their relationship was a consummated plural marriage. Although in starkly different ways, both Anne Dudley Bradstreet and Augusta Adams Cobb successfully and courageously flouted social mores of the times.

A Cobb and a Pierpont Get Married. Augusta's grandson, named Albert Wheelwright Cobb, was my greatgrandfather. Albert graduated from Harvard in 1872 and joined his father's business, A. A. Cobb (Albert Adams Cobb) & Co., located at 70 State Street in Boston. In the fall of 1873, Albert traveled extensively in Europe, shopping for his father and for the family. Several lengthy letters that he wrote back to his family still survive. They chronicle his six months of travels in Spain, Italy and France, and list his purchases, which included whale-bone corsets, leather gloves, and fabric. Somewhere in Italy, he bought several paintings, bringing them back to be framed in Boston.

When Albert returned home to Boston, he married Caroline Sutton Pierpont, and they moved to Chicago in 1875. Albert and Caroline (the couple in the center of Pappy's ancestral chart) were Granny's parents and my great-grandparents. Albert started several businesses in Chicago—selling gunpowder, importing and selling dry goods and groceries, and finally making and selling chocolate.

Albert went bankrupt when his chocolate business went down during the Banker's Panic of 1907 and the resulting deep recession. Although the elder two sons had graduated from Harvard in 1900, the younger sons were not so lucky and had to go to work rather than to college. The family had to give up their cook and their maid. As the only daughter still at home, my grandmother took over the cooking at the age of fifteen.

After the bankruptcy, the Cobbs sold their home in Lake Forest and bought a small farm near Guilford, Connecticut, nearer their extended families. They moved to the farm with the youngest three children. I can see in photos taken on the farm that they were not too distressed by this turn of events. The family appears to be having great fun as they learn how to handle farm equipment and care for animals, including pigs, cows and horses.

My mother remembered her grandparents, Albert and Caroline, well. Her grandmother was the seventh child of Judge John Pierpont and Sarah Lawrence. John was the Chief Justice of the Vermont Supreme Court. They lived in the town of Vergennes. I saw a portrait of him in Vergennes in 1954, hanging in the public library. Sarah's wedding dress has been passed down through the generations, most recently to Carrie, my daughter. Sarah could not have been much taller than about four feet, ten inches. They had many children, probably about ten, most of whom died in infancy and are buried behind a church in Vergennes.

Elizabeth (Granny) was born on March 2, 1892 in Chicago. She had dark brown hair, brown eyes, and was a delicate child. She was named after the much-admired wife of one of her father's childless brothers. Mom said she wore a size 4 1/2 AAAA shoe, an interesting piece of trivia to be passing on. She was a musical child and had a lovely voice. In those days, family and friends frequently gathered around the piano and someone would sing a solo, or they would sing and harmonize together. Elizabeth began singing to entertain family and friends when she was young.

Her favorite was a long ballad entitled "Lord Lovell" about a young bride and groom who were celebrating their wedding with a feast and a game of "hide and seek." The bride ran into the attic and hid in an old trunk. The lid snapped closed and could not be opened again from the inside. She was not found for many years and Lord Lovell grieved and mourned for a long time. One day, he opened the trunk and there was his bride's skeleton arrayed in her beautiful wedding dress. Why do I remember that song?

We have a beautiful sepia-tone photograph of the Cobb family, including Auntie Nin, sitting on the large porch of their home in Lake Forest taken in about 1896. My grandmother is wearing a frilly white lace dress and looks to be about four or five years old. She was the seventh child of the seventh child as Caroline was also a seventh child. According to Granny, this distinction conferred supernatural powers and, from all reports, she did have a highly developed sense of intuition.

Arthur and Elizabeth Meet and Marry
Granny's sister, Nancy, and her Army officer husband were stationed with my grandfather at Fort D. A. Russell. Nancy

was pregnant and her mother, Caroline, sent Granny to help her sister with the children and the birth of the new baby. My grandparents' fateful meeting thus occurred on an Army post in Wyoming.

Pappy was twenty-eight years old, eight years older than Granny. Nancy warned her little sister that Arthur was a "ladies' man and too old for you." Her concerned big sister went on to tell Granny that the life of an Army wife was difficult, dangerous, full of travel and time alone. She believed that this life would be too much for the gentle and beloved "baby" of the family.

Nancy's warnings went unheeded. By all the accounts, it was love at first sight. The southern Cavalry officer and the gentle New Englander made an unlikely match, he descended from the Confederacy, and she from abolitionists. Arthur and Elizabeth began writing to each other after she returned to her family's farm in Guilford. The correspondence continued for more than two years as Pappy pursued his Army career and frequent reassignments. Her parents hoped the relationship would end. It didn't.

They were married in January 1914 in Guilford. Arthur took Elizabeth directly to Douglas, Arizona on the Mexican border, where he was assigned TDY. There are photographs that indicate that Granny was in Douglas at the cavalry post, Camp Henry J. Jones, a couple of years before Poncho Villa's raid in which several civilians were killed. Camp Jones had been established to maintain control over the Mexican border.

The couple honeymooned on the way back to Wyoming, his permanent station. During the honeymoon, they rode horseback and camped near Mt. Evans in the Rocky Mountains. This is probably the genesis of a family love affair with Colorado. It must have been a deliriously happy time for them both. Many years later, they specified in their wills that their ashes were to be dropped over Mt. Evans. But Pappy, in old age, decided that they should be buried at West Point. Their children honored both these wishes. Dad flew over Mt.

Evans and dropped half their ashes. The remaining ashes are buried at West Point under a handsome stone engraved "Wilbourn."

In July 1914, Pappy was ordered to Fort Riley, Kansas, to teach at the Cavalry School, from which he had graduated a few years earlier. As soon as possible when they arrived for their new assignment, they were expected to visit the commanding officer and his wife to leave Pappy's calling card and a calling card engraved with both their names. The next day, Granny was to call on the wife of the commanding officer and leave her calling card. At some later date, they would come for a scheduled visit and again leave calling cards. This somewhat convoluted social ritual was mandated throughout the Army, although no longer practiced by the time I was growing up.

The newlyweds moved into large brick officers' quarters on Post where Mom was born on November 20, 1915. Evidently it was a difficult birth. Many years later, I saw tears in Pappy's eyes after Granny died. He pointed to her bed and told me that she had done all her suffering in that bed, beginning with my mother's birth and ending with the last days before she died.

Orders to Combat on the Mexican Border

In March 1916, Pappy was ordered to accompany Gen. "Black Jack" Pershing on what was called the Punitive Expedition to Columbus, New Mexico. Mexican bandits headed by Francisco "Pancho" Villa had become a problem, raiding towns along the border area. In early March 1916, Villa and his followers raided Columbus, killing 17 Americans and burning the town. President Woodrow Wilson ordered General Pershing to take 4,000 troops from the 12th Cavalry stationed in Wyoming into Mexico to find and take Villa prisoner. When this order was given, there were only about 5,000 officers in fifteen cavalry regiments in the entire Army. That number was soon increased to twenty-five regiments as a result of the problems with Villa. After Uncle Bobby died, I found in Pappy's papers a brief piece from the New York Times. The date on the article is March 27, presumably in 1916. It reads as follows:

> *That service with the American Army in Mexico is not comfortable can be seen from the appearance of the men who are returning from the front. Today one arrived, who passed his friends actually unrecognized until he had spent much time with the barber and under the camp shower bath. He was Lieutenant Wilburn (sic), of the Twelfth Cavalry, whose home is in Lexington, Virginia. He had been at the front and along the line of communication longer than any of the other men who have returned, and had been in charge of the supplies from the field bases at Casas Grandes to the front, and to a new base being established at El Valle, thirty-five to forty miles southeast of Casas Grandes. When he reached camp, the Lieutenant had a quarter of an inch growth of beard and he was the color of chalk from the fine alkali dust amid which he had been working.*

A Mystery. Long after my grandfather's death, I found a typewritten report among a small number of papers included in Uncle Bobby's files, which had belonged to Pappy. Five pages were typed with handwritten corrections, and no heading. There is no information as to the identity of the person who experienced the frightening ordeal described, but Pappy was probably the typist. He learned to type early in his career long before there were many people with that skill. The typing was clearly done on an old typewriter. We can only surmise that he saved the account because it was of some significance to him personally.

The mysterious story involves four Americans riding a train from Mexico City up to cross the border into the United

States during the uprising in Mexico. One of the Americans is identified only as an elderly woman, another as a Mrs. Burr, another a woman doctor named Dr. Haile and the fourth is the teller of the tale, a West Point graduate. The train is attacked by bandits, including generals De la O, and Pimienta. The writer decides that his West Point ring must be hidden in Mrs. Burr's bodice. The other Americans are removed from the train and held in a makeshift camp. The writer is taken by General de la O, apparently to be held for ransom or killed.

The account details the writer's hair-raising escape, running bare foot for miles while the bandits' search narrowly misses his hiding places. All the Americans make it back across the border alive with a great deal of important information to help the United States deal with the situation. Someday we will no doubt learn more details about this mystery.

Some family members have indicated that they heard, or read somewhere, a similar account, and that it was the experience of Gen. MacArthur, Gen. Pershing, a military attaché to Mexico, or of a classmate of Pappy's. Duty on the Mexican border was difficult and hazardous. Pappy shared little of his experiences with his wife and children. As a military officer, he felt that it was his duty to shield them from fear for his safety. He also firmly believed in his duty to protect the confidentiality of sensitive information. The answer to the mystery might be found in newspaper accounts from the Mexican front during those weeks, unless the Army felt the need to keep the information secret and was successful in doing so.

On the Rails and Roads. Mom gave me a little book that belonged to Granny entitled, *The Care and Feeding of Children*, by L. Emmett Holt, M.D., published in 1915. On the fly leaf, Granny faithfully recorded every journey made by my mother from her birth in 1915 until the family moved to San Antonio in 1937, where she met and married my father. This list succinctly describes the nomadic military life into which my mother was born. Most of the travels described were following Pappy from Army post to Army post when he was ordered on temporary duty or permanent change of station.

Mom's first trip was by train to visit her grandparents in Guilford by way of Chicago. Mom was four months old in March 1916. They left by train soon after Pappy was sent on TDY back to the Mexican border. They stayed with Granny's brother Charlie and his wife, Margaret, in Chicago for a couple of weeks before going on to Guilford.

Back to the Mexican Border
When Pappy was ordered back to New Mexico in the fall of 1916, Granny and the baby embarked on another long train ride to join him. He prepared a little adobe house for her, with a secret room hollowed out in the dirt floor, entered by a trap door, where they could hide from any marauding Mexican bandits. He placed a carpet over the trap door.

Mom told me the following two stories, which took place while Pappy was commanding an all-black unit on the Mexican border, and which were repeated for years throughout the old Army. One day, as an eagle flew overhead, Pappy drew his pistol and fired a shot. Eagles were not endangered at the time and there was no law against killing them. The eagle fell to the ground, with a bullet hole right through an eye. The word spread like wildfire. Pappy told Granny that he would be careful never to allow his marksmanship to be tested again. He'd fired a lucky shot and planned to keep his reputation as the best shot in the Army.

I think this next story survived because it's shocking. In the barracks tent one night, one of the troops was drunk and began terrorizing the unit, waving around a loaded pistol and threatening his fellow soldiers. Pappy was notified of the disturbance and came running. Upon entering the barracks, he shouted to the soldier to drop his weapon. The soldier turned and drunkenly aimed at my grandfather, who shot the soldier dead on the spot. That story would probably not have made it into the newspapers.

After seven months in Columbus, New Mexico, my mother and grandmother returned to Guilford to spend the summer. Soon afterwards, General Pershing was ordered to Europe to lead the American Expeditionary Forces in World War I and gave up the quest to find Pancho Villa. In September, Pappy, Granny and baby were reunited at Ft. Riley, but it was not long before new orders arrived.

New Assignments, New Babies, and More Travels

Pappy was promoted to Captain in May 1917 and assigned to the Aviation Section of the Signal Corps to establish a flight training facility at Kelly Field near San Antonio. With a toddler in tow and seven months pregnant with her second child, Granny joined Pappy. Fearing another difficult birth, she was determined that Pappy be there for the delivery. He was. Aunt Danny was born in December 1917 in San Antonio. I guess they had expected a boy, whom they would have named Daniel. They named the baby Elizabeth, but always called her Danny.

From San Antonio, Pappy was transferred to the Air Service and sent to Wilbur Wright Field near Dayton, Ohio (now Wright-Patterson Air Force Base), and then to Chanute Field near Rantoul, Illinois, to organize the training schools for aviation mechanics. The Army Air Corps was born, and Pappy was there to help lead the effort. Granny followed him with two baby girls in January 1918 and stayed there for nine months before Pappy was again reassigned.

In October 1918, he was transferred out of the Air Service at his strong request, promoted to Lt. Colonel of the Infantry and ordered to join the 810th Pioneer Infantry at Camp Green, North Carolina mobilizing for combat duty overseas. One month later, the Armistice was signed. Despite his efforts, Pappy had missed the First World War. Fortunately, the family also missed the Spanish Influenza that swept around the world as the war ended, killing millions, including more of our soldiers than had died fighting.

My grandparents were reunited in North Carolina in January 1919. I can hardly imagine the challenges Granny faced, traveling around the country with two babies, by train, and horse and buggy. What did she do about laundry? I hope her two babies were healthy and good sleepers. Trains were dirty and sooty and did not provide showers or tubs. Although I remember her as genteel and fragile, she must have been strong and determined, and she must have loved my grandfather very much.

A little more than a month later, they moved down to Camp Jackson in South Carolina where Lt. Col. Wilbourn was assigned on TDY with the Quartermaster Corps to dispose of the Army's mules. I think some were sold, but many more were shot and buried in a mass grave.

There are some fading black-and-white photographs from their stay there on which Granny carefully recorded the time and place. I imagine it was hot in South Carolina in July. They decided that she should travel back to Connecticut to spend the rest of the summer with her parents. Granny and her babies left for Guilford on July 18, 1919.

On the way north, they made the only visit Mom remembered to her paternal grandparents' home. The train stopped in Roanoke, Virginia, and they rode in a horse -drawn buggy to Lexington. Mom was almost four and the visit with her grandparents lasted about a week. She remembered that her grandmother, Hester Jane, was a good cook but she had no memory of her grandfather. Pappy was busy and preoccupied with his career, and Granny took time when he was away to visit her parents rather than his. I've also picked up hints that his family was more "blue-collar" than hers, and she may not have been comfortable with them.

They returned to Ft. Riley in the fall of 1919, when Granny was six months pregnant with my Uncle Bobby. He was born at Ft. Riley on January 6, 1920, and the youngest child, Anne, was born in 1921, also at Ft. Riley. Granny traveled the following summer with all four children to Connecticut. There are many photos of happy adults and laughing children taken during that summer.

Mom sometimes told this story on her sister. She and three-year-old Danny attended Sunday school at Ft. Riley. One Sunday the Chaplain asked if the children knew any prayers. Danny, always the family clown, said that she knew a prayer. When asked what it was, Danny said, "Roses are red, violets are blue, you're funny in the head cuz I fooled you!" and laughed. The Chaplain, lacking a sense of humor, delivered a sermon in which he tsk-tsked that there was a woman in the church whose little child knew only one prayer—and he repeated what Danny had said. It was a small community and everyone in the church knew who he was talking about. Granny rose, slowly walked out, and never attended a Post Chapel service again. Furthermore, she never had any of her children baptized.

Granny's relatives in New England were abolitionists, so she had liberal views about race, which differed from Pappy's, influenced as they were by his Southern upbringing. In the "Old Army," as we affectionately called Pappy's days in uniform, officers were assigned enlisted personnel to serve as cooks and orderlies. Usually, they also had maids and nannies, who were often black or Latino. This created the ingredients for another story Mom told about Danny, in which her use of a racial slur (no doubt picked up from the white maid) led to a trip upstairs and a mouth washed out with soap while her sister and brother were made to watch so they didn't miss the lesson. "We never use that word in this house, young lady!" Granny declared.

When I first heard this story, as a child, I was interested to learn that even back in 1920, this was considered a bad word, despite Mark Twain's use of it in my favorite books, *Tom Sawyer* and *Huckleberry Finn*.

Much later in her life, Granny became a devout Christian Scientist, as did Aunt Danny. My mother was baptized a Roman Catholic when she was in her fifties. After his Alzheimer's diagnosis, Uncle Bobby asked to be baptized a Catholic. A priest friend of ours came to his nursing home in Virginia and baptized him.

I wonder what my grandmother and great-grandmother thought in August 1920, when the 19th Amendment to the U.S. Constitution was ratified, giving women the right to vote decades after the 15th Amendment recognized that right for black men. Progress was being made, but slowly. When Augusta Adams Cobb first arrived in Utah with Brigham Young, she had the right to vote in that territory, then lost it when Utah became a state, in 1896. An amendment to the Constitution that would let women vote had first been introduced in Congress in 1878. It was defeated then and reintroduced every single session for the next 40 years. I wish I had had the chance to ask Granny whether she was excited about being able to vote. But as a military dependent, it's possible she never got to exercise that right. Because of their frequent moves, military families rarely qualified as voting residents any state.

Caroline Cobb Dies. In June 1923, Granny decided to send Mom, then age seven, on the train with Mrs. Patton (the mother of Gen. George Patton) to spend the summer with her grandparents. By then they had sold the farm in Guilford and moved to Cohasset, Massachusetts. This was a fateful visit and I think it left deep scars on my mother's little spirit.

Her grandparents, Albert and Caroline Cobb, lived in a small Cape Cod cottage in view of the water. Albert had a sailboat and one day he took Mom out sailing. While they were gone, Caroline fell down the stairs. When they returned from the sail, they found her unconscious. She never regained consciousness.

Mom saw her grandmother a few days before she died, and remembered that her head was swollen and bruised black and blue. Granny went into deep mourning for a year, wearing black and spending much time alone in her room.

The following summer, Granny took her four children back to Cohasset to stay a while with her widowed father, Albert. This was her last trip to Cohasset with the children. I hope Albert had other family nearby during his last years alone.

Horse Sense. My grandfather was famed throughout the Army as an expert horseman, skilled in breaking and training the Army's horses to jump and compete in dressage, horse dancing, as performed most famously by the Lipizzaner stallions. An expert and devoted polo player, he required that all his children learn to ride as soon as they could walk. Their first riding experiences were on a pony, a mean one according to Mom. The pony would turn around and bite them for no apparent reason. Not surprisingly, the younger three children did not like to ride.

Mom, on the other hand, displayed a natural ability and her father praised her excellent "seat" in the saddle. She was required to ride every day in the riding ring. Pappy carefully tutored her, and she went on to win blue ribbons at horse shows when she was still in her early teens. Granny won dressage competitions on horses Pappy had trained, and he won jumping competitions. Both won blue ribbons in Madison Square Garden. Mom told us that Pappy said that you cannot be considered a good rider until you've been thrown from, or fallen off, a horse at least seven times. Mom fell many more times than seven, once suffering a bad fall that left her unconscious for several days with a severe concussion.

I grew up with colorful expressions that reflected Mom's life in the Cavalry. For example, when we were needlessly hurrying, we were cautioned to "hold your horses!" If we were feeling happy or frisky, we were "feeling our oats." When one of us was believed to be passing up a good thing, they shrugged and said, "You can lead a horse to water, but you can't make him drink." If you were bound and determined to carry out some action, and nothing would stop you, you had "the bit in your teeth." If a horse can manage to get the bit in his teeth, the rider has lost control. The horse was then "hell-bent for leather." Those who deserved severe punishment, such as the many drivers who annoyed Pappy, "should be horse-whipped!"

Giving someone "his head" and using a "loose rein" meant you trusted him. Encouragement was stated as "Get on that horse and ride him!" and that phrase could also be an order. If someone was called a "high stepper," he or she was well turned out, spiffy and sprightly. When horses galloped hard, their tails flew high in the air behind them, thus, the meaning behind "hightailing it out" of someplace. When one was all dressed and ready to go, one was "booted and spurred." If someone was accused of "riding roughshod" over something, they were inadequately prepared, being reckless and possibly causing harm, as when a horse was poorly shod. I'm not sure where the excuse "I have to see a man about a horse" came from, but I always knew that was a polite way to say, "I have to visit the toilet."

A Soldier and a Scholar. After Pappy graduated from the Army's Command and General Staff College, at Fort Leavenworth, he was asked to stay on as an instructor. Mom remembered huge maps spread across a wall in his study as he prepared diagrams of various battles during the Spanish American and Civil Wars. Pappy taught strategy and tactics at the Staff College. In 1928, he was ordered to attend the Army War College, which later became the National War College, in Washington, D.C. The family moved into a development of brick apartment buildings called Cathedral Mansions on

Massachusetts Avenue near the National Cathedral, which was in the early stages of construction.

Georgia and Viginia: 1929-1932

By 1929, the Wilbourns had acquired an automobile, in which they drove to Pappy's new assignment at Ft. Oglethorpe, Georgia, where he took command of a cavalry squadron. I wish I knew more about that first car! Much of their travel from then on was by car, rarely more than 30 miles per hour, three in the front and three in the back.

As the Depression deepened, Pappy was ordered from Ft. Oglethorpe to Fredericksburg, Virginia, to map the Civil War Battlefields for the National Battlefield Monuments Commission, with a pay cut and an uncertain future in the Army. His title was Secretary of the Commission.

The family found an old farmhouse outside Fredericksburg, a small town in those days. The farm was named Altoona and has since been replaced by an interstate highway entrance ramp. Granny was in her element. Mom said that they teased her unmercifully as she began dressing to look like a farm wife. They decided that Altoona would be a proper farm and they dug a vegetable garden, raised chickens, pigs, and cows, and acquired a horse. Pappy cultivated the large vegetable garden. Corn on the cob was a favorite and Granny was required to have a pot of water boiling on the stove before Pappy would pick the corn.

Soon after they moved to Altoona, a small black boy came by asking for work. Granny offered him a job caring for the chickens. Isaac was a couple of years older than my Uncle Bobby, who would have been ten or eleven years old. The two boys became inseparable, camping in the woods nearby, hunting squirrels, fishing in the river, and of course teasing Bobby's sisters.

The boys were together one day when Granny and Pappy were gone and Bobby found one of Pappy's loaded pistols. He was showing off to Isaac, twirling it around his finger, as Wyatt Earp might have done, when it went off and a bullet tore into his horse's foot. A vet removed the bullet and, amazingly, the horse healed, and the children were able to ride him again. Bobby, however, never heard the end of it. Mom repeated the story often to tease her brother.

I have seen a black and white photo of Bobby and Isaac, grinning, with their arms about each other's shoulders, Isaac a head taller than Bobby. In about 1941, Bobby was a freshman at the University of Virginia. On a break, he found a ride to Fredericksburg. After many inquiries, he found Isaac working as a janitor in a warehouse. With a joyful smile and open arms, he greeted Isaac who looked alarmed, shook his head and began backing off. "Don't you remember me," Bobby asked. "I'm Bobby!" Isaac said, with a worried look in his eye, "Yes sir, I remember you," and backed further away. Bobby told me that sad story one day as he talked about his childhood. Long after his decline into Alzheimer's disease, I could always get a smile out of him if I asked him if he remembered Isaac.

While at Ft. Leavenworth, Mom's excellent horsemanship had earned her a horse, a mare named Manita. Pappy bought the horse for her when they were visiting Colorado in 1925. The stable from which Manita was purchased is now the stable on the Air Force Academy grounds, where Mom rode when Dad was the Superintendent of the Academy 45 years later.

Mom loved Manita and rode her to win numerous blue ribbons and silver trophies. When Pappy was transferred from Ft. Leavenworth to Washington in 1927, the parting of girl and horse had been sad. In fact, it was so sad that my grandparents found a way to bring the horse to Fredericksburg. Manita arrived at Altoona on Christmas morning with a large red bow tied around her neck.

When the family moved on from Fredericksburg in August 1933, Manita went north to the stables at Ft. Myer, Virginia. Three years later, Mom went to the Ft. Myer stables to see Manita. To the amazement of the stable hands, Manita made it clear that she had been Mom's horse, licking her all the way from her head to her feet.

In 1933, the Roosevelt Administration asked Pappy to leave the Army and take over as director of the National Battlefield Parks Commission, which was to be relocated in the Department of the Interior in Washington. Pappy was not fond of Roosevelt and was even less fond of the person for whom he would be working, Harold Ickes. He declined the offer and stayed in the Army. He had been promoted to Lt. Colonel, U.S. Cavalry, in June 1932 for the second time. His promotion to Lt. Col. in 1918 during the First World War had been a temporary promotion; he was demoted to major after the Armistice.

I think their years in Fredericksburg were particularly happy for the Wilbourn family. From the path Pappy's career took, however, I wonder if he wasn't more the scholar and academic than the soldier. He enjoyed instructing and mapping the battlefields. During his three years in Fredericksburg, he made his mark in the reconstruction of the Fredericksburg, Antietam and Petersburg Civil War battlefields. He also acquired, surveyed, and constructed access roads and supervised the erection of monuments at Fredericksburg, Chancellorsville, The Wilderness, Spotsylvania Court House, and Petersburg.

Ft. Ethan Allen, Vermont: 1933
New orders sent the Wilbourns from Fredericksburg to Ft. Ethan Allen near Burlington, Vermont, in August 1933. Pappy's new assignment was to command the 1st Squadron, 3rd US Cavalry. Granny was delighted to be near Vergennes, where her mother had been born. Mom, who was blossoming into a beautiful young woman, began attending Trinity College, a Catholic school in Burlington. Then she fell in love

with a young Cavalry officer of whom Granny disapproved. Mom told me that Granny complained that he drank too much, and she hatched a plan to disrupt the romance.

Granny sent Mom by train for a "short" visit to help her Aunt Peggy in Washington in May 1935—a ruse, it turned out. Her parents would not allow her to return home to Vermont. The love affair faded away.

To Fort Sam Houston, San Antonio, Texas: 1936

In April 1936, Pappy was ordered to Ft. Sam Houston in San Antonio to take over command of the Organized Cavalry Reserves for the Eighth Corps Area. Mom's history would soon become part of my own. When there were no quarters available on the Post, they moved into a rented house in Alamo Heights.

Mom tried to get a job with the YWCA, but they declined to hire her, saying that she didn't need a job because she was living with her family and her father had a job. There were too many women who desperately needed the jobs. The YWCA staff asked her to volunteer her time to teach women typing and shorthand, so she taught there for a year.

Final Assignments

In 1940 Pappy was reassigned from Ft. Sam Houston to Fort Brown near Brownsville Texas, as commander of the 12th Cavalry, an all-black unit. In 1941, he was sent back to San Antonio to the Eighth Corps Area where he served as Inspector General. However, the Corps Headquarters was transferred to Dallas in 1943, taking Pappy away from San Antonio until he retired in February 1944.

I think Pappy had every expectation of being promoted to general. But his Army career included several assignments that would have been avoided, if possible, by a career-minded officer. Most importantly, he missed World War I while he was assigned to establish aircraft maintenance training for the Army Air Corps. Maybe he was better at following orders than manipulating the system. Whatever the explanation, Pappy watched while his subordinates, men he had instructed and trained, were promoted above him.

Uncle Bobby may have suffered as a result of his father's disappointment. Bobby remarked one evening that when he returned from the Philippines, Pappy refused to listen to any of his war stories. Having fought heroically with the First Cavalry, Bobby was deeply hurt by this. I wonder whether Pappy's lack of interest in his son's experiences in World War II may have reflected disappointment in his own lack of combat experience.

But for Mom and his grandchildren, it was a gift that Pappy was there in San Antonio during World War II and not away fighting, as were the rest of the men in the family. Although he may have had his moments of bitter disappointment, I never sensed them.

After we left San Antonio in early 1946, I saw little of my grandparents. Fortunately for me, Pappy was a wonderful letter writer and we corresponded frequently throughout my childhood until a couple of years before he died. He often sent me cartoons from "The New Yorker," which I remember puzzling over, trying to understand why they were funny.

Their Last Days

My sister was in high school and living with them at the time of Granny's death. Mary told me that one day she came in from school, and a love song from Wagner's opera "Tannhauser" was playing on the record player. The lovers are singing as they realize that their love is doomed and that the heroine, named Elizabeth, is to die. Pappy was hugging Granny and sobbing. The experience of seeing Granny so ill, and then to see her die, must have been extremely traumatic for my sensitive sixteen-year-old sister living so far from her parents.

I remember the last letter I received from Granny. She must have known that she was dying from breast cancer, but no one in the family knew, not even Pappy. Because she was a Christian Scientist, I wonder if she expected to be miraculously healed. In her last letter, she complimented me on being such a good military wife in the service of our country. It was a terrible shock when we received word that she had died. I was 19 and my first-born was five months old. My parents were in Saudi Arabia. No one traveled to San Antonio for her funeral.

Sometime in about 1961 or 1962, Pappy became too disoriented from the early stages of dementia to stay in Texas living alone. Bobby brought him to Washington to live with him, but this arrangement worked for only a short time. Pappy would wander and was often found trying to get back to San Antonio to see again "the love of my life."

Early one morning in 1965, while I was living in Hawaii, I received a telephone call from a Western Union operator. He told me that he had bad news and asked me if I wanted him to read to me a telegram that had just arrived. With my heart in my throat, I said, "Yes, please, of course." He read a telegram from Mom telling me that my dear Pappy had died in a nursing home in Annapolis.

Clockwise from top left: Pappy as a young cavalry officer; Pappy showing his equestrian skill at the Cavalry School at Ft. Riley, Kansas, 1912; Granny with her four children (my mother is at bottom right).

Chapter Seven
My Father's Stories:
The Army Doctor and the Irish Nurse

The Clarks and the Gannons

My paternal grandparents were Albert Patton Clark and Mary Catherine Gannon. I didn't know them except from Dad's books about them, which he prepared in his old age with Carrie's help. He wanted all his descendants to know about the parents he loved and respected. I also learned about them from the stories he and his sister told. They both spoke lovingly of their parents. I knew my grandmother's cousin, MC Butler, well and she also had much to say. But I wish I had asked more questions.

The Clarks came from Pennsylvania and environs north, from a mix of English, Irish, Scottish and Dutch ancestors. The Gannons and the Connaughtons (also spelled Connoughton), my Dad's maternal ancestors, came from County Roscommon in Ireland. We don't know where Dad's grandfather's family, the McAvoys, came from. We found their name spelled McAvoy and McEvoy. The proper spelling is with an "A" since that is the way their names are spelled on the gravestones. All our Irish ancestors came to America during the Irish Potato Famine sometime between 1848 and 1850. We believe they sailed from Sligo on the west coast of Ireland, the closest port to County Roscommon. They were fortunate to come to Maryland, a state settled by Roman Catholics, avoiding some of the prejudice against the Irish found in New York and Boston.

Albert Patton Clark, Colonel, United States Army Medical Corps. My Dad's father, Albert, grew up in Washington, D.C. He was the youngest of three. Dad said his grandfather, Herman, was a crusty old guy and they weren't close. But he loved his grandmother, Julia Hipple. She was gentle and kind to him during the ten years he lived near them in Chevy Chase, Maryland. His Aunt Anne and Uncle Joe, and his grandparents, cared for him and his sister during the hard year their mother was in Walter Reed Hospital with Rheumatoid Arthritis, an autoimmune disease with no known cure.

Albert was more than six feet tall, fair-skinned, with piercing blue eyes, a handsome man who loved the outdoors. As a teenager he walked from Washington to Niagara Falls. He went to medical school at George Washington University and was a member of Sigma Chi Fraternity. He worked at Garfield Hospital in Washington where he met his future wife. After graduating from GWU, he attended the Army Medical School and was commissioned a Second Lieutenant in the Army Medical Corps in 1911.

Mary Catherine Gannon (Polly), Governess, Photographer, Nurse. Mary Catherine Gannon was also from Washington, D.C. Her mother, Annie McAvoy Gannon, died soon after the birth of her fifth child when Mary Catherine was five years old. Her father, Timothy, remarried soon after. The new stepmother was hard on Mary Catherine's little brother, Bernie, so Mary left with him and walked from Washington to their aunt's home in Maryland. MC, my grandmother's cousin, told me that their aunt, whom they all called Aunt Mary, raised her two sisters' four orphaned children after both sisters died following childbirth.

Aunt Mary had lost her only child as an infant, and her husband in a construction accident building the Willard Hotel. She later married Will Pierce, who helped her raise her three nieces and a nephew. There were so many Mary Catherines in the extended family that they decided to call my grandmother Polly. Her cousin became just MC.

Aunt Mary sent Polly to a Catholic girls' school and she became an excellent pianist under the tutelage of the nuns. She grew into a tall woman with lovely blue-grey eyes and auburn hair. She had an independent streak and traveled extensively throughout Europe as a governess to one or more wealthy families.

Polly was an excellent photographer and developed her own photographs. She later graduated from nursing school at George Washington University. Polly and Albert met and fell in love while they were both working at Garfield Hospital. They were married in June 1911. I don't know whether my grandfather knew that she was ten years older than he was. Dad didn't learn this until after she died.

Albert and Polly Join the Army

Polly penned a brief memoir of her years as an Army wife. She makes it clear that she loved being in the Army and was thrilled with all the varied assignments. Despite being invalided from the time her children were young, she never once mentions her disease or the chronic pain she endured for twenty years until her death. In addition to being a talented musician and an accomplished photographer, she had a quirky, Irish sense of humor. Her memoir was published in the Army-Navy Register in 1939 shortly after she died.

She called their next assignment, to Ft. Williams in Maine, "...a right-little-tight-little artillery post." Near Portland, their quarters looked over the sea with a lighthouse in the near distance. Her first child, Mary, was born there. When they received much hoped-for orders to Hawaii in 1912, where my father would be born a year later, she wrote, "We got going, walking six inches above the ground. The ship they were to sail on, the Sherman, was, "...as big as the river boats at home, and we were going halfway to China!"

A good Army wife, she quickly turned each new set of quarters into a home. The quartermasters in those days allowed Army wives a lot of latitude for creativity and Polly took advantage of this freedom to re-invent each new space. When the children were small, she hung a swing from the living room ceiling, which Dad loved. An avid reader, Polly

256

found a quote about home in an 1844 poem by Leigh Hunt that so moved her that she penned it in gold leaf and black ink on parchment. It hung in each of our many homes, and Dad made copies that hang in many of his children's and grand-children's homes today:

> *"For there are two Heavens Friend, both made of Love. One inconceivable even by the other so divine it is. The other far on this side of the Stars, by Men called Home."*

The Doctor and His Family in World War I

Albert left for France and the Great War in June 1917, assigned to the Medical Company of the Railroad Engineer Regiment. In a letter dated in November, he says he was sent to the front at Belleau Wood, where the British were engaged. A year later, in June 1918, the United States would suffer more than 9,000 killed and wounded in fighting at Belleau Wood. While at the front Albert attended the wounded in the trenches and learned first-hand of the difficulties of getting medical supplies to the field.

In late November 1917, he was transferred to Gen. Pershing's headquarters in Chaumont, France. In one of his letters home, he said: "It is a relief to be away from the big guns and constant air fights for a while to say nothing of all the mud, cold and wet." After his reassignment, he goes on to say, "I have been given a fine position and am in charge of all medical property business pertaining to our forces here." He would spend the next year and a half in Chaumont. The French awarded him their Legion d'Honneur for his work during the War.

I came across the following poem written after "the war to end all wars," as World War I was called. It painfully applies to that war, and all wars.

Suicide in the Trenches by Seigfried Sassoon
(1886-1967)

I knew a simple soldier boy
who grinned at life in empty joy,
Slept soundly through the lonesome dark
and whistled early with the lark.
In winter trenches, cowed and glum,
with crumps and lice and lack of rum,
He put a bullet through his brain,
and no one spoke of him again.
You smug-faced crowds with kindling eye
who cheer when soldier lads march by,
Sneak home and pray you'll never know
the hell where youth and laughter go.

Home from the War

Albert's first assignment after the war was to Washington to serve on the general staff. Finding a house was a challenge. According to my grandmother's memoir, "People were sleeping in bathtubs and on top of pianos." When they finally found a house in Chevy Chase at #10 Oxford Street, my grandmother was suffering from the condition that would plague her until she died.

Although she does not say so in her memoir, I learned from Dad and MC that their reunion after the war was stressful for my grandparents. Dad remembered conflict over her cooking, and especially her "frites," which were not up to the standards he had enjoyed in France. That might explain why Dad would never eat French fries. And one morning she accidentally put powdered borax in his cereal instead of powdered sugar. "Fireworks ensued," she wrote.

The years from 1919 until 1928 were not easy ones for my Dad or his sister, Mary. They remembered the year that their mother was in Walter Reed as traumatic. They were bounced between the grandparents and their father's sister and her husband, who had no children and little patience. By the time their mother was released from the hospital, they were way behind in school. She kept them home for a year and taught them herself using the Calvert School, a Baltimore-based system for home-schooling children.

Dad was a quiet little boy and had a hard time when he finally entered Blessed Sacrament School in Chevy Chase. His mother said that he was late to school, "... three times in a month, or three times in a week, which meant suspension . . . [One] day he was late coming home, half an hour, one hour, two hours. By that time, I had disorganized the doctor's office, the school system, the telephone service. About five o'clock a very tired little boy came trailing up the street. 'Well,' he said. 'I was late and for the third time; so I didn't see any use going in at all. I had my lunch; so, I went down to Rock Creek (miles away!) and sat on a big stone out in the water.'"

I have a small schoolbook of my Dad's in which a childish scrawl complains, "Poor little Albert." He told me that being a redhead sometimes made him a target for bullies. He was given many unkind nicknames and hated to be called "Red." Because his carrot top was so noticeable, he was easily picked out of a crowd and blamed for things he had not done.

His dislike of being called "Red" was to remain with him throughout his life. When he arrived at the house for my wedding to Ted, he was greeted by Ted's brother Bob, also a redhead. "Hi, Red!" Bob said. Eyeing Bob's own carrot top, Dad chuckled and replied, "You're the only one in this room who could get away with calling me that!"

Albert may not have been a patient father when his son was young, but he wrote many encouraging and loving letters when Dad was at West Point, and while he was a POW during World War II. His letters to Dad during the war illustrate his concern for the poor nutrition of the POWs. He advised sucking on rusty nails to get iron and chewing on charcoal to heal diarrhea. He sent vitamins to Mom to include in the Red Cross packages.

One of my grandfather's assignments during the Depression was to tour and inspect the Civilian Conservation Corps (CCC) camps. He took Dad along. His father's instruction on how to build a sanitary privy was useful when Dad arrived in the filthy Stalag Luft III POW camp. Many of the POWs and the German guards were sick, some with dysentery. Dad showed them how to build sanitary latrines to avoid the flies and the stench. His grateful fellow POWS dubbed the latrines "Clark's Crap in Comfort" (CCC) privies.

Orders to San Antonio

The Clark family happily greeted their 1928 orders to San Antonio. My grandfather, by then a flight surgeon, was assigned as the first commander of the School of Aviation Medicine at Brooks Army Medical Center. My grandmother reported that, "We all settled down in this land that we love for a breathing spell. The children made friends enough to last them as long as they live."

Aunt Mary loved to drive and ultimately taught two of my children to drive. She and my Dad pooled their money and bought a second-hand Ford, fixing it up with a new top, seat covers, battery, horn, tires and two coats of paint. Dad could drive but Mary was not allowed. Their father insisted that she was not "temperamentally" suited to drive.

My grandmother reports in her memoir how Mary managed to learn. ". . . begging, bullying and bribing everyone we knew, old, young and 'middling' to let her drive just five minutes or just to the corner or just to the gate." She was soon able to prove to her father that she could drive. Then she drove too fast one day, and the MPs gave her a ticket and called her father. She was unhappily grounded for a month.

It was during my grandfather's second assignment at Ft. Sam Houston that Dad and Mom met. They were married in October 1937. My grandmother's memoir ends eight months before she died. The last words in her memoir were, "There'll be no more orders for us. We'll miss them a great deal I think." She died in the hospital at Fort Sam Houston in 1938, five months before I was born.

The Widowed Doctor Marries Again

There were more orders for my grandfather. And he married again, a divorcee named Ruth Kinsella Hill who had a young daughter, Anne. They spent most of WWII at Ft. Lewis, Washington. He commanded McCraw General Hospital as it grew over four and a half years from 350 beds to 3,500 beds with large psychiatric and burn units. He retired from the Army in May 1946. He and Ruth bought the house in San Antonio that we lived in during the war.

Ruth had been married previously to an Army officer and West Point graduate. I suppose that their divorce and her subsequent remarriage to my recently widowed grandfather was grist for the gossip mill. Anne, her daughter, told me that Ruth had a problem with alcohol.

Albert Clark holding Dad at Ft. Derussy, with Diamond Head in the background.

My grandfather was aware of this and always kept the alcohol locked away and the key hidden. This way, he ensured that she stayed a moderate drinker throughout their eight years together.

In July 1946, only two months after they had moved to San Antonio, my grandfather suffered a sudden heart attack and died in the room that had been my bedroom. His death was traumatic for Anne, who was only 12 years old at the time and always considered him to be her father. She had no memory of her biological father. When he died, my parents went to San Antonio to help Ruth, and to attend the funeral

My grandfather and grandmother with Aunt Mary and Dad.

and witness his burial beside my grandmother in the National Cemetery at Fort Sam.

Anne grew up to be an excellent student and a talented pianist. She married a Mexican lawyer she met while attending Rice University and moved to Mexico City. They had five beautiful children. Ruth followed her daughter to Mexico City and died in a Mexico City hospital. We stayed in touch with Anne and enjoyed numerous visits with her. She died early in 2022, surrounded by her loving children.

Chapter Eight
Our Family's Irish Story

Many Americans of Irish descent feel pulled by Ireland. I have wondered whether it might be an errant gene, somewhat like the gene for red hair, which skips a generation or two and unexpectedly reappears. But more likely, it's the gripping stories passed down to children and grandchildren like me.

I didn't know my Irish grandmother, Mary Catherine Gannon, nicknamed Polly, except in my mind's eye. My child's imagination imbued her with sacred characteristics, and I felt her presence as an angel watching over me. She had been a Catholic and a nurse and had played the piano. I prayed to her sometimes. I felt loved by her and was intrigued by all things Irish. The stories of Irish history had hooked me, and I determined that one day I would go there.

My father took my son Bill to Ireland in search of our Irish roots. They were unsuccessful and disappointed. Ted and I decided to continue the search in Ireland a few years later. MC had given me some critical clues during visits when I was in high school—a few scanty pieces of information-- meager, enticing hints of what must have been a bitter drama. My great-great-grandmother, Sarah Connaughton, had come from a place called Lismacool in County Roscommon. Sarah had loved it so much that, after they came to America and had some money saved, they bought a farm outside of Baltimore and called it Lismacool. My great-grandfather, Timothy Gannon, had a baby brother, Maurice, who stayed behind in Ireland with their parents. The Gannons had lived on a small dairy farm near the town of Elphin in County Roscommon.

MC told me that Sarah and Tim had known each other in Ireland. They emigrated in about 1850, probably on the same ship and most likely from Sligo, the Atlantic port nearest to County Roscommon. He was about ten years younger than she and came to America as a child. He grew up to marry Sarah's daughter, Annie. Annie died when her daughter, my grandmother, was five. Tim died before his grandson, my father, was born. That was really all that MC knew about our Irish ancestors.

They left Ireland fleeing a terrible famine caused by the potato blight. More than a million Irish starved to death and more than a million immigrated to America and Australia. They had few choices but to leave or starve. It was the lucky ones who managed to get passage out of Ireland, terrible though conditions were on many of the ship that carried them. Families were broken. Loved ones were separated forever: parents from children, brothers and sisters from each other, husbands from wives.

Our First Trip to Ireland, September 1990

We began our search at the County Roscommon Heritage Center in Strokestown, where we found parish records from the nineteenth century of three Gannon families from the county. Two Maurices and a couple of Timothys, and several Marys and Catherines were noted on the records. There were also a couple of Sarah Connaughtons. Baptisms had been registered in three different parishes within a radius of about seven miles around Elphin. However, no modern map identified any of these parishes, nor was there any sign of a place named Lismacool.

The Heritage Center director suggested that we go to a pub in Elphin and talk to the old people. Then she said, smiling, "Look for a place that feels like home." We drove to Elphin with copies of the records and of an ancient map that identified the parishes and a townland called Lismacool, connected by roads that weren't on the modern map. Many of the old townlands had disappeared as their residents fled the famine.

On our way to Elphin we stopped to ask a woman if she knew where Lismacool was. She looked perplexed, until I went on to say that my great-great-grandmother had lived there. Then she smiled knowingly and spent ten minutes repeating a confusing series of right and left turns to be taken on unmarked and partially paved roads, saying that might be where Lismacool had once been located.

We followed her directions as best we could, looking carefully at the nineteenth century maps, and finally came to the stretch of road where she'd directed us. Looking out over the rolling green pastures, the grey stone fences, the sheep, the silence, I realized that it felt like home. It looked like farm country in Maryland and Virginia.

Spotting an old fellow walking in the gate of a nearby farm, we approached him and asked. "This is Lismacool," he said. "It starts up the road there at the top of the hill, where you see that tree; and it goes down the road a piece, past the next curve to the old school." He told us that there had been some Connaughtons living there but they'd moved away, to Dublin he thought. We took a photograph of an ancient stone farmhouse long since abandoned, maybe by an Irish family lucky enough to get passage to America.

We stopped at a pub in Elphin to look for some old folks. It was late in the morning as a tired woman poured me a cup of tea, and Ted a pint of Guinness. I asked her if there were any Gannons around, saying that I was a Gannon from America. She perked up and took us outside to show us where a John Gannon lived right next door, and described where two more Gannon families lived, one on the road to Carrick, the other on the road to Boyle. "John's car isn't there," she told us, "so he isn't home."

The next day we drove through Elphin again and saw that John Gannon's car was parked in front of his house. Ted stopped and I hesitantly knocked on the door, which was opened by a big bear of a guy, probably in his sixties, who insisted that we come in. Opera was playing on the stereo. We went upstairs and were joined by his brother, Pat Gannon.

265

They told us that we weren't related because their family name had been Kilgannon from Sligo. Some ancestor had gotten involved in the "troubles," they explained, and had changed the family's name to Gannon.

When I mentioned the name Maurice Gannon, he told us he knew him. He explained that, although the name is spelled as the French do, they pronounce it Morris as the English do. He promptly stood up and said that he would take us there on his way to check his cows in a nearby pasture. I suggested that we telephone first. John laughed. "Maurice doesn't have a phone," he said.

We followed John out of Elphin, past the bronze monument to Roscommon's dead heroes, past the Shankhill Cemetery, to a one-room cinderblock farmhouse with a donkey grazing in the front yard. John banged loudly on the front door, pushed the door open, and announced, "Maurice, I've got some relatives from America here to see you. Remember me, Maurice, I'm John Gannon." We heard a gruff reply, followed by shuffling and banging noises. Were we intruding on someone who couldn't possibly be a relative? An interminable two or three minutes passed, and John came to the door, beckoning forcefully for us to come in.

We stepped inside. The room was dominated by a floor-to-ceiling open fireplace in which burned a couple of generous chunks of peat despite the warmth of the September day. An old man in a black suit and an almost-white shirt sat by the fire looking at us curiously and obviously annoyed. His black beret was snatched from his head by John just as we entered and placed on his knee. John repeated to him that I might be a relative from America. The old man sat up a little straighter, pondered the situation momentarily, grunted and reluctantly stuck out a pale freckled hand to shake mine.

John invited us to sit down on the straight-backed chairs he had hastily arranged in front of the fireplace. I took a deep breath and said something about my great-grandfather being a Gannon who had a brother named Maurice Gannon

266

who had stayed in Ireland after he went to America. Maurice looked at me intently for a minute, thinking, and said that his father had been named Maurice and had had a brother named Tim who went to America. My eyes opened in startled surprise. I said that my great-grandfather had been named Timothy. Maurice gave a slow lop-sided grin and stuck out his hand again, this time with a bit of a flourish, for another, heartier, shake.

We had never expected to find a living relative. We had been looking for gravestones. I wondered how this Maurice could be old enough to be the son of my great-grandfather's brother. I asked him how old he was. He didn't remember but said that he'd been born in about 1905. Eighty-five, we all said at once. Then he said that his father had not married until late in life and had died at 75 leaving four young children, of which he was the oldest. I started adding backwards out loud, as they all stared at me. It worked out. This old fellow was the son of Timothy's brother who had stayed behind in Ireland, my first cousin twice removed. I was stunned speechless, and on the verge of tears.

I finally recovered enough presence of mind to ask some questions. Had he known his father's parents? No, they had been dead a long time before he was born. He'd known his mother's family. She had been Catherine Hanley. Did he know when Tim had gone to America, and with whom? A question that we had pondered for many years: who did

John Gannon at Tiermore

he go with? Maurice said he didn't know exactly when they went, but Mary Catherine, Tim's older sister, had taken him with her and her husband, a man he thought was named McDonnell.

He knew this, he said, because his father had told him that when her husband died in America, Mary Catherine had sent his gold watch back to the family in Ireland. I had trouble following what Maurice was saying with his heavy brogue and missing teeth. He noticed that I hadn't understood and said to John, "Tell her! Tell her what I said!" He was eager for me to hear about this event that had occurred long before he was born, but so important that he had been told and remembered it all his life. He went on to tell me that he thought that Mary Catherine had married again but he didn't know to whom.

As I thought about a widow in a strange country sending her deceased husband's gold watch back to the family in Ireland, I felt the tears rising to the surface. This may have kept them from starvation during the famine that had lasted for several years.

I had more questions. Had his father gone to school? No, his father had never been to school or learned to read and write. Where were his parents buried? His father was buried in the Shankhill Cemetery, and he didn't know where his grandfather had been buried. His mother and grandmother were buried behind the church in Elphin.

What color was his father's hair? "Sandy blond," they both said at once. All of them had been tall, fair-haired and fair-skinned. Had he ever married? No, Atty had married, but had never had children. Neither Jack nor Mary Cate had ever married. There had been a dramatic and understandable dip in the birth rate in Ireland during and following the famine. The decline in the population of Ireland was still evidenced by the abandoned farmhouses and villages that dotted the countryside.

Maurice was the only one of the four Gannon children still alive. Did he live here alone? "Yes, but a young fella stops by now and then to tidy up." There was no television, no radio, no other signs of the modern world's more common means of passing time. What did he do all day? Perhaps, because we had stepped into another time and place, I took no

268

notice of those things at the time. It was "all of a piece," as the saying goes. I looked around the room again and realized that my great-grandfather had probably been born in this room, in front of this very fireplace.

When we rose to go. I went over to shake Maurice's hand. With the white skin and multitude of freckles, it looked just like my father's hand. I looked right into his eyes, determined to get a good, close look. They were startlingly blue. He shook my hand, looked at me quizzically, and slapped his hat back on his head as we turned to leave. We drove off toward Dublin, dazed, silent, remembering too late all the questions I hadn't asked, the photographs we hadn't taken, and pondering the curious twists and turns life takes.

The Enduring Legacy

There were reasons we'd managed to find Maurice. A simple one has to do with the Irish propensity for naming their children after their forebears. Also, Maurice Gannon is an uncommon name, unlike Patrick O'Brien, or a hundred other Irish names. Another reason has to do with the Irish tendency to stay put. The land itself seems to have a curious hold on the Irish, perhaps rooted in Ireland's history.

A more emotional reason has something to do with why so many Irish went to America, the immensity of the pain of the broken families, and the broken relationship with the land of their fathers and mothers. When they said goodbye and turned their faces toward Sligo or Cork, it wasn't to be forever. Often, they hoped for, planned for, longed for, their return. This is hauntingly clear in the songs of the Irish immigrants in America. "I'll take you home again, Kathleen, across the ocean wild and wide, to where your heart has always been..." was written in 1876 in America, about 25 years after the Great Famine.

This longing was enhanced by the gritty urban ghettos where so many of them ended up and was passed on to their children, their grandchildren and their great-grandchildren.

We troop back to Ireland in curious droves, driven by much that is out of our conscious awareness. Thus, in a sense, we go back for them. If it were otherwise, why would we know what we know? Why would we want to look for these ancestors and their graves? And why would the Irish be so delighted to help us in our searches? Why would we all care so much?

Maurice died three months after our visit. His last days were filled with visits from the "Church ladies" and from John. We corresponded with John for several years and went back in the summer of 1995. We found Maurice's grave behind the church in Elphin, beside his brother Atty's and my great-great grandmother's grave. We visited their graves again with Kiley a few years later.

The farm that had been of such value to the Gannon family for who knows how many generations was not inherited by any Gannons. My father could have claimed it, as according to Irish law the grandchildren of anyone born in Ireland can claim Irish citizenship. But Maurice intended it to go to the neighbor who had kindly looked in on him during the years he lived there alone.

The Luck of the Irish
My great-grandparents, Sarah Connaughton and Paul McAvoy probably met on the ship that brought them from Sligo to Baltimore. I can see them all now, in my mind's eye, as they made their way on foot to Sligo, Mary Catherine with her husband and her brother Tim, and Sarah Connaughton. They had a long walk carrying belongings on their backs. But maybe their father brought them in a wagon pulled by a donkey.

According to MC, Paul was an expert horseman and managed the stables of a wealthy citizen of Baltimore. The family lived in the gatehouse at the entrance to the mansion. They had five children: Annie, Julia, Mary Catherine, and two sons. Both sons died young, one in a horse-related accident when he was a teenager. Sarah and Paul are buried in the old Catholic cemetery in Baltimore near where they had lived. Two of their daughters, Annie McAvoy Gannon (my great-grandmother) and Julia McAvoy Butler, died following childbirth.

Annie McAvoy and Timothy Gannon, our links to Ireland.

While I am grateful for the legacy of our many English ancestors, I am also proud to be descended from our courageous Irish ancestors. I love an Irish Blessing from *Beannacht* by John O'Donohue (1956-2008) and I pass it on to all readers of this book. It reads in part:

*On the day when the weight deadens on your shoulders,
and you stumble,
May the clay dance to balance you.
May the nourishment of the earth be yours,
May the clarity of light be yours,
May the fluency of the ocean be yours,
May the protection of the ancestors be yours.
And so may a slow wind work these words of love
around you,
An invisible cloak to mind your life.*

PART V

In Loving Memory

The deeper that sorrow carves into your being, the more joy you can contain. -Kahlil Gibran

Remembering My Brother, Pat

Pat was so much a part of my life for his 65 years that I have a hard time separating memories of him from the story of my own life. He was my best friend from further back than I can remember. He was generous and kind to me and made me laugh. Sadly, as an adult, he developed some anger issues. He felt that he'd suffered injustice, first as the son in a military family, and then when the Vietnam War was badly executed and cost him so many friends. And he did have friends, those who understood and loved him, and his fellow pilots who admired his skill and courage.

Pat was always there for me and my children. He went out of his way to visit us as our family grew from one baby to four. He loved my kids. He thought they were smart and funny and loved gently teasing them and telling them tall tales. When I needed money to buy the house from Bud, Pat sent me a check for exactly the amount I needed, no questions asked. When Carrie needed money for a down payment on her first car, she asked Pat. He sent her the money and kept his promise never to tell me. She was the one who finally told me.

After Pat retired and moved to Colorado Springs near Mom and Dad, they called him to fix things and take them to doctors' appointments. Soon after moving to Colorado, Pat found a nasty-looking mole on his left thigh—melanoma. After the initial surgery, he had extensive tests every three months for five years. At the five-year mark, he was considered extremely lucky—a survivor. But fifteen years later, the melanoma returned, with a vengeance.

Pat began thinking about the afterlife. He was one of few people I ever knew who understood Einstein's Theory of Relativity. He could have majored in physics instead of philosophy. He thought God might be in the black holes in space, and our souls were actually energy that joined God at death. He hoped we'd get a do-over, maybe on another planet.

After suffering through three week-long, excruciating chemotherapy sessions and weeks in the hospital, he began an experimental treatment in Denver, which gave him another year. But he knew the cancer had won in November 2005, even before the doctor called. He cooked Thanksgiving dinner for Dad, Kathleen and Edward with his right eye swollen from a tumor. He told Kathleen he must have gotten something in his eye. On December 18, 2005, he died in a hospice facility.

We had Pat's funeral Mass at the Air Force Academy in January. His pilot friends came from all over the States. A few months later, he was buried with full military honors in Arlington National Cemetery. His friends came to that as well. After the ceremony, they went back to his grave, huddling over it, softly singing in unison. When we asked them what they'd been singing, they laughed and said, "Throw a nickel on the grass, save a fighter pilot's ass." Oh yes, I thought, I'd heard that song in many Officers' Club bars. So we all trooped over to his grave and threw more nickels on it. Now, every time we visit his grave, we drop nickels on it.

His friends had a plaque made commemorating his service as a Marine as well as his service as an Air Force fighter pilot. Pat's plaque, the only one like it, hangs on the wall of the Marine Memorial in San Francisco. Kathleen, Edward, Ted and I went when his friends dedicated it.

Pat was a good man, and a wonderful brother. Like all of us, he had his failings, but he laughed often, was strong and brave, and cried in movies. I miss him. I so regret that he

273

never found the true love he was looking for. Some of his life was just plain unfair. But as he often said, "No one ever promised us that life would be fair." Sometimes I see Pat in Kathleen and Edward, some of their facial expressions and mannerisms. The memory of his chuckle brings him back for a moment. He'd appreciate being remembered that way.

My Eulogy for Pat, January 13, 2006

My brother, Pat, was born into a "duty, honor, country, shoulders back, chin in, yes sir/no sir stiff upper lip" military family. He was among three generations in his family to put on a uniform and serve his country in war and in peace. Pat believed with all his heart in liberty and justice for all, no matter the color of their skin or the language they spoke.

A graduate of Georgetown University, Pat's degree was in Philosophy. He was a thoughtful and spiritual man who believed in, and loved, God, beauty, goodness and truth. One of his favorite books was "Coming of Age in the Milky Way" by Timothy Ferris. He read all of Stephen Hawking's books on the workings of the universe and the origin of life. Pat was fascinated by Einstein's theory of relativity.

Pat was a good father to his children, and also their friend. He was always there for our parents. He was a good brother to me, and he was my dear, best friend from as far back as I can remember. He was also a caring uncle to all his nephews and his niece. Pat loved deeply, laughed often and knew how to make others laugh. In fact, he was the only one who could make our mother laugh during her last painful days. Pat was very good doing what he loved doing—flying. His life was cut short, but he lived a full life.

Pat was a man of extraordinary fortitude, a valiant fighter for his country, and for his life. His last three years were difficult, but he lived them with courage, optimism, and

My brother, Pat, was a Marine (above), then a fighter pilot who flew 400+ combat missions in Vietnam.

good humor, most of the time, and continued to love and care deeply for his children, his parents and for all his extended family. Often a man of few words, he nevertheless knew the most important words of all. He taught his family how to open those stiff upper lips and say I love you. I love you Pat.

Remembering Mom and Dad

They were married for 65 years and were deeply in love as they began their journey together. Their love comforted them both during the bleak years of Dad's imprisonment in as a POW in World War II, which were Mom's years as a single mother of three.

In his professional life, Dad was considered fair, honest, and kind, a man of integrity. He expected nothing less than the best from his colleagues and subordinates. Those who were found by him to be dishonest, unkind or unfair were in serious trouble.

Mom could have earned a PhD in history or literature with all the knowledge she gleaned from her voracious appetite for books. She was a creative genius with knitting and sewing needles, making her own clothes and sewing for my sister and me. She was only 40 when we children were put in boarding schools. I was 16, Pat was 15, and Mary was 13. Despite Mom's beauty, intelligence, and creative talent, she is identified only as "wife of General A.P. Clark," on the stone marker over her grave, a military wife's limited identity.

My Eulogy for Mom

Although many of you have known her for a long time, I'd like to tell you some things about my mother that you might not know. She was an Army brat through and through. Her father was a Cavalry Officer who had graduated from both the Virginia Military Institute and West Point. You can be sure he was a disciplinarian. He was also an excellent horseman, and he taught her to ride. She won blue ribbons in the ladies' classes when she was only 14 years old. Fort Riley, Fort Leavenworth, Fort Ethan Allen, Fort Oglethorpe, Fort Sam Houston--all places my mother called home in her early years. She was the oldest of four and was graced with exceptional beauty. I'll bet she was the most beautiful young woman my father had ever seen when she caught his eye in San Antonio. They were married there in 1937 and she continued the nomadic military life, with energy and grace.

I don't remember many new assignments that she didn't greet with enthusiasm, except for the orders that took my father to England and the Second World War. It was only a short five years after they were married that she received the telegram: "We regret to inform you that your husband is missing in action." Four long weeks later, she learned that he was a prisoner of war in Germany. During the following three years she fought with all her might to obtain the Red Cross help that the POWs needed.

Mother loved the ballet and classical music. She was an avid reader, a self-educated expert in world history, literature and poetry, much of which she committed to memory. We have all been treated to lengthy recitations of her favorite poems. She was also an artist with knitting needles and a sewing machine, making us beautiful clothes and knitting us gorgeous sweaters over the years.

I am grateful for all the wonderful books she read to us as children, and for her intellectual curiosity. She passed on a valuable legacy. I'd like to read a stanza from "The Reading Mother," which I came across recently. "You may have tangible wealth untold, caskets of jewels and coffers of gold. Richer than I you can never be – I had a mother who read to me."

She lived a fortunate life, with three healthy children, a successful husband whose career allowed her to travel widely and share many happy experiences. She was also fortunate in her eight beautiful grandchildren, and nine exceptional great-grandchildren. She was very proud of all of us.

My mother's last years have been hard as she gradually lost her sight and had to give up her knitting and reading, and then her mobility. She faced these difficulties with courage. We are certain that she is now at peace with our loving and merciful God. We ask your prayers for our father and for all of us who loved her.

Losing Dad: After Mom died, Dad picked up the pieces and went on with his life. He had already started his book about his experience as a POW in World War II, with the help of good friends. He bought a computer and learned how to use email. He typed his book on his computer when he was in his early 90s.

He kept getting up every day, got dressed, walked with his walker or cane to the dining room at Liberty Heights, grimaced quietly with pain, stood as straight as he could, and looked his friends in the eyes as he tried to hear their conversations and respond.

Then one day in March 2010, a nurse called from a hospital to tell us that he was in grave condition due to a doctor's medication error. Ted and I rushed from Virginia to his bedside in Colorado Springs. When I turned on my cell phone during a stop in Denver, I had a voice-mail message. I clicked on the message and heard, "Carolyn, your Dad was a great man." "Oh no!" I whispered. "She said 'was.' We didn't make it in time." We couldn't hold his hand and say good-bye.

His would be the third funeral for us to plan and hold at the Air Force Academy. To the Academy, Dad's was the most important. He had been their superintendent for four years. The Academy requested that we schedule it before the cadets left for Spring break so they could be involved. We agreed on St. Patrick's Day, appropriately, as Dad was proud of his Irish heritage. It was a solemn affair with a P-51 fly-by, and four F-18s screaming overhead in the missing-man formation. Even the stiffest upper lips trembled at the sight and sounds of the fly-by.

My Eulogy for Dad

Dad was a military brat born into the same "yes sir/no sir, chin in, shoulders back, stand at attention, no excuses sir" family that my sister and brother and I were born into. We learned self-discipline, persistence, determination and courage from him. Dad experienced what he felt was the greatest failure of his life, when he was shot down over the English Channel soon after the United States entered World War II and was forced to surrender to the enemy. But he turned that failure into success, he survived. He struggled with stage fright, public speaking was difficult for him, but he overcame his fear and developed self-confidence. He never shrank from a challenge. He climbed to the tops of many mountains but never forgot the view from the valley. He loved and laughed and sang and danced and told stories. Dad had more than a little Irish in him.

My mother, Carolyn Wilbourn Clark (1915-2002), and my father, Albert Patton Clark (1913-2010).

He was a talented artist, a skilled woodworker, and he could fix almost anything, often using duct tape, glue, coat hangers or rubber bands. He was always a good scout. Be prepared, he'd say. He sailed and taught himself to navigate by the stars in case that were ever necessary, and indeed it was. But that's another story. He worked hard and played hard. He loved God and was a devout Catholic all his life. He valued truth and beauty. Duty, honor, country, the West Point motto, ever remained his watch words, his mantra. He dearly loved the Air Force Academy.

To me, he embodied courage itself. He lived with almost constant pain for the past several years, but he never lost his determination to get up each day and keep going. He experienced many losses. His parents died when he was still a young man; and he lost his sister, his wife, his son and many dear friends over the years, but he never became bitter or indulged in self-pity. He was an example for us all on how to live a full life and age with dignity.

This is the end of an important chapter in my life and the lives of our wonderful extended family. Our father's life was immeasurably enriched by you, by the cadets, by his friends at Liberty Heights where he has lived during the last 18 years, and by his military and civilian colleagues. My sister and I are very grateful for your being here today to honor him. Thank you.

Afterwards: The months passed and I mourned for him, for Pat, and for my mother. We went on about our lives, but I felt only half there. The weekend after Veterans' Day, we went to Florida with friends. I caught a cold and was in my room when I heard fighter jets flying overhead. Outside, I looked up and there was an F-86 screaming by, performing in an air show just across the river. I sat on the deck, blowing my nose and watched as the airplanes flaunted their stuff, performing acrobatic maneuvers, ancient biwings as well as modern jets. There was a flight of four P-51 Mustangs, followed by a flight of four F-18s. The sound was so familiar. Hadn't we just heard it a few months back at Dad's funeral?

Just as I thought the show had ended, two aircraft flew at low altitude straight across our field of view in front of the deck: A P-51 Mustang with an F-4 Phantom in its wing. The P-51 was, no doubt, flying as fast as it could and the F-4 so slow that I thought it might stall. My heart skipped a beat, and tears welled. I thought, "There goes my father with my brother on his wing!" It was a sign. I'll never forget them, I'll never stop missing them, but they're both okay.

Memories of Bobby and Lily

We loved each other. There were no expectations, only love and support that was always there. We could be our authentic selves, strong and weak, smart and confused, and we knew that we were accepted just as we were.

Uncle Bobby was my mother's only brother but we dropped the "Uncle" early on. Bobby was the Wilbourn sibling who tried to stay in touch. He cared about his sisters and their kids, never having had any of his own. I am sure that he knew how important he was to me and to my children, and then to Ted. He was a combination father and grandfather during the 25 years we lived close by, the years we needed each other the most.

Bobby and Lily were there for the special occasions during those years: birthdays, Thanksgivings, Christmases, Easters, and just to hang out on a weekend evening. He taught Hal and Bill to sail and took us on many lovely sails around the Chesapeake. He taught us to discuss and argue and sometimes our feelings were hurt. Many times, he would take a position that he knew would elicit controversy. When we all vehemently disagreed, he'd finally say, "Well, that was my position to begin with. Glad you see my point!" He confronted us without mincing words when he felt we needed it.

When he first told us that something was wrong with his brain, we dismissed his concerns as normal senior moments. It didn't seem possible that this bright, passionate man could possibly succumb to the dreaded "Big A," Alzheimer's disease. Many months later, when he called me at work to tell me the diagnosis, he sighed and said, "Everyone wants to think that they have earned some sort of a guarantee against these things, but of course no one has."

Lily was a loving and devoted wife when he was sick. We visited him often and watched helplessly as he experienced increasing disability and indignity as the cruel disease progressed. But there was still much of the Bobby we loved inside. He chuckled and laughed, sometimes at his own private jokes. His brow still furrowed as he talked, a fragmented trail of words that reflected his vast vocabulary and masterful command of the English language. Sadly, the sentences were indecipherable. But we knew that he was talking about politics, religion, the economy, moral values and family relationships—all the issues that had occupied his active mind for so many years. We would look him in the eyes and nod. He seemed satisfied that we were listening and understood. He still recognized us. I noted this one day in my journal:

His fingers picked up little pieces of nothing off the table, off the floor, and out of the air, carefully carrying them around, and then handing them to Ted to free his hands to hold a glass of water. The other residents drifted over, trying to join us, trying to get others to move so they could sit with us, grabbing our arms, thinking I was a daughter, Ted a husband, that they knew us from somewhere, but couldn't remember our names. Today he sadly asked, "Why can't people just have a clean death?"

In May 1997, Bobby wandered out an unlocked door into the garden where we had been sitting with him. He fell on the concrete, hit his head and couldn't get up. He lay there for several hours in the dark before they found him. He died a couple of days later at the age of 77. His ashes were placed in the Columbarium at Arlington National Cemetery with full military honors. We had a memorial service in the little Ft. Myer Chapel, attended by about 50 people, including a large group of family members.

Lily had an admirable capacity to laugh at herself. We teased her mercilessly about her accent. She could never say "beach." It always came out "bitch," as in, "I love the bitch." But she had quirks that drove us nuts. She suffered a chronic case of buyer's remorse, shopping in stores and on the phone, returning 90% of what she bought. Having been raised in the Middle East, she believed in bargaining and had no respect for advertised prices. She was an expert at haggling, even with utility companies, and was often successful. She spoke with a decided Greek accent and never completely conquered English pronunciation and syntax. People would give up arguing with her and let her have her way. She was so smart she could convince them that she wasn't.

Uncle Bobby Wilbourn with Lily in Maine.

After Bobby died, Lily moved into a ground-floor apartment in a beautiful retirement community on the banks of the Chesapeake. One or the other of us talked to her on the phone at least once a week and visited every couple of weeks when we weren't traveling. She often asked Ted for investment advice, which she promptly ignored. She loved to play the market and managed to lose $100,000 over her last 15 years.

When she finally became fatally ill, she was not prepared to surrender. "Tear up that advanced directive," she said while lying in the hospital bed. "I'm not giving up!" The doctor told me to talk to her and tell her she had to sign the DNR or she would suffer terribly. But I couldn't. So he did. She finally gave up the good fight on September 25, 2012. We placed her ashes beside her beloved Robert's in the Columbarium. We miss her. This poem was printed on the handouts for both of their memorial services.

SEA FEVER by John Mansfield (1878-1967)

I must go down to the seas again, to the lonely sea and the sky,
And all I ask is a tall ship and a star to steer her by,
And the wheel's kick and the wind's song and the white sail's shaking,
And a grey mist on the sea's face and a grey dawn breaking.
I must go down to the seas again, for the call of the running tide
Is a wild call and a clear call that may not be denied;
And all I ask is a windy day with the white clouds flying,
And the flung spray and the blown spume, and the sea-gull's crying.
I must go down to the seas again to the vagrant gypsy life,
To the gull's way and the whale's way where the wind's like a whetted knife;
And all I ask is a merry yarn from a laughing fellow rover,
And a quiet sleep and a sweet dream when the long trick's over.

Memories of Aunt Mary and Uncle Abe

Dad's sister and her husband, Aunt Mary and Uncle Abe, were dear to all of us during our years in northern Virginia. I never called her just Mary. She was either Aunt Mary, or her children's name for her, Mother L.

When I brought Ted over to meet her and Uncle Abe, she thanked him for "helping Carolyn to become a real live girl again." I wouldn't have chosen those words, but we knew what she meant. She could tell that I was happy and was acutely aware of the contrast between "back then" and now. She made my corsage and held a reception for us at their home when we got married.

Aunt Mary was an artist. She appreciated color, texture, line, balance, harmony and form. Like my Dad, she needed to find a place for everything that was lovely. Did she ever love clothes! A skilled seamstress, she couldn't throw away even a scrap of beautiful fabric or yarn. She created works of art, clothes for herself and her loved ones. Rarely did she ever wear something that came right off the rack, or straight from a catalog. She mixed and matched, added her own touch, making her outfits uniquely her own creations.

Uncle Abe and Aunt Mary made the perfect military couple. A graduate of West Point with a master's degree in engineering from Princeton, Uncle Abe had retired as a Lt. General in the Army Corps of Engineers. Aunt Mary had eagerly followed him wherever he was assigned—Okinawa, North Africa, Italy. She soaked up the local culture wherever they were assigned and expertly entertained exactly as a good Army wife should. She threw herself into supporting his career and I'm sure she earned compliments in his efficiency reports. They both were very good parents to their three

With Mary and Abe, November 1979

children, modeling a respectful and loving marriage as the kids grew into adulthood.

When Ted and I dropped by for a drink, Ted would go downstairs with Uncle Abe and they would pour drinks and chat. Ted would happily listen to his stories, sometimes not for the first time. I would go with Aunt Mary, Ted would bring us each a drink, wine for me and a martini for her, and she

285

and I would talk. She also read voraciously and always had a new book or newspaper article to discuss when we visited them, which was often.

Uncle Abe kept on playing golf, often alone, even after he stopped keeping score and moved so slowly that he let anyone behind him play through. While mowing the lawn one day in July 1999, he slowly fell over and died in the shade of a tree. Not such a bad way to go.

Aunt Mary died suddenly at her home in Alexandria. I was shocked. She had looked so beautiful just a few days before. But, at 89, she also had been blessed in her swift parting from the earthly beauty that had so delighted her.

Their deaths left a hole in our lives. Life is short. It flies by while we're not looking. Only as we lose those we love do we realize that we should show our love more often for those we still have.

"Though we need to weep your loss,
You dwell in that safe place in our hearts."
-John O'Donahue

Loss is the price of having loved. Grief is love's souvenir.

Appendix 1
The Telegrams

The telegram Mom received when Dad was shot down:

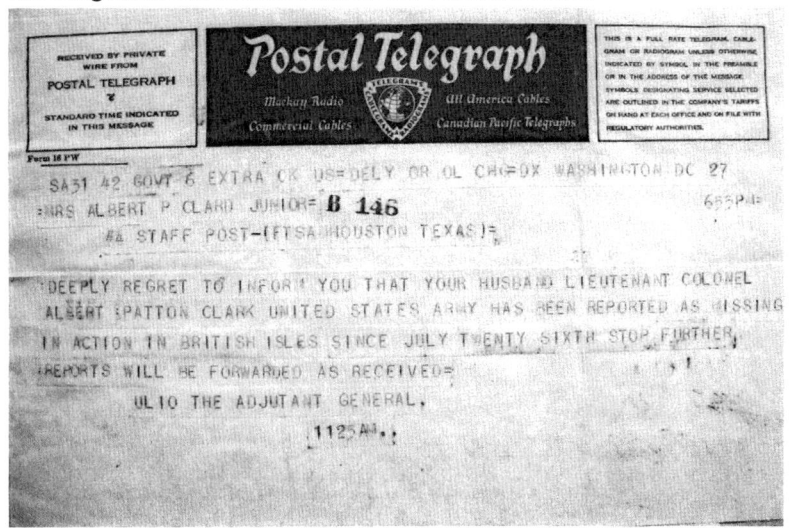

And three years later, the good news that he had been liberated:

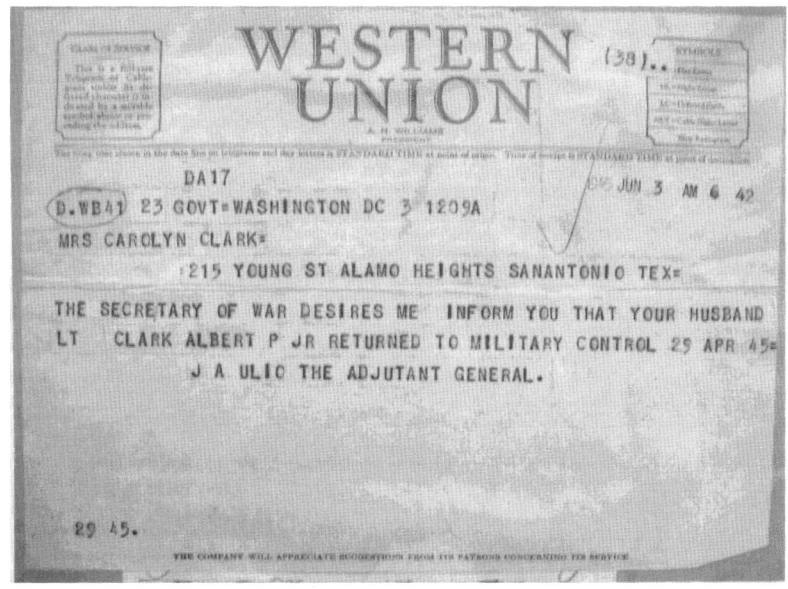

Appendix 2
Glossary:
Words Every Military Brat Knows

AP, Air Police, personnel with police and security responsibility on an Air Force Base

Army Air Corps, in 1947 became the U.S. Air Force

Base is an Air Force installation; a **Post** is what we call an Army installation

Base Exchange (BX) or Post Exchange (PX), a store on a military installation that sells uniforms and offers household products and clothing at reduced prices

Below the zone, early promotion of an officer given for outstanding performance

Bird Colonel, a full colonel whose insignia is eagles pinned on each shoulder

BOQ, Bachelor Officers' Quarters; **VOQ**, Visiting Officers Quarters

Boot camp, training for new recruits, often involving harsh discipline

Brat, a child of military personnel

Buck private, the first rank given to a new recruit, thus the lowest

Class VI Store, where military personnel can buy alcoholic beverages at reduced prices

(The) Colors refers to the American flag

Commissary, a grocery store on a military installation; usually offering products at reduced prices

Corpsmen, military personnel working in dispensaries or hospitals

Cross-country, a short trip to gain flight time and stay proficient in the aircraft

Deploy, leave as a unit on a military assignment for which one has trained, often in anticipation of combat

Dead-stick landing, an emergency landing after an aircraft has lost power

Dependents, wives of military personnel and their children under 18

Demobilization, the process by which troops are processed out of the military into civilian life, for example after a war, or from a combat unit to another unit

Dispensary, where medical care and medications are provided to military personnel and dependents outside of a hospital setting

Ditch, to escape an aircraft in trouble, often in water, causing it to be lost

Flight line, the location of the hangars, parked aircraft, and runways

Fly-By, usually an honor flight of aircraft that fly low and slow over a parade, funeral or important event

Fraternization, usually meaning inappropriate socialization between officers and enlisted personnel or their dependents

Hold baggage, household items that may be needed on a temporary basis, often carried in the area of troop ships called "The Hold;" usually accompanying a transfer or change of station

Insignia, pins and patches that denote rank on a uniform; on the shoulders, sleeves, chest, hat and/or helmet

KIA, Killed in Action

Maneuvers, practice for combat

Mess dress, the formal uniform, complete with decorations (medals); the "mess" is the dining hall. In the old Army, officers dined in formal uniform

MIA, Missing in Action

O Dark Thirty, very early in the morning, as in "wheels in the well at O dark thirty," a very early take-off

On the economy, living off the Post or Base in a civilian community

Pass muster, to pass an inspection carried out to make certain that all regulations have been met

P's and Q's, "Watch your P's and Q's" was often said to children years ago warning them to behave, but having many other possible meanings

PCS, Permanent Change of Station, permanent move to a new location, which may end up being only a few months or as long as four years, rarely longer.

POW. Prisoner of War

Pull alert duty, to be assigned temporarily to stand guard, as against a surprise attack

PX, Post Exchange, store on an Army Post offering merchandise at reduced prices

Quartermaster Corps, personnel responsible for maintaining military equipment, quarters and furniture for military personnel and their families living on or near a military installation; responsible for items to be requisitioned for military or personal use; also responsible for equipping personnel assigned to special duties

Quonset huts, first manufactured in 1941 to temporarily house World War II sailors and soldiers; widely used on military installations, constructed of corrugated steel

Quarters, homes for personnel on a military post or base

MP, Military Police, personnel on an Army Post with police and security responsibility

Requisition, to request government property for official or personal use, to be returned in good condition

Retreat, a bugle call signaling troops to retreat from the battle; also, 5:00 PM on a military installation when the flag is lowered

Reveille, a bugle call signaling troops to advance into battle; also, time to get up in the morning

RHIP, rank hath its privileges, often invoked if someone claims "unfair"

R & R, rest and recuperation

Short-arm Inspection, a surprise inspection, usually held at night with flashlights, to identify troops suffering from venereal disease; no longer practiced

Slot position in a flight of four aircraft flying in a diamond configuration, with a lead aircraft, one on each wing of the lead, and the fourth in the last, or slot, position

Space Available, or Space-A, riding without a reserved space on a military or contracted aircraft after all reserved seats have been filled.

Stand at attention, to stand straight, feet straight ahead and together, hands at one's side, shoulders back, chin in, eyes straight ahead, straight face (no frowns or smirks!)

Straighten up & fly right, used as a correction order, as also in "get with the program"

Strikers, personnel with the responsibility to turn on, or strike the match, to operate coal furnaces in military housing

Taps, last bugle call at night, or over a grave site

TDY, Temporary Duty, temporary move to a new location and/or to carry out new responsibilities

Time hog, a pilot who flies more and longer flights than required, in order to accrue extra flight time

Tour, short for "tour of duty," or military assignment

Twenty-one Gun Salute, honor given at burial involving seven uniformed personnel firing three times each in unison, thus 21 shots fired

VIP Quarters, temporary quarters for visiting dignitaries

VOQ, Visiting Officers Quarters

WAC, WAF, Women's Army Corps, Women's Air Force

Watch Words, secret words given to identify a soldier on watch or guard duty, and/or to identify his replacement

Wheels up & in the well, the aircraft is off the ground and in the air, used to describe a precise point in time

White-glove inspection, a thorough inspection theoretically leaving "white gloves" clean

ZI, Zone of the Interior, military lingo for the U.S. mainland

Appendix 3
The Military Code of Conduct

This is the Code of Conduct that my father, and American combatants, swear to abide by.

I.   *I am an American fighting in the forces which guard my country and our way of life. I am prepared to give my life in their defense.*

II. *I will never surrender of my own free will. If in command, I will never surrender the members of my command while they still have the means to resist.*

III. *If I am captured, I will continue to resist by all means available. I will make every effort to escape and aid others to escape. I will accept neither parole nor special favors from the enemy.*

IV. *If I become a prisoner of war, I will keep faith with my fellow prisoners. I will give no information or take part in any action which might be harmful to my comrades. If I am senior, I will take command. If not, I will obey the lawful orders of those appointed over me and will back them up in every way.*

V.   *When questioned, should I become a prisoner of war, I am required to give name, rank, service number and date of birth. I will evade answering further questions to the utmost of my ability. I will make no oral or written statements disloyal to my country and its allies or harmful to their cause.*

VI. *I will never forget that I am an American, fighting for freedom, responsible for my actions and dedicated to the principles which made my country free. I will trust in my God and in the United States of America.*

Appendix 4
Where I've Lived: My Address List

I still remember all the homes I've moved into and out of. My childhood memories follow me to my dolls' hiding places, outside into the new mown grass, up to the branches of the trees I climbed, and down the alley ways I rode my bicycle. The times in between homes fill my memory bank with long hours on the highway, stays in motels, visits with extended family, and searches for new homes.

After I was married, I remember so many details of the homes I lived in from my efforts to arrange furniture and decorate them with what I had. We'd move again soon. Why buy new stuff that might not work in the next house? I remember my children's rooms in which I kissed them each goodnight, and rooms decorated for all the Christmases and birthday parties. I remember cleaning all those houses, the kitchens and bathrooms, the floors, the carpets, the windows, the wood-work and baseboards, and sometimes the walls.

Selfridge Field, Michigan, October 1938-December 1941
Officers' Quarters, Selfridge Field; near Mt. Clemmons, a suburb of Detroit
Fort Sam Houston, Texas, December 1941-October 1942
Officers' Quarters Number 4, Fort Sam Houston near San Antonio
San Antonio, Texas, October 1942-January 1946
215 Young Street (renamed Claiborne Way), Alamo Heights
Barksdale Field, Louisiana, January 1946-January 1947
Officers' Quarters, Barksdale Field was near Shreveport
Norfolk Naval Station, Virginia, January 1947-July 1948
Officers Barracks, Armed Forces Staff College near Norfolk
Langley Field, Virginia, July 1948-January 1950
Officers' Quarters, 38B Bryant Avenue near Hampton

Baldwin, Long Island, New York, January-June 1950
On the economy
Mitchell Field, Long Island, New York,
June 1950-January 1951
Officers' Quarters, Mitchell Field near Hempstead
Colorado Springs, Colorado, February-July 1951
1335 North Tejon Street
Washington, D.C.,
3505 Lowell Street, August 1951-August 1953
4704 Albemarle Street, August 1953-June 1955
Chaumont, Haute Marne, France,
July 1955-December 1956
17 rue Decres, Chaumont
St. Blaise, Switzerland, October 1955-June 1956
Petit Beau Site, La Chatelainie Boarding School for Girls, near
Neuchatel
Paris, France, October 1956-March 1957
Numero 1, rue Maréchal Harispe, 16ème Arrondissement
Wiesbaden, Germany, March-June 1957
Weurttemberg Strasse 16, Aukamm
Chaumont Air Base, France, June-November 1957
Trailer # 37, Chaumont Air Base, Haute Marne, France,
Albany, Georgia, November 1957-January 1958
85-B Turner City
Apple Valley, California, August-October 1958
Chief Desert Lodge, near Edwards Air Force Base
Niceville, Florida, January 1958-February 1959
1009 Christie Drive, off Bayshore Drive
San Jose, California, February-April 1960
7084 Bark Lane, with Al and Bev
Las Vegas, Nevada, April-June 1960
Motel 6
North Las Vegas, Nevada,
2204 Perliter Street, June-October 1960
3209 Wright Street, October 1960-April 1961

Nellis Air Force Base, Nevada, April 1961-February 1962
Officers' Quarters, 6 Meissner
Washington, D.C., February-May 1962
4704 Albemarle St., Washington, DC
Aiea, Oahu, Hawaii, June 1962-June 1964
99-1822 Aiea Heights Drive
Hickam Air Force Base, Oahu, Hawaii,
June 1964-May 1966
Officers' Quarters, 108 Ilima Lane
Montgomery, Alabama, July 1966-June 1967
1107 Marlowe Drive
Hampton, Virginia, June 1967-July 1970
24 Wendell Drive, Tide Mill Farms
Montgomery, Alabama, July 1970-June 1971
Audubon Road
Alexandria, Virginia
6304 Crestwood Drive, June 1971-July 1973
6106 Larstan Drive, July 1973-November 1986
5816 Colfax Avenue, November 1986 - present

About the Author

Carolyn Clark Miller is the daughter of a World War II Prisoner of War, Air Force fighter pilot and Lieutenant General, and the granddaughter of two Army Colonels, one a Cavalry officer and the other a medical doctor. She was married to an Air Force officer for 20 years. As a military dependent for the first 38 years of her life, she was inspired to write of her family's experiences growing up in the military service of her country: first by her brother, Pat Clark, who wrote a novelized version of his service in Southeast Asia during the Vietnam War entitled: *Last Wolf Home*; and by her father, Albert P. Clark, who wrote a memoir entitled: *33 Months as a POW in Stalag Luft III: An American Airman Tells His Story*. She lives with her husband in Alexandria, Virginia, and spends her summers at Lake Almanor, California.